A CATALOGUE OF VAIṢṆAVA LITERATURE

The reader should note that the following roll (reel) numbers from the original collection, due to technical difficulties, were not included in the present Catalogue: 8 through 30; 64 through 77; 79 through 90; and roll "C". They are housed together with the original microfilms of the complete collection in the Archives of the American University Bender Library in Washington, D.C., USA. It is our hope that these priceless writings from India's religious heritage may eventually be retrieved and made accessible through digital enchancement. Thereafter, a supplemental Catalogue can be produced if there is scholarly interest in doing so.

A CATALOGUE OF VAIṢṆAVA LITERATURE

On Microfilms in
The Adyar Library, The Bodleian Library,
& The American University Library

CHARLES S.J. WHITE

MOTILAL BANARSIDASS PUBLISHERS
PRIVATE LIMITED • DELHI

First Published: Delhi, 2004

ISBN: 81-208-2067-3

MOTILAL BANARSIDASS
41 U.A. Bungalow Road, Jawahar Nagar, Delhi 110 007
8 Mahalaxmi Chamber, 22 Bhulabhai Desai Road, Mumbai 400 026
236, 9th Main III Block, Jayanagar, Bangalore 560 011
120 Royapettah High Road, Mylapore, Chennai 600 004
Sanas Plaza, 1302 Baji Rao Road, Pune 411 002
8 Camac Street, Kolkata 700 017
Ashok Rajpath, Patna 800 004
Chowk, Varanasi 221 001

Printed in India
BY JAINENDRA PRAKASH JAIN AT SHRI JAINENDRA PRESS,
A-45 NARAINA, PHASE-I, NEW DELHI-110 028
AND PUBLISHED BY NARENDRA PRAKASH JAIN FOR
MOTILAL BANARSIDASS PUBLISHERS PRIVATE LIMITED,
BUNGALOW ROAD, DELHI 110 007

In memoriam

DR. S. JAYASREE

2001

Financial and Other Assitance from

- Smithsonian Institution
- The American University
- The Bhaktivedanta Archives
- Mr. Robert Cohen (Brahmatirtha Das)
- Hridayananda Dasa Goswami
- The Oxford Centre for Vaiṣṇava and Hindu Studies
- Dr. Charles S.J. White
- Mr. Pavan Kumar Singh for computer donation
- All organizations and persons that allowed us to microfilm their books and manuscripts.

CONTENTS

FOR INQUIRIES, REGARDING VAIṢṆAVA LITERATURE MICROFILMS' AVAILABILITIES, PLEASE CONSULT

The Adyar Library
The Theosophical Society
Adyar, Chennai (Madras), 600 020
INDIA

•

The Bodleian Library
Oxford University, Oxford,
OX1 3BG, U.K.

•

The American University Library
4400 Massachusetts Ave., N.W.
Washington, D.C. 20016
U.S.A.

PREFACE

The Materials presented here form a part of the original Vaiṣṇava Literature Conservation Project, funded by a grant from the Smithsonian Institution and the Institute for Vaiṣṇava Studies. Dr. Graham M. Schweig, Ph.D., Director, Indic Studies Program; Associate Professor of Religious Studies; Senior Editor, *Journal of Vaishnava Studies*, Department of Philosophy and Religious Studies, Christopher Newport University, Virginia, while still a graduate student, together with colleagues, originated the proposal to the Smithsonian Institution that began this endeavour. Mr. Gregory Jay (Gaurakeshava) was the Operations Manager in India. Francine Berkowitz directed the South Asia grants of the Smithsonian Institution. The total extent of the present Catalogue includes 1679 entries. The organization of the files and the preparation of the first entries in the Catalogue received support from the American Institute of Indian Studies and the Institute for Vaiṣṇava Studies. We wish to express special thanks to the Director General of the American Institute of Indian Studies, Dr. Pradeep Mehendiratta, for supplementary financing. Our deep appreciation goes to Mrs. Radha Burnier, International President of the Theosophical Society, and to Mrs. Parvati Gopalaratnam, the Librarian of the Adyar Library, for allowing us to deposit a complete set of the microfilms in the Adyar Library and to carry out the organization of the files (numbering twenty-five volumes, and the immediate source of the Catalogue), the printing from the microfilm reader-printer, and preliminary work connected with the preparation of the Catalogue. Thanks are also due to the Honorary Director of the Adyar Library, Dr. K.K. Raja for his support of this work. Dr. William Deadweiler and Mr. Robert Cohen made special contributions to creating the Catalogue project. Mr. R. Laxman and Ms. K. Jayasree, and other members of the Adyar Library staff, were of great assistance in the preparation of the Catalogue files. We thank Dr. V.K. Chari for his help in Telugu consultation. Mr. S. Venkatesh, in-charge of the computer section of the Adyar Library, and Mr. Christopher Raj gave indispensable aid in the printing of the Catalogue draughts. Our deepest thanks go to Srimati Savitridasi, who created the diacritical marks for the typing of the Catalogue and, also, provided the alphabetized index. Thanks to Gopiparanadhana Dasa for his assistance in formatting the diacritical text. We appreciate, too, the cooperation of The American University Librarian Ms. Patricia A. Wand and The Archivist Mr. George D. Arnold, assisted by Mr. Ignacio Moreno and Mr. Christopher Lewis of Media Services. Thanks go also to Dr. Gillian Evison and Ms. Lesley Forbes, of the Bodleian Library of Oxford University, for their assistance in making the microfilms available in the United Kingdom. I also express my thanks to Mr. Shaunaka Rishi Das of the Oxford Centre for Vaiṣṇava and Hindu Studies for his cooperation and to Dr. Allen W. Thrasher, Senior Reference Librarian of the Southern Asian Section of the Library of Congress, who kindly agreed to review the Catalogue.

The work rendered by Dr. S. Jayasree in annotating and Mr. S.A. Lokesh in transcribing data on the microfilms in this Catalogue was of utmost importance. The microfilm titles, listed in the Catalogue, are available for consultation in the Libraries, as mentioned in the front of the book.

DR. CHARLES S.J. WHITE
Principal Investigator

ABBREVIATIONS

B	:	Printed Book
PM	:	Paper ms
PL	:	Palm leaf ms
D	:	Devanagari
GR	:	Grantha
KAN	:	Kannada
MAL	:	Malayalam
NA	:	Nandinagari
O	:	Oriya
TA	:	Tamil
TE	:	Telugu
TU	:	Tulu
BL	:	Bengali
H	:	Hindi—(Braj Bhāṣā)
GUJ	:	Gujarati

(Sequences 1, 1; 1, 2, etc., 2,1; 2,2 etc. refer to the roll numbers and the works in order on individual rolls.)

INTRODUCTION*

I

The purpose of the Catalogue of Vaiṣṇava Literature aims to preserve the literatures of Vaiṣṇava traditions and make them accessible to scholars in India and the West through microfilm technology. Although this project is still in progress, I would like to present to you at this time what the project is, what it involves, and what we have achieved.

The Vaiṣṇava Literature Microfilm Project came to be known by the nickname, "The Matsya Project." As you know, the Matsya, incarnation of Kṛṣṇa, is described in the Bhāgavata Purāṇa as having saved the Vedas from the waters of devastation. We cannot claim to be engaged in such an ambitious project as the one Matsyāvatāra undertook. However, we hope that this project will contribute to the preservation of some of India's great spiritual literature, and increase the knowledge and appreciation of India's culture and ancient civilization.

Since this is a conference to celebrate the life and work of A.C. Bhaktivedanta Swami Prabhupada, Founder-Ācārya of the International Society for Krishna Consciousness, let me make a few references at this point as to how he might relate to this project, arising, as it did, originally from the Institute for Vaiṣṇava Studies, an ISKCON- inspired organization.

In this connection I remember my first contact with the devotees of Swami Prabhupada in Philadelphia in the late

* The Introduction was originally prepared as a Conference Paper, Autumn 1995. It does not completely reflect the state of the materials discussed–in the present time period. Nevertheless, it does give historical background to date.

1960s. In a store-front temple in Philadelphia's Center City I saw for the first time the Hari-Kṛṣṇa style manifested. I and my students came for the evening āratī. We observed the pūjā, the chanting and dancing. We ate a sampling of the temple prasād and we listened to a lecture by the youthful temple leader on a Hindu text—I believe it was the Bhagavad Gītā. The memorization of the sacred text, the expounding of an authoritative commentary, and a more personal exegesis of the import of the text for one's life: these were notable elements to observe in that formative period of ISKCON life and, I believe, have developed and flourished in the subsequent generations. Indeed, ISKCON devotees have studied for baccalaureate, masters' and doctors' degrees on the basis of their introduction to the rich intellectual tradition of India in the daily life of an ISKCON temple. Hence, the intellectual character of Bhaktivedanta's movement was evident from the very beginning. It could scarcely be otherwise, given the high-caste modalities of the ISKCON movement, and the models of sampradāya organization from which ISKCON arose—and with which, in a sense, it competed.

Sanskrit literacy and competency are among the hallmarks of high-status identity in the Hindu religious milieu. From the point of view of the Western devotees in the movement, the challenge of Sanskritization fitted the counter-culture origins of ISKCON in a very positive way. As any student knows, the mastery of a literature—all the better if it is memorized as well—is normally an irrevocable possession that helps one define one's own competence and intellectual self-worth, not only for one's self but as against the other.

All of the historical Vaiṣṇava sampradāyas developed great depth of knowledge and interpretive sophistication not only in the teachings of their own ācāryas—though that was of major importance—but also, in varying degrees, of other viewpoints. As well as argumentation of theological points, there was no doubt cross-fertilization in this process. Swami

Prabhupada recognized this himself, for example in his commentary on Caitanya-caritāmṛta, Antya-Līlā 2. 95 he wrote:

> A Vaiṣṇava should study the commentaries on Vedānta-Sūtra written by the four sampradāya-ācāryas, namely Śrī Rāmānujācārya, Mādhvācārya, Viṣṇusvāmī and Nimbārka, for these commentaries are based upon the philosophy that the Lord is the master and that all living entities are His eternal servants. One interested in studying Vedānta philosophy properly must study these commentaries, especially if he is a Vaiṣṇava. These commentaries are always adored by Vaiṣṇavas.

In his day-to-day contact with his close disciples, Swami Prabhupada was asked questions regarding the study of the whole corpus of Vaiṣṇava literature. The above quotation could be matched by others in which he advised the study of all of the Vaiṣṇava Vedānta teachers and teachings. In respect to the present project, it was Swami Prabhupada's wish that at some time in some format, a university should arise in which the Vedānta philosophy would be the focus of the curriculum, leading up to the granting of a Ph.D. degree. His original thought, I believe, was that this university would be located in Mayapur and be incorporated into the University of Calcutta system.

Even if that particular idea was modified, it became evident in those discussions that one could not have a university program without a significant library. The Matsya project, the founding of the Institute for Vaiṣṇava Studies and the undertaking of the Vaiṣṇava Literature Conservation Projects, with external funding and external academic cooperation, were and are the steps taken in that direction although of necessity with a wider application than the boundaries per se of the Bhaktivedanta Sampradāya.

With so much else going on in the ISKCON movement, including the death of the Ācārya Founder and subsequent retrenchment and reorganization, the goal of an independent academic entity at the highest level may have been obscured but not forgotten. My own recruitment into these projects was a kind of link in the chain of circumstances described above. Dr. William Deadweiler (Ravindra Swarupa Dasa) translated the concept of the university into that of an Institute for Vaiṣṇava Studies on american soil. From him (now) Dr. Graham Schweig (Garuda Dasa) became the actual agent for the foundation of the Institute. My role became that of academic sponsor and liaison between the religious and academic communities, but with the preponderance of my responsibility the professionally academic one, which brings me to the discussion I would like to present here today.

II

When we undertook the photographic work in the early 1980s, our specific task in the field was to photograph rare books and manuscripts from the Rāmānuja, Mādhva, Nimbārka, Vallabha, and Gauḍīya traditions, as well as works of other sampradāyas and individual authors. A small team of photographers and researchers spent a total of eighteen months working in India, locating, identifying and photographing numerous hand-printed, paper and palm-leaf manuscripts as well as some printed editions from these Vaiṣṇava traditions. These works were found in the collections of traditional Vaiṣṇava families, monasteries and academic institutions. In many cases these collections were very extensive. But even in the small collections, there had to be a specific way of determining what was to be filmed.

Private collections included that in the possession of Dr. K.T. Pandurangi, former head of the Sanskrit Department of the Bangalore Jñānabhāratī University. We also photographed at the Parimala Research and Publishing house near Bangalore. I photographed in the Mādhva religious centers at Udipi in the Pejwar, Palimar, Puttige and Krishnapura Maṭhs and also at the Udipi Sanskrit College. We photographed at the Rāmānujite centers in

Melkote at the Sanskrit College and the Academy of Sanskrit Research. We also did extensive microfilming in the Oriental Manuscript Library in Mysore and the Government Oriental Manuscript Library in Madras (Chennai) and in the Dr. Swaminatha Iyer Library in Madras (Chennai) and at the Vrindavan Research Institute in Vrindaban.

In the first few months of the field work, during which time the actual needs and requirements of the project became clear, we developed and refined practical and scholarly procedures for determining which texts to film for accomplishing the ultimate goal of making these literatures accessible. Here the term "accessible" is key; for it is on a conception of "accessibility" that the method of research and evaluation was developed. "Accessibility" here refers to three different levels of achieving access to literary works: the first was to identify and locate endangered Vaiṣṇava works; the second was to analyze the degree of accessibility of the texts found; and the third was to microfilm and present the works in easily available microforms. We eventually adopted the term "conservation" to indicate the overall goal of the microfilming project.

Identifying works of the subject field of literature is the first level. Such identification required consultation with librarians and scholars who knew the specific works of a tradition thoroughly, in order to form a comprehensive bibliography and to determine the location of these works. We referred to the identification of the individual works within a particular tradition as the "breadth" of a tradition's literature.

Exactly where the Vaiṣṇava field of literature ends and the literature of the Hindu complex of religious traditions begins is, of course, not precise; for the Vaiṣṇava traditions are inextricably a part of the cultural context within which they are found. However, some works within a tradition have more historical and philological importance than others, and some have more religious and philosophic significance. In addition to these types, there are texts which are not immediately within the boundaries of the tradition, but which are essential for understanding the texts proper to the tradition.

The team in the field kept a master search list which not only identified the works of particular traditions and their various locations, but also indicated priorities for filming. Therefore, a system of classifying works, according to their relation with the tradition, was devised as the first level in the evaluation of texts. In consultation with the Indian experts, the letter symbols "A", "B" and "C" were assigned to the texts on the search list.

"A" works represented that part of the literature which formed the foundation, or nucleus of a tradition. Such works stand out in the literary history of a sect, and are regarded by the members of the sect as the most important. An "A" work is most likely to have been well-preserved by the tradition. Therefore, filming of multiple editions in the "A" category might be less urgent than those in the "B" category, except in the cases where an additional edition is determined to be particularly important, or when previously unknown or undiscovered "A" works are found.

"B" works are not as central as "A" works, but, as we mentioned, are not necessarily less important. They are frequently discussions and elaborations of the ideas in "A" works. This category of works is usually the largest in any tradition, and although they may be considered by the sect as less important than the "A" works, they are often essential texts for understanding the history of the sect as well as other important historical data. The "B" works of the Vaiṣṇava traditions are the least known and have been the most neglected.

"C" works lie outside the tradition, but are needed to understand the "A" and "B" works. These will usually be classical texts, viz certain purāṇas, upaniṣads and vedāṅgas, which are often presented with sectarian commentaries, or works from other schools of thought to which an "A" or "B" work is a development or a response.

The second level of evaluating the accessibility of Vaiṣṇava texts requires that we identify the different editions of a particular work. Since the number of works in any tradition is greatly increased by the number of varying editions that one finds for each work, and since it is impossible to film every edition of every work, considerations had to be given to the variations between editions and to what made one edition more desirable than another. The number of editions and variations of a particular work are what we refer to as the "depth" of a tradition's literature. Of course, it would be ideal to record every edition as well as every scrap of every work to aid scholars in putting together critical editions. But this was beyond the means of the present project.

Editions of works vary greatly. Age, authenticity, language, script, legibility, physical condition, and form constituted the different factors by which one edition could be evaluated as more accessible—and hence, more "conserved"—than another edition.

All of the variables under each of these seven accessibility or conservation factors are in an order of preference. If a manuscript were judged to be very old and close to the original, this made for better conservation. The language and/or script in which the text was found, the exact content or authenticity of the work, the age, legibility, etc., all had to be considered together to determine the accessibility of each work. In some cases, however, several editions of a work were filmed, e.g., the Bhāgavata Purāṇa.

The practical issue arises as to how these various factors of conservability could be determined by any one scholar, for there were thousands of possible works from various sects within the Vaiṣṇava tradition, which were spread all over India and found in numerous languages and scripts. To be guided in these crucial questions of accessibility, the field methodology included collaboration with expert Indian academic and Vaiṣṇava scholars. It was with their assistance and knowledge that accessibility factors were analyzed.

The third level of achieving access and conservation had to do with the technical microphotographic procedures. (I wish to set aside, for the moment, the technicalities of the cameras and films themselves, the variations in voltage, the failure of electricity, the use of portable generators and the like, as not germane to my purpose here today.) I would like to sketch a picture for your imagination or mind's eye of the step-by-step procedures in the field work:

1. The Field Director consulted with scholars to define the breadth of the tradition's writings, and he began to form a comprehensive bibliography, to which more works might be added as the work proceeded. On this search list, the location, the importance, and the "breadth" category "A", "B", or "C" was indicated.
2. The next step was to gain permission from the proprietors of collections for filming—in some cases government officials—and to research the holdings in such collections if there were no catalogue.
3. With the help of a pandit/scholar (in many cases the librarian of the collection), we compiled a working bibliography of the particular collection to determine the quality of various editions, i.e., the depth analysis and which of those texts should be filmed.
4. The Operations Manager, Mr. Gregory Jay (Gaurakeshava), travelled with the photographic team to the site of filming, installed the equipment, made living arrangements for the team personnel, and scheduled times for filming.
5. The project's bibliographer worked closely with the local pandit, taking down all the basic bibliographic informations and entering it onto the project's bibliographic record sheet.
6. The bibliographer established a bibliographic control number for the text and entered it onto the bibliographic record sheet. This control number, which indicated the tradition, author, work, edition

and number of the microfilm roll, was helpful to the present task of creating the finite catalogue.

7. The pandit checked the manuscript for any missing pages, as well as to see that the pages were in correct order. If there were any unusual aspects observed by the pandit, then the bibliographer made note of them on the record sheet.
8. The bibliographer gave the microfilm photographer the bibliographic record sheet along with the manuscript to be filmed. The bibliographic record was photographed first, then each folio of a manuscript, or the opened two pages of a book, were filmed.
9. The photographer had the task of turning the folios or pages for long hours. He checked again for irregularities in the folio or page order. Simultaneously he made sure that the thickness of the book or pile of manuscript folios remained within the depth-of-field range of the camera. He also was concerned to watch the fluctuation of the electrical current as indicated in the camera stabilizer.
10. While the photographer filmed, the bibliographer registered the author and title of the work being filmed, along with its control number in an alphabetically arranged card catalogue. This catalogue contained all the works filmed, and was checked for previously filmed materials to prevent unnecessary duplication. Then the bibliographer, with the aid of the librarian, began to prepare the next text to be filmed. In the case of palm-leaf manuscripts—once we had discovered the technique, somewhat late in the first year of the project —preparation might entail oiling each individual palm-leaf to make the script more visible to the camera by producing a greater contrast between the script and its background.
11. The bibliographer also kept a master author list, which was simply an easy reference list of all the bibliographic control numbers which have been assigned to different

authors. Each time the work of a new author was filmed, the new author number was registered on this list.

12. After the day's filming, the equipment had to be stored safely. Often the on-site librarian or pandit helped with this and other security aspects of the filming work.
13. The operations manager directed the above procedures, attempted to solve the problems which arose, and improved the overall efficiency of the work. When rolls of film were completed, he developed the films.
14. The operations manager inspected the films to determine whether there were "major" or "minor" defects in the work, which could be of three kinds: defects from human error, from technical photographic problems, or from problems in the processing of film.
15. When twenty rolls of film had been developed and inspected, they were delivered to the field director who dispatched them to the U.S. (in those days via the diplomatic pouch) for further editing, bibliographic organization and other archival work. This was the final step in the field work. (I am indebted to [then] Mr. Graham Schweig for aspects of the conceptualization of Part II.)

III

Ten years passed. In the interval the Smithsonian grant was renewed at about $50,000.00, which would have enabled us to photograph a considerably larger number of Vaiṣṇava works. However, due to a change in Government of India regulations as applied to this project, we were not able to renew Government of India authorization at that time. Smithsonian kept our funds aside for some time, but eventually they were applied to other projects.

In 1992 I made a brief trip to India and met with Dr. Pradeep Mehendiratta, Director General of the American

Institute of Indian Studies. He suggested that the time might be propitious to request permission from the Government of India to renew the project. Once the permission had been granted, he advised, then it would be possible to request funding. I followed his advice and the authorization was granted by the GOA in the spring of 1993. After that I launched numerous requests for funding with practically no success until, finally, in July of 1994 The American Institute of Indian Studies granted me a short-term award with stipend and research support for four months. (Since it had previously seemed likely that I would be able to bring some kind of closure to the VLCP, during the fall of 1993 and the spring of 1994 I was able to obtain from the American University College of Arts and Sciences a research grant to support a student's work in entering on diskettes the alphabetical catalogue referred to above.)

Thereafter, with the realization that I could not undertake anything like the large scale project of the original Smithsonian grant, I decided that the most useful thing to do in India would be to begin annotation of selected works from the existing microfilm collection. India would be the place where I could find the technical linguistic competence to be able to carry out such work. Thus, when I finally left for India in February of 1995, I brought with me over one hundred microfilm rolls of the duplicate set that had been made from the originals on file in the archives of the Bender Library of the American University. Some of these films had been reviewed by Mr. Brian Marvin over a several year period; so I had the results of his evaluation of film quality to start my own work through his annotations on the file boxes of the microfilms.

My first idea had been to go to Pune to the Deccan College language centre for assistance from its staff. However, projected costs for the work there proved too prohibitive in the terms of my small AIIS award; hence, I changed the venue to the Adyar Library and Research Centre of the

Theosophical Society in Madras where I had frequently visited previously and was well-acquainted with both living and working conditions.

My work began at the Adyar Library and Research Centre under the sponsorship of Dr. K. Kunjunni Raja, the Honorary Director of the Library, and retired Professor of Sanskrit of Madras University. I had thought to start out by selecting a hundred works from the two to three thousand in the collection for close description and annotation. I examined the Adyar Library manuscript catalogues and consulted with Dr. Raja on a daily basis to determine the best procedure to accomplish this. The Adyar Library had acquired a Minolta Reader-printer of recent vintage. This was in the microphotography section of the Library. The microphotography section was currently not in production because of problems with a camera. As a consequence, I had nearly exclusive use of the facility throughout the period of the the four-month grant.

In the first couple of weeks of my work there I tried the approach of having a Sanskrit scholar to copy out the first and last pages of the works for the later annotation. The person who was training for this work suddenly left because of a family illness. This gave me the opportunity to reconsider the purpose and methodology of the project. Since we had both printed works and manuscripts to deal with, it was obvious that there were different concerns of accessibility and dissemination.

For some weeks subsequently, I worked by myself in the microfilm lab, progressing through the works in numerical order. I began to see that what was actually needed in this phase of the project was to do a complete survey—insofar as possible—of the whole collection. (The meticulous work of the alphabetical bibliography, referred to above, was difficult in some ways to coordinate with the bibliographic records of the actual film rolls.)

The procedure of establishing the "Finite Catalogue," as I have come to call it, gradually emerged as follows:

1. We set the goal of photocopying the bibliographic record page and the first and the last one or two pages of each work itself; to provide information regarding the author, commentators—if any—scribe, and the like. (A considerable amount of the research money for the project went toward paying the Adyar Library its customary photocopy charge of Rs. 1.50 per frame. I also paid for Minolta service charges during the period of the grant.)
2. These pages were then gathered together in files, according to roll number and roll sequence number. (The number of works varies from roll to roll, depending on their length.)
3. We made a series of files and numbered them in Roman numeral sequence.
4. When all the rolls we had, had been seen, and the printouts filed appropriately, we counted the number of works to appear in the initial catalogue: 1,045 (now 1,679).
5. We surveyed the number of different languages by works and indicated this with the aggregate number of works per file. It is a common phenomenon in South India for Sanskrit to be written in other scripts besides Devanāgarī. We include among our collection examples of this in Tulu-Malayalam, Telugu, Grantha and Kannada. We also have vernacular works in Hindi, Braj Bhāṣā, Bengali, and Gujarati to name some of them.

In the course of developing the "Finite Catalogue," I hired Mr. S.A. Lokesh to do the printing of bibliographic record pages and first and last pages and to be general research assistant. Although not a Sanskritist, he was a young scholar with excellent command of English and with good knowledge of Tamil, Marathi and Sanskrit. Dr. S. Jayasree was hired to check the accuracy of author and title against the bibliographic records and sample pages in Sanskrit. She also reads Grantha and Hindi. Other scholars will be needed for reviewing records in Telugu, Bengali, Gujarati, as mentioned above; since not all of the Vaiṣṇava works are in Sanskrit, irrespective of the script.

Although the project has been temporarily interrupted, progress has already been made in entering data by hand into notebooks from which the finite catalogue will be created. The formula used is that of the Adyar Library Manuscript Catalogue system. (Because of Government of India regulations for funding purposes, the Adyar Catalogue is printed in columns across two pages—spread-sheetwise. This will probably not be done in the present catalogue):

1. Serial number
2. Roll and roll sequence number
3. Author
4. Title
5. Commentator
6. Material (palmleaf, paper, et. al.)
7. Language
8. Script
9. Size (length and width)
10. Folios
11. Pages/leaves
12. Condition and age
13. Additional particulars

Since we have already preserved the books and manuscripts of this collection through microphotography, some of the Adyar Library categories should be interpreted as applying to the special conditions of microphotographed works. (In actual fact, the Catalogue, as it now exists, includes mainly information under numbers 1 to 8 in the list above but not always in every instance.)

In conclusion I should say that the second phase of this microfilm project, called Vaiṣṇava Literature Conservation Project II, is not finished. I left India in July to return to the United States for the following, among other reasons: (a) the AIIS grant was nearly finished—although on the eve of my departure, an unexpected additional month's stipend, sans research expenses, was allocated at Smithsonian request. When I return, I will somehow have to manage to complete the work to the fullest extent possible with available funding, which I have been seeking to augment; (b) I felt that I needed, at least, a laptop computer and diskettes to enter the catalogue in a format that could be scrutinized by my Indian collaborators on the scene. I am happy to report that, since my return, through the good offices of Dr. William Deadweiler and the BBT, a laptop has been given to me on loan, with Words Perfect 5. 1 installed so the I can do that work more efficiently at the most convenient location. I am very grateful for that. (c) While working at the Adyar Library, I became aware of certain other aspects of American-Indian cooperation in the area of library resources, and while in the United States, in these past several months, I have tried to develop some of that area of the overall issue of conservation and accessibility, including the Vaiṣṇava Literature conservation Projects.

I am sure that everyone here will agree that Bhaktivedanta Swami Prabhupada's insight and intuition, regarding the intellectual flowering of his own Kṛṣṇa devotees and followers, should not be forfeited. This small project, I believe, has a positive roll to play in this, as well as in more general ways. In his introduction to the Śrīmad Bhāgavatam, Prabhupada wrote:

> Many devotees of Lord Caitanya like Śrīla Vṛndāvana Dāsa Ṭhākura, Śrī Locana Dāsa Ṭhākura, Śrīla Kṛṣṇadāsa Kavirāja Gosvāmī, Śrī Kavikarṇapūra, Śrī Prabodhānanda Sarasvatī, Śrī Rūpa Gosvāmī, Śrī Sanātana Gosvāmī, Śrī Raghunātha Bhaṭṭa Gosvāmī, Śrī Jīva Gosvāmī, Śrī Gopāla Bhaṭṭa Gosvāmī, Śrī Raghunātha Dāsa Gosvāmī and in this latter age within [the last] two hundred years, Śrī Viśvanātha Cakravartī, Śrī Baladeva Vidyābhūṣana, Śrī Śyāmānanda Gosvāmī, Śrī Narottama dāsa Ṭhākura, Śrī Bhaktivinoda Ṭhākura and at last Śrī Bhaktisiddhānta

Sarasvatī Ṭhākura (our spiritual master), and many other great and renowned scholars and devotees of the Lord, have prepared voluminous books and literatures on the life and precepts of the Lord. Such literatures are...based on the śāstras...the Vedas, Purāṇas, Upaniṣads, Rāmāyaṇa, Mahābhārata and other histories and authentic literatures approved by the recognized ācāryas. They are unique in composition and unrivaled in presentation, and they are full of transcendental knowledge. Unfortunately, the people of the world are still ignorant of them, but when these literatures come to light the world, and when they are presented before thinking people, then India's glory and the message of love will overflood this morbid world, which is vainly searching after peace and prosperity by various illusory methods not approved by the ācāryas in the chain of disciplic succession.

A CATALOGUE OF VAIṢṆAVA LITERATURE

0001 Īśāvāsyopaniṣat Khaṇḍārtha (with text); *Rāghavendra Yati;* B; 1, 1; SKT, D.

0002 Kāṭhakopaniṣat Khaṇḍārtha (with text); *Rāghavendra Yati;* B; 1, 2; SKT, D.

0003 Ṣaṭpraśnopaniṣat Khaṇḍārtha (with text); *Rāghavendra Tīrtha;* B; 1, 3; SKT, D.

0004 Aitareyopaniṣat Khaṇḍārtha (with text); by a disciple of *Bhārakarī Veṅkaṭavarāhācārya;* B; 1, 4; SKT, D.

0005 Chāndogyopaniṣat Arthasaṅgraha (with text); *Rāghavendra Yati*; B; 1, 5; SKT, D.

0006 Bṛhadāraṇyakopaniṣat Bhāṣyārthasaṅgraha (with text); *Rāghavendra Yati*; B; 1, 6; SKT, D.

0007 Kāṭhakopaniṣad Bhāṣyaṭīkā or Kāṭhakavyāsa Tīrthīya Ṭīkā; *Vyāsa Tīrtha*; B; 1, 7; SKT, D; 1905 A.D.

0008 Ātharvaṇa Bhāṣya Ṭīkā; *Vyāsa Tīrtha Yati;* B; 1, 8; SKT, D; 1903.

0009 Māṇḍūkya Bhāṣya Ṭīkā; *Vyāsa Tīrtha Muni;* B; 1, 9; SKT, D; 1904 A.D.

0010 Talavakāra Upaniṣad Bhāṣya Vivaraṇa; *Vedeśa Tīrtha Bhikṣu;* B; 1, 10; SKT, D; 1907 A.D.

0011 Kāṭhaka Upaniṣad Bhāṣya Ṭīkā; *Vedeśa Bhikṣu*; B; 1, 11; SKT, D; 1905 A.D.

0012 Bṛhadāraṇyaka Bhāṣya Ṭīkā (Para Brahma Prakāśikā); *Raghūttama Yati*; B; 1, 12, SKT, D; 1907 A.D.

0013 Aitareya Bhāṣya Ṭīkā (Aitareya Bhāṣyārtha Ratna Mālā); (Tāmraparṇī) *Śrīnivāsa*; B; 1, 13, SKT, D; 1908 A.D.

0014 Ātharvaṇa Upaniṣad Bhāṣya Vivaraṇam; (Umarji) *Kṛṣṇācāryasūri*; B; 1, 14; SKT, D; 1903 A.D.

0015 Ṣaṭpraśna Bhāṣya Ṭīkā Vivaraṇa; *Maṅkāla Dharmācārya*; B; 1, 15; SKT, D; 1907 A.D.

0016 Taittirīya Upaniṣad Bhāṣya Ṭīkā; *Śrīnivāsa Tīrtha*; B; 1, 16; SKT, D; 1905 A.D.

0017 Māṇḍūkya Upaniṣad Bhāṣya Vivṛti-Padārthadīpikā; *Śrīnivāsa Tīrtha*; B; 1, 17; SKT, D; 1904 A.D.

0018 Bhagavad Gītā Bhāṣya with Prameya Dīpikā (with two Ṭippaṇīs); *Madhva*; B; 1, 18; SKT, D; 1887 A.D.

0019 Bhagavad Gītā Bhāṣya with Prameya Dīpikā (or) Gītā Bhāṣya Prameya Dīpikā); *Madhva*; B; 1, 19.

0020 Bhagavad Gītā Bhāṣyaprameya Dīpikābhāvaratna Kośa; *Sumatīndra Tīrtha*; B; 1, 20; SKT, D.

0021 Gītātātparya Pañcikā with Nyāya Dīpa (with a Ṭippaṇī); *Madhva*; B; 1, 21; SKT, D; 1905 A.D.

0022 Gītātātparya Pañcikā with Nyāya Dīpa (with Ṭippaṇī); *Madhva*; B; 2,1; SKT, D; 1905 A. D.; (Continuation of 0021).

0023 Bhagavad Gītā with Vivṛti; *Rāghavendra Yati*; B; 2, 2; SKT, D; 1905 A.D.

0024 Bhāgavata with padaratnāvalīṭīkā; *Vyāsa*; B; 2, 3; SKT, D; Śaka 1790, 1868 A.D.

0025 Bhāgavata Ṭippaṇī; *Satyadharma Yati*; B; 2,4; SKT, D.

0026 Śrīmad Bhāgavatam; *Kṛṣṇadvaipāyana Vyāsa*; B; 3, 1; SKT, D; Śaka 1850, 1928 A.D.

0027 Nyāyasudhā; *Jayatīrtha;* PM; 3, 2; SKT, D.

0028 Nyāyasudhā; *Jayatīrtha*; PM; 3,3 SKT, D; (Continuation of 0027).

0029 Bhāgavata Ṭippaṇī (Sajjanahita); *Ceṭṭi Veṅkaṭādri*; B; 3, 4; SKT, D; Śaka 1850, 1928 A. D.

0030 Śrīmad Bhāgavata Ṭippaṇī-Mandanandinī; *Vyāsatattvajña Tīrtha*; B; 3, 5; SKT, D; 1928 A. D.

0031 Śrīmad Bhāgavata Ṭippaṇī- Padamuktāvalī; *Limverī Śrīnivāsa*; B; 3, 6; Śaka 1850, 1928 A. D.

0032 Śrīmad Bhāgavata Ṭippaṇī-Mandabodhinī; *Śeṣa* (*Disciple of Chalārī Narasiṁhācārya*); B; 3, 7; SKT, D; Śaka 1850, 1928 A. D.

0033 Śrīmad Bhāgavata Ṭippaṇī; *Śrīnivāsa Tīrtha*; B; 3, 8; SKT, D; Śaka 1850, 1928 A.D.

0034 Ṛk Sūcī: Alphabetical Index of the Mantras from Mantrārtha Mañjarī; B; 3, 9; SKT, D; Śaka 1874, 1907 A.D.

0035 Ṛg Bhāṣya; *Madhva/Ānanda Tīrtha*; B; 3, 10; SKT, D; Śaka 1824, 1902 A.D.

0036 Ṛg Bhāṣya Ṭīkā; *Jayatīrtha Bhikṣu*; B; 3, 11; SKT, D; Śaka 1823, 1901 A.D.

0037 Ṛg Bhāṣya Ṭīkā Vivṛti; *Chalārī Narasiṁhācārya*; B; 3, 12; SKT, D; Śaka 1824, 1902 A.D.

0038 Śrīman Mantrārtha Mañjarī; *Rāghavendra Tīrtha*; B; 3, 13; SKT, D; Śaka 1824, 1902 A.D.

0039 Nyāya Vivaraṇam; *Raghūttama Tīrtha*; B; 3, 14; SKT, D.

0040 Kāṭhakopaniṣad Khaṇḍārtha; *Rāghavendra Yati*; B; 3,15; SKT, D.

0041 Kathā Lakṣaṇa Vivaraṇa; *Jayatīrtha Bhikṣu*; B; 3, 16; SKT, D.

0042 Māyāvādakhaṇḍana Vivaraṇa; *Jayatīrtha Bhikṣu*; B; 3, 17; SKT, D.

0043 Māyāvādakhaṇḍana (Mandāra Mañjarī) Ṭīkā Bhāvaprakāśikā; *Vyāsa Yati*; B; 3, 18; SKT, D.

0044 Māyāvādakhaṇḍana Pañcikāvyākhyā; *Śrīnivāsa Tīrtha*; B; 3, 19; SKT, D; Śaka 1818, 1896 A.D.

0045 Prapañca Mithyātvānumāna Khaṇḍana (Mandāramañjarī) (Bhāvaprakāśikā); *Vyāsa Yati*; B; 3, 20; SKT, D; Śaka 1818 1896 A.D.

0046 Prapañca Mithyātvānumāna Khaṇḍana Vivaraṇa; *Jayatīrthabhikṣu*; B; 3, 21; SKT, D; Śaka 1818, 1896 A.D.

0047 Tattva Viveka Vivaraṇam; *Jayatīrthabhikṣu*; B; 3, 22; SKT, D; Śaka 1818, 1896 A.D.

0048 Pramāṇa Paddhati Bhāva Dīpa; *Rāghavendra Yati*; B; 3, 23; SKT, D.

0049 Prapañca Mithyātvānumāna Khaṇḍana Pañcikā; *Śrīnivāsa Tīrtha*; B; 3, 24; SKT, D; Śaka 1818, 1896 A.D.

0050 Tattva Saṁkhyāna Vivaraṇa; *Jayatīrtha Bhikṣu*; B; 3, 25; SKT, D.

0051 Upādhikhaṇḍana Vyākhyāvivṛti; *Śrīnivāsa Tīrtha*; B; 3, 26; SKT, D; Śaka 1818, 1896 A.D.

0052 Talavakāropaniṣadkhaṇḍārthaḥ; *Rāghavendra Yati*; B; 3, 27; SKT, D; Śaka 1819, 1897 A.D.

0053 Pramāṇalakṣaṇa Ṭīkā (Nyāya Kalpalatā); *Jayatīrtha Bhikṣu*; B; 3, 28; SKT, D; Śaka 1820, 1898 A.D.

0054 Pramāṇalakṣaṇa Ṭīkā (Bhāvadīpa); *Rāghavendra Yati*; B; 3, 29; SKT, D; Śaka 1820, 1898 A.D.

0055 Ṣaṭpraśna Bhāṣya Ṭīkā; *Jayatīrtha*; B; 3, 30; SKT, D.

0056 Kāṭhaka Upaniṣad Bhāṣya Ṭīkā; *Vyāsa Tīrtha*; B; 3, 31; SKT D; 1905 A.D.

0057 Talavakāropaniṣadkhaṇḍārthaḥ; *Rāghavendra Yati*; B; 3, 32; SKT, D; 1907 A.D.

0058 Talavakāra Upaniṣad Bhāṣyavivaraṇam; *Vedeśa Tīrtha Bhikṣu*; B; 3, 33; SKT, D; 1907 A.D.

0059 Talavakāra Upaniṣad Bhāṣya Vivaraṇa; *Vyāsatīrtha*; B; 3, 34; SKT, D; 1907 A.D.

0060 Kāṭhaka Upaniṣad Bhāṣya Ṭīkā (Padārthakaumudī); *Vedeśa Bhikṣu*; B; 3, 35; SKT, D; 1905 A.D.

0061 Ṣaṭpraśna Bhāṣya Ṭīkā Vivaraṇam; *Maṅkāla Dharmācārya*; B; 3, 36; SKT, D; 1907 A.D.

0062 Tattvasaṁkhyāna Ṭippaṇī; *Satyadharma Yati*; B; 3, 37; SKT, D.

0063 Taittirīya Upaniṣad Bhāṣya Vivaraṇa; *Vyāsa Tīrtha*; B; 3, 38; SKT, D; 1905 A.D.

0064 Īśāvāsya Bhāṣya Ṭīkā Vivṛtiḥ; *Raghunātha Tīrtha*; B; 3, 39; SKT, D; 1907 A.D.

0065 Śrī Sadācāra Smṛti Ṭīkā with Vākyārthavivṛti; *Ānandatīrtha*; B; 3, 40; SKT, D; Śaka 1804, 1882 A.D.

0066 Śrīmad Brahma Sūtra Bhāṣya Ṭīkā Tattva Prakāśikā; *Jayatīrtha*; PM; 3, 41; SKT, D.

0067 Śrīmad Brahma Sūtra Bhāṣya Ṭīkā Tattva Prakāśikā; *Jayatīrtha*; PM; 4, 1; SKT, D; (Continuation of 0066).

0068 Bṛhadāraṇya Bhāṣya Ṭīkā Parabrahma Prakāśikā; *Raghūttama Tīrtha*; B; 4, 2; SKT, D; 1907 A.D.

0069 Śrī Vyāsagadyaṁ; *Yadupatyācārya*; B; 4, 3; SKT, D.

0070 Sattattvaratnamālā Vyākhyā; *Ānandatīrtha* s/o *Śrīmadviṭṭhalācārya*; B; 4, 4; SKT, D; 1918 A.D.

0071 Aitareya Bhāṣyārtha Ratnamālā; *Tāmraparaṇī Śrīnivāsa*; B; 4, 5; SKT, D; 1908 A.D.

0072 Gītā Tātparya Nirṇaya Nyāya Dīpakiraṇāvalī Ṭippaṇī; *Śrīnivāsa Tīrtha*; B; 4, 6; SKT, D; 1905 A.D.

0073 Tattvaprakāśikā Vākyārthamañjarī; *Śrīnivāsatīrtha*; B; 4, 7; SKT, D.

0074 Nyāyaratnāvalī with Prakāśasaṅgraha; *Vādirājatīrtha*; B; 4, 8; SKT, D.

0075 Kapilagītā (with Ṭīkā and Artha in Kannada); *Kṛṣṇa Dvaipāyana Vyāsa*; B; 4, 9; SKT, D; Śaka 1836, 1914 A.D.

0076 Śrīmat Saṁgraha Rāmāyaṇa (with Vyākhyā); *Nārāyaṇa Paṇḍita Ācārya*; PM; 4, 10; SKT, D; c. 1830 A.D.

0077 Vāgvaikharī; *Vijayīndra Bhikṣu*; PM; 4, 11; SKT, D; c. 1700

0078 Nārāyaṇopaniṣad Ṭippaṇī; *Śrī Dhīrendra Tīrtha*; PM; 4, 12; SKT, D; c. 1780.

0079 Śārīraka Mīmāṁsā (Rāmānuja Bhāṣya Anusārī); *Vijayīndra Bhikṣu*; PM; 4, 13; SKT, D.

0080 Tātparya Candrikā Adhikaraṇamālā; *Vijayīndra Tīrtha*; B; 4, 14; SKT, D.

0081 Viṣṇu Stuti Vyākhyā; *Vijayīndra Yati*; PM; 4, 15; SKT, D.

0082 Para Tattva Prakāśikā; *Śrī Vijayīndra Tīrtha*; PL; 4, 16; SKT, NA.

0083 Bheda Vidyā Vilāsa (Opposition to Narasiṁhāśrama Muni's Bheda Vikāra); *Śrī Vijayīndra Tīrtha*; PL; 4, 17; SKT, NA; c. 1600 A.D.

0084 Vāda Mālikā; *Śrī Vijayīndra Tīrtha*; PL; 4, 18; SKT, NA; c. 1600 A.D.

0085 Tarka Tāṇḍava Vyākhyā; *Śrī Vijayīndra Tīrtha*; PL; 4, 19; SKT, NA; c. 1652 A.D.

0086 Māyāvāda Khaṇḍana Vyākhyā Mandāra Mañjarī; *Vyāsarāja (Tīrtha)*; PL; 4, 20; SKT, NA.

0087 Mithyātvānumānakhaṇḍana Mandāra Mañjarī; *Vyāsarāja (Tīrtha)*; PL; 4, 21; SKT, NA.

0088 Upādhi Khaṇḍana Mandāra Mañjarī; *Vyāsarāja (Tīrtha)*; PL; 4, 22; SKT, NA.

0089 Tarka Tāṇḍava Vyākhyāna-Nyāyadīpa; *Śrī Rāghavendra Tīrtha*; PM; 4, 23; SKT, D; c. 1660 A.D.

0090 Tarka Tāṇḍava Vivaraṇavivṛti-Nyāyadīpa (Continuation of 0089); *Śrī Rāghavendra Yati*; PM; 5, 1; SKT, D; c. 1660 A.D.

0091 Bhāvaratnakośa on Jayatīrtha's Prameyadīpikā?; *Sumatīndra Tīrtha?*; PM; 5, 2; SKT, D; c. 1720 A.D.

0092 Bhāvaratnakośa on Bhaṭṭabhāṣyaṭīkā (First Part, Second Chapter Only); *Mudduveṅkaṭakṛṣṇa*; PM; 5, 3; SKT, D.

0093 Nyāyamauktikamālā; *Śrī Vijayīndra Tīrtha*; PM; 5, 4; SKT, D. c. 1580 A.D.

0094 Narasiṁhastuti with Vyākhyā 'Ekāvalī'; *Trivikrama Paṇḍitācāryaḥ*; PM; 5, 5; SKT, D; c. 17th century.

0095 Bhāvavarṇana on Tattvasaṅkhyāna Vyākhyā; *Vijayīndra*; PM, 5, 6; SKT, D; c. 1500 A.D.

0096 Bhāgavata Vyākhyā; *Sudhīndra Tīrtha*; PM; 5, 7; SKT, D; c. 1620 A.D.

0097 Ṛgbhāṣya Ṭīkā; *Jayatīrtha*; PM; 5, 8; SKT, D; c. 14th century.

0098 Tattvodyota Ṭippaṇī; *Vijayīndra Tīrtha*; PM; 5, 9; SKT, D; c. 1600 A.D.

0099 Māṇḍūkya Upaniṣad Khaṇḍārtha; *Rāghavendra Tīrtha*; PL; 5, 10; SKT, NA.

0100 Ātharvaṇa Upaniṣat Khaṇḍārtha; *Rāghavendra Tīrtha*; PL; 5, 11; SKT, NA.

0101 Kāṭhakopaniṣad Khaṇḍārtha; *Rāghavendra Tīrtha*; PL; 5, 12; SKT, D.

0102 Ṣaṭ Praśna Upaniṣad Khaṇḍārtha; *Rāghavendra Tīrtha*; PL; 5, 13; SKT, D.

0103 Taittirīya Upaniṣad Khaṇḍārtha; *Rāghavendra Tīrtha*; PL; 5, 14; SKT, D.

0104 Parimala: (on Nyāya Sudhā of Jayatīrtha); *Rāghavendra Tīrtha;* PL; 5, 15; SKT, D.

0105 Bhāva Dīpā on Tattva Prakāśikā of Jayatīrtha; PL; 5, 16; SKT, D.

0106 Nirdoṣatva Vāda; *Veṅkaṭa Varāhācārya of Bhāskara Family*; PM; 5, 17; SKT, D.

0107 Īśāvāsya Bhāṣya Ṭīkā; *Jayatīrtha*; PM; 5, 18; SKT, TU.

0108 Māyāvāda Khaṇḍana Ṭīkā; *Ānandatīrtha*; PM; 5, 19; SKT, TU.

0109 Bhedojjīvanakāśikā; *Kāśītimannācārya*; PM; 5, 20; SKT, TU.

0110 Upādhikhaṇḍana Ṭīkā on Tattvaprakāśa by Ānandatīrtha; *Jayatīrtha*; PM; 5, 21; SKT, TU.

0111 Mandāra Mañjarī on Jayatīrtha's Tattvavivekaṭīkā; *Vyāsatīrtha*; PM; 5, 22; SKT, TU.

0112 Mandāra Mañjarī on Māyāvādakhaṇḍanaṭīkā; *Vyāsayati*; PM; 5, 23; SKT, TU.

0113 Mandāra Mañjarī on Jayatīrtha's Upādhikhaṇḍanaṭīkā; *Vyāsayati*; PM; 5, 24; SKT, TU.

0114 Tattvasaṅkhyāna Ṭippaṇī; *Upādhyāya*; PM; 5, 25; SKT, TU.

0115 Mandāra Mañjarī on Jayatīrtha's Mithyātvānumānakhaṇḍana; *Vyāsayati*; PM; 5, 26; SKT, TU.

0116 Vādāvalī; *Jayatīrtha*; PM; 5, 27; SKT, TU.

0117 Bhagavad Gītā; *Kṛṣṇa Dvaipāyanavyāsa;* PM; 5, 28; SKT, TU.

0118 Ṣaṭpraśnopaniṣadbhāṣyaṭīkā; *Jayatīrtha*; PM; 5, 29; SKT, TU.

0119 Vādāvalī; *Jayatīrtha*; PM; 5, 30; SKT, TU.

0120 Pramāṇa Paddhati; *Jayatīrtha*; PM; 5, 31; SKT, TU.

0121 Prameya Dīpikā on Madhva's Gītābhāṣya; *Jayatīrtha*; PM; 5, 32; SKT, TU.

0122 Pavamāna Sūkta; PM; 5, 33; SKT, D.

0123 Tīrtha Prabandha; *Vādirāja Tīrtha*; PM; 5, 34; SKT, TU.

0124 Viṣṇustuti with Vyākhyā (Viṣṇusaṁstavasadvyākhyāpradīpaḥ); *Trivikrama Paṇḍitācārya*; PM; 5, 35; SKT, TU.

0125 Bhārata Vyākhyā; *Vimala Bodha*; PM; 5, 36; SKT, TU.

0126 Tattvaprakāśikā; *Jayatīrtha*; PM; 5, 37; SKT, TU.

0127 Śrīmad Bhāgavata (Cantos 9 & 10); *Kṛṣṇa Dvaipāyana Vyāsa*; PM; 5, 38; SKT, TU.

0128 Śrīmad Bhāgavata; *Kṛṣṇa Dvaipāyana Vyāsa*; PM; 6, 1; SKT, TU. continues 5, 38.

0129 Māyāvāda Khaṇḍana (Pañcikā) Bhāvaprakāśikā; *Vyāsatīrtha/Vyāsayati*; PM; 6, 2; SKT, D.

0130 Prapañca Mithyātvānumāna Khaṇḍana (Pañcikā) Bhāvaprakāśikā; *Vyāsatīrtha*; PM; 6, 3; SKT, D.

0131 Tattvaviveka (Pañcikā) (Bhāvaprakāśikā); *Vyāsatīrtha/Vyāsayati*; PM; 6, 4; SKT, D.

0132 Tattva Viveka (pañcikā) Ṭīkā (Bhāvaprakāśikā); *Vyāsatīrtha/Vyāsayati*; PM; 6, 5; SKT, D.

0133 Nṛsiṁhakavacamālāmantra from Nṛsiṁhapurāṇa; *Kṛṣṇadvaipāyana Vyāsa*; PM; 6, 6; SKT, D.

0134 Lakṣmīnṛsiṁhasahasranāma Stotram; *Kṛṣṇadvaipāyana Vyāsa*; PM; 6, 7; SKT, D.

0135 Ādityahṛdaya of Bhaviṣyottara Purāṇa; *Kṛṣṇadvaipāyana Vyāsa*; PM; 6, 8; SKT, D.

0136 Yamaka Bhāratam; *Madhvācārya/Ānandatīrtha*; PM; 6, 9; SKT, D.

0137 Māṇḍūkyopaniṣad and Kaṭhalakṣaṇa; *Madhvācārya*; PM; 6, 10; SKT, D.

0138 Īśavāsya Bhāṣya Ṭīkā-Vivaraṇa (of Ānandatīrtha's Yajñīya Mantra Bhāṣya); *Jayatīrtha*; PM; 6, 11; SKT, D.

0139 Tattvodyota; *Madhvācārya/Ānandatīrtha*; PM; 6, 12; SKT, D.

0140 Rāmāyaṇa Sundarakāṇḍa; *Vālmīki*; PM; 6, 13; SKT, D.

0141 Kṛṣṇāmṛta Mahārṇava; *Madhvācārya/Ānandatīrtha*; PM; 6, 14; SKT, D.

0142 Nṛsiṁha Stuti Vyākhyā; *Viśvapati Tīrtha*; PM; 6, 15; SKT, D.

0143 Nakhastuti and Harivāyustuti (Vyākhyā); *Viśvapati Tīrtha*; PM; 6, 16; SKT, TU.

0144 Śivastuti Vyākhyā; *Viśvapati Tīrtha*; PM; 6, 17; SKT, TU.

0145 Āśvalāyana Śrauta Sūtra (Pūrva Ṣaṭka); *Āśvalāyana*; PM; 6, 18; SKT, D.

0146 Gṛhya Pariśiṣṭa; *Āśvalāyana*; PM; 6, 19; SKT, D.

0147 Pramāṇa Paddhati Ṭīkā; *Rāghavendra Tīrtha/Yati*; PM; 6, 20; SKT, D.

0148 Āśvalāyana Śrauta Sūtra (Uttara Ṣaṭka); *Āśvalāyana*; PM; 6, 21; SKT, D.

0149 Bhāgavata (Seventh Canto) Ṭīkā (Vijayadhvajīya); *Vijayadhvaja Tīrtha*; PM; 6, 22; SKT, D.

0150 Bhagavad Gītā Tātparya Nirṇaya Ṭīkā Nyāya Dīpikā; *Jayatīrtha*; PM; 6, 23; SKT, D.

0151 Candrikā; *Vyāsatīrtha*; PM; 6, 24, SKT, D.

0152 Dvādaśa Stotra; *Ānandatīrtha*; PM; 6, 25; SKT, D.

0153 Bhagavad Gītā; *Kṛṣṇa Dvaipāyana Vyāsa*; PM; 6, 26; SKT, TU.

0154 Kaṭhalakṣaṇa Vivaraṇam; *Jayatīrtha*; PM; 6, 27; SKT, TU.

0155 Caturtha Skandha Tātparyanirṇaya Prakāśa Ṭīkā; *Śrīnivāsa*; PM; 6, 28; SKT, D.

0156 Vāyustuti with Pratiśloka Mūlavedamantra; PM; 6, 29; SKT, D.

0157 Daśamaskandha Tātparya Nirṇayaprakāśa Ṭīkā; *Śrīnivāsa*; PM; 6, 30; SKT, D.

0158 Veṅkaṭa Giri Māhātmya from Bhaviṣyottara Purāṇa; *Kṛṣṇa Dvaipāyana Vyāsa*; PM; 6, 31; SKT, TU.

0159 Viṣṇurahasya; PM; 6, 32; SKT, D.

0160 Bhāgavata Tātparya Nirṇaya; *Madhvācārya/ Ānandatīrtha*; PM; 6, 33; SKT, D

0161 Brahmasūtrabhāṣya; *Madhvācārya*; PM; 6, 34; SKT, TU.

0162 Brahmasūtra (with Praiṣoccāraṇa); *Kṛṣṇa Dvaipāyana Vyāsa*; PM; 6, 35; SKT, TU.

0163 Vādāvalī Ṭīkā Bhāva Dīpikā; *Rāghavendra Tīrtha/Yati*; PM; 6, 36; SKT, D.

0164 Dvādaśa Stotra; *Madhvācārya/Ānandatīrtha*; PM; 6, 37; SKT, D.

0165 Ārādhanā Prayoga (Nāgara Khaṇḍa); PM; 6, 38; SKT, D.

0166 Ṛṣi Pañcamī Vrata Kathā of Bhaviṣyottara Purāṇa; *Kṛṣṇa Dvaipāyana Vyāsa*; PM; 6, 39; SKT, D.

0167 Ananta Kathā of Bhaviṣyottara Purāṇa; *Kṛṣṇa Dvaipāyana Vyāsa*; PM; 6, 40; SKT, D.

0168 Āditya Hṛdaya Stotram of Bhaviṣyottara Purāṇa; *Kṛṣṇa Dvaipāyana Vyāsa*; PM; 6, 41; SKT, D.

0169 Veṅkaṭeśa Sahasranāma from Brahmāṇḍa Purāṇa; *Kṛṣṇa Dvaipāyana Vyāsa*; PM; 6, 42; SKT, D.

0170 Svarṇa Gaurī Kathā of Skanda Purāṇa; *Kṛṣṇa Dvaipāyana Vyāsa*; PM; 6, 43; SKT, D.

0171 Ṣaṣṭi Pūjā; PM; 6, 44; SKT, D.

0172 Māyāvāda Khaṇḍana Pañcikā Ṭīkā; *Śrīnivāsa Tīrtha*; PM; 6, 45; SKT, D.

0173 Pramāṇa Paddhati Ṭīkā; *Puṇyaśravaṇa Tīrtha*; PM; 6, 46; SKT, D.

0174 Āmaśrāddha (Āśvalāyana Śrauta Sūtrokta Śrāddha Saṅkalpa Vidhi); PM; 6, 47; SKT, D.

0175 Bhāgavata Navama Skandha Ṭīkā (Pada Ratnāvalī); *Vijayadhvaja*; PM; 6, 48; SKT, D.

0176 Tantra Dīpikā; *Rāghavendra Tīrtha*; PM; 6, 49; SKT, D.

0177 Mahābhārata Tātparya Nirṇaya; *Madhvācārya/Ānandatīrtha*; PM; 6, 50; SKT, D.

0178 Potṛtva Prayoga; PM; 6, 51; SKT, D.

0179 Hautram; PM; 6, 52; SKT, D.

0180 Gopālasahasranāma of Saṁmohana Tantra; PM; 6, 53; SKT, D.

0181 Dvādaśa Stotra; *Madhvācārya/Ānandatīrtha*; PM; 6, 54; SKT, D.

0182 Taittirīya Caula Prayoga and Upanayana Prayoga; PM; 6, 55; SKT, D.

0183 Rukmiṇī Vivāha Kathā of Bhāgavata, (58th chapter of tenth canto); *Vijayadhvaja*; PM; 6, 56; SKT, D.

0184 Karmanirṇaya; *Madhvācārya/Ānandatīrtha*; PM, 6, 57; SKT, D.

0185 Ananta Kathā of Bhaviṣyottara Purāṇa; *Kṛṣṇa Dvaipāyana Vyāsa*; PM; 6, 58; SKT, D.

0186 Karma Nirṇaya Ṭīkā; *Jayatīrtha*; PM; 6, 59; SKT, D.

0187 Hariścandropākhyāna of Mahābhārata (Āraṇya Parva); *Kṛṣṇa Dvaipāyana Vyāsa*; PM; 6, 60; SKT, D.

0188 Aitareya Āraṇyaka; PM; 6, 61; SKT, D.

0189 Ṛṣi Pañcamī Kathā of Bhaviṣyottara Purāṇa; *Kṛṣṇadvaipāyana Vyāsa*; PM; 6, 62; SKT, D.

0190 Viṣṇusahasranāma Nāmāvalī from Mahābhārata (Anuśāsanika Parva); *Vyāsa*; PM; 6, 63; SKT, D.

0191 Ṇatva Tattva Vibhūṣaṇam (explanation of cerebral 'Ṇa' in 'Nārāyaṇa'); *Anantācārya*; PM; 6, 64; SKT, TU.

0192 Nyāya Sudhā; *Jayatīrtha*; PM; 6, 65; SKT, D.

0193 Nyāya Sudhā; *Jayatīrtha*; PM; 6, 66; SKT, D.

0194 Śiṣṭatātparya Candrikā; *Raghunātha Yati*; PM; 6, 67; SKT, D.

0195 Śiṣṭatātparya Candirkā; *Raghunātha Yati*; PM; 7, 1; SKT, D.

0196 Prapañca Mithyātvānumāna Khaṇḍana Pañcikā Bhāva Prakāśikā; *Vyāsa Yati*; PM; 7, 2; SKT, D.

0197 Māṇḍūkyopaniṣad and Kaṭhalakṣaṇa by Ānandatīrtha; *Madhvācārya*; PM; 7, 3; SKT, D.

0198 Veṅkaṭeśa Māhātmya from Āditya Purāṇa; *Kṛṣṇa Dvaipāyana Vyāsa*; PM; 7, 4; SKT, TU.

0199 Mādhava Stava Rāja of Vāyupurāṇa; *Kṛṣṇa Dvaipāyana Vyāsa*; PM; 7, 5; SKT, D.

0200 Vyākhyā on Ānandatīrtha's Ṣaṭpraśnopaniṣad Bhāṣya; *Jayatīrtha*; PM; 7, 6; SKT, D.

0201 Ṛgveda Pada Ṭīkā (or Pāṭha); PM; 7, 7; SKT, D.

0202 Māṇḍūkyopaniṣad Bhāṣya; *Ānandatīrtha*; PM; 7, 8; SKT, D.

0203 Gītā Bhāṣya; *Ānandatīrtha*; PM; 7, 9; SKT, D.

0204 Brahma Vaivarta Purāṇa Rahasya; *Kṛṣṇa Dvaipāyana Vyāsa*; PM; 7, 10; SKT, D.

0205 Pramāṇa Paddhati Ṭīkā (Bhāvadīpa); PM; 7, 11; SKT, D.

0206 Śrī Bhāṣya; *Rāmānujācārya*; PM; 7, 12; SKT, D.

0207 Nyāyavivaraṇa Ṭīkā; *Jayatīrtha*; PL; 7, 13; SKT, TU.

0208 Gītā Vivaraṇam; PL; 7, 14; SKT, TU.

0209 Mahābhārata Tātparya Nirṇaya Bhāvaprakāśikā; PL; 7, 15; SKT, TU.

0210 Nyāya Sudhā Vyākhyārtha Candrikā; *Vidyādhīśa Tīrtha*; PL; 7, 16; SKT, TU.

0211 Nyāya Sudhā Vyākhyārtha Candrikā; *Vidyādhīśa Tīrtha*; PL; 7, 17; SKT, TU.

0212 Mahābhārata (Bhīṣmaparva and Droṇaparva); *Kṛṣṇa Dvaipāyana Vyāsa*; PL; 7, 18; SKT, TU.

0213 Mahābhārata (Śānti Parva); *Kṛṣṇa Dvaipāyana Vyāsa*; PL; 7, 19; SKT, TU.

0214 Vāyu Purāṇa; 31, 1; SKT, D.

0215 Śrī Bhāgavata-Ṭippaṇī; *Satydharma Yati*; B; 31, 2; SKT, D; 1936 A.D.

0216 Harivaṁśa with Ṭīkā, (Contains Viṣṇuśatanāma Stotram from Viṣṇupurāṇa, and Santānagopāla Mantrānuṣṭhāna Vidhiḥ); *Kṛṣṇa Dvaipāyana Vyāsa*; B; 31, 3; SKT, D; 1954 A.D.

0217 Śiva-Mahāpurāṇa-Vidyeśvara-Saṁhitā; *Kṛṣṇa Dvaipāyana Vyāsa*; B; 31, 4; SKT, D; 1954 A.D.

0218 Bhāgavata-Ṭippaṇī; *Yadupati (Yādavārya)*; B; 31, 5; SKT, D.

0219 Bhāgavata-Ṭippaṇī; *Yadupati (Yādavārya)*; B; 32, 1; SKT, D.

0220 Viṣṇu-Dharmottara-Mahāpurāṇa; B; 32, 2; SKT, D; 1912 A.D.

0221 Śrī Mahā-Bhāgavata; *Kṛṣṇa Dvaipāyana Vyāsa*; B; 32, 3; SKT, D; 1913 A.D.

0222 Nyāya Sudhā with Śeṣavākyārthacandrikā Ṭippaṇī; *Vidyādhīśa Tīrtha*; B; 32, 4; SKT, D.

0223 Śrī Bhaviṣya Mahāpurāṇa (Brahma Parva); *Kṛṣṇa Dvaipāyana Vyāsa;* B; 32, 5; SKT, D.

0224 Śrī Bhaviṣya Mahāpurāṇa (Brahma Parva); *Kṛṣṇa Dvaipāyana Vyāsa*; B; 33, 1; SKT, D.

0225 Aitareya Brāhmaṇa; B; 33, 2; SKT, D; 1909 A.D.

0226 Ṛg Veda Sarvānukramaparibhāṣā (Ṛksaṁhitā Pariśiṣṭa); B; 33, 3; SKT, D.

0227 Nayacandrikā; *Traivikramācārya*; B; 33, 4; SKT, D.

0228 Śrīman Nyāya-Sudhā-Ṭippaṇī; *Rāmacandra Bhikṣu*; B; 33, 5; SKT, D.

0229 Tātparya Candrikā; *Vyāsa Yati*; PM; 33, 6; SKT, D.

0230 Kūrma Mahāpurāṇa; *Kṛṣṇa Dvaipāyana Vyāsa*; B; 33, 7; SKT, D; 1926 A.D.

0231 Brahma-Vaivarta Mahāpurāṇa (Prakṛti Khaṇḍa and Śrī Kṛṣṇa-Janma Khaṇḍa); *Kṛṣṇa Dvaipāyana Vyāsa*; B; 33, 8; SKT, D; 1931.

0232 Bhāgavata Tātparya Nirṇaya with Ṭīkā (Dīpikā); *Madhvācārya*; B; 33, 9; SKT, D; 1890 A.D.

0233 Bhāgavata Tātparya Nirṇaya with Ṭīkā (Dīpikā); *Madhvācārya*; B; 34, 1; SKT, D; 1890 A.D. (Continues 33, 9)

0234 Tantra-Dīpikā; *Rāghavendra Yati*; PM; 34, 2; SKT, D.

0235 Bhagavad Gītā with commentary by Śrīdhara Svāmī; *Kṛṣṇa Dvaipāyana Vyāsa*; B; 34, 3; SKT, D; 1900 A.D.

0236 Taittirīya Saṁhitā; B; 34, 4; SKT, D; 1899 A.D.

0236b Sarasabhāratīvilāsa; *Vādirājatīrtha*; B; 34, 5; SKT, D; 1882 A.D.

0237 Mantrārtha Mañjarī; *Rāghavendra Yati*; B; 34, 6; SKT, D; 1902 A.D.

0238 Ṛg Bhāṣya with Ṭīkā; *Madhvācārya*; B; 34, 7; SKT, D; 1901 A.D.

0239 Madhva Vijaya with Ṭīkā Bhāvaprakāśikā and Mandopakāriṇī; *Nārāyaṇa Paṇḍita Ācārya (s/o Trivikrama Paṇḍita Ācārya)*; B; 34, 8; SKT, D.

0240 Gītā Tātparya Nirṇaya with Nyāya Dīpikā Ṭippaṇī and Nyāyadīpikākiraṇāvalī; *Madhvācārya*; B; 34, 9; SKT, D; 1905 A.D.

0241 Guru-Bhāva-Prakāśikā and Rukmiṇīśa-Vijaya with Ṭīkā; *Vādirāja Tīrtha*; B; 34, 10; SKT, D; 1892 A.D.

0242 Rukmiṇīśa Vijaya with Ṭīkā Bhāva Prakāśikā; *Vādirāja Tīrtha*; B; 35, 1; SKT, D; 1892 A.D.; (Continues 34, 10)

0243 Upanyāsaratnamālā; *Vādirāja Tīrtha*; B; 35, 2; SKT, D; 1954 A.D.

0244 Vaikuṇṭha Varṇana; *Vādirāja Tīrtha*; B; 35, 3; KAN, D; 1893 A.D.

0245 Commentary on Madhva's Atharvaṇopaniṣad Bhāṣya (Vivaraṇa); *Vyāsa Tīrtha*; B; 35, 4; SKT, D; 1902 A.D.

0246 Ṛg Bhāṣya with Ṭīkā; *Madhva/Ānandatīrtha*; PM; 35, 5; SKT, KAN.

0247 Madhva-Siddhānta Sāra (Padārtha Saṅgraha Vyākhyāna); *Padmanābha Tīrtha*; B; 35, 6; SKT, D; 1893 A.D.

0248 Nyāya Ratnāvalī with Commentary, Prakāśa Saṅgraha; *Vādirāja Tīrtha*; B; 35, 7; SKT, D.

0249 Pramāṇa Lakṣaṇa with Ṭīkā Gītānyāya Kalpalatā; *Madhva/Ānandatīrtha*; PM; 35, 8; SKT, TU.

0250 Karma Nirṇaya; *Madhva/Ānandatīrtha*; PM; 35, 9; SKT, TU.

0251 Ṛg Veda Caturthāṣṭakaḥ; PM; 35, 10; SKT, TU.

0252 Mahābhārata Tātparya Nirṇaya Ṭīkā (Bhāvaprakāśikā); *Bhātirāja Tīrtha*; PM; 35, 11; SKT, TU.

0253 Aṇumadhva Vijaya with Ṭīkā; *Nārāyaṇa Paṇḍitācārya*; PM; 35, 12; SKT, D.

0254 Upaniṣad-s and commentaries; *Madhva*; PM; 35, 13, SKT, D.

0255 Tattvodyota Ṭīkā; *Jayatīrtha*; PM; 35, 14, SKT, TU.

0256 Tantra Dīpikā; *Rāghavendra Tīrtha*; PM; 35, 15; SKT, TU.

0257 Skanda Purāṇa, Sahyādri Khaṇḍa, Apara Bhāga, "Mañjula Kṣetra Māhātmya;" B; 35, 16; SKT, D; 1920 A.D.

0258 Aitareya Brāhmaṇa; B; 35, 17; SKT, D; 1925 A.D.

0259 Nyāya Ratnāvalī; *Padmanābha Tīrtha Bhaṭṭāraka*; B; 35, 18; SKT, D.

0260 Vādāvalī and Vādāvalī Bhāvadīpikā; *Jayatīrtha* and *Rāghavendra Yati;* SKT, D; 35, 19; 1904 A.D.

0261 Aitareya Bhāṣyārtharatnamālā; *Śrīnivāsācārya*; B; 35, 20; SKT, D; 1908 A.D.

0262 Pramāṇa Paddhati with Ṭippaṇī (Bhāvadīpa); *Jayatīrtha*; B; 35, 21; SKT, D; 1897 A.D.

0263 Śrī Kṛṣṇāmṛta Mahārṇava; *Madhva*; B; 35, 22; SKT, D; 1881 A.D.

0264 Dvādaśa Stotra with Ṭīkā; *Madhva*; B; 35, 23; SKT, D; 1890 A.D.

0265 Śrīnivāsatīrthīyaṭippaṇī (Commentary on Māyāvāda Khaṇḍana of Madhva); *Śrīnivāsa Tīrtha*; PM; 35, 24; SKT, D.

0266 Karṁa Nirṇaya Pañcikā with Vivaraṇa; *Jayatīrtha* and *Śrīnivāsa Tīrtha*; B; 35, 25; SKT, D; 1900 A.D.

0267 Bhagavad Gītā Bhāṣya; *Madhva/Ānanda Tīrtha*; PM; 35, 26; SKT, D.

0268 Nyāyavivaraṇa Ṭīkā; *Jayatīrtha*; PM; 35, 27; SKT, TU.

0269 Ratna Saṅgraha; *Raghunātha*; PM; 35, 28; SKT, TU.

0270 Aghanirṇaya Vyākhyā; *Venkaṭeśa*; PM; 35, 29; SKT, TU.

0271 Śanaiścara Stotram; PM; 35, 30; SKT, TU.

0272 Ṛg Veda Mantra Saṁhitā; B; 35, 31; SKT, D; 1924 A.D.

0273 Ṛg Veda Mantra Saṁhitā; B; 36, 1; SKT, D; 1924 A.D.; (Continuation of 35, 31).

0274 Nyāya Vivaraṇa with Bhāvoddhāra; *Ānandatīrtha*; B; 36, 2; SKT, D; 1917 A.D.

0275 Tattva Saṅkhyāna Ṭīkā-Bhāvadīpa, (also Contains Tattva Saṅkhyāna Śrīnivāsatīrthīya Ṭippaṇī by Śrīnivāsa); B; 36, 3; SKT, D; 1896 A.D.

0276 Sarva Mūla Granthāḥ, contains Bhāgavatatātparyanirṇaya; *Madhva*; B; 36, 4; SKT, D.

0277 Adhyātmarasarañjanī; *Jayatīrtha*; B; 36, 5; SKT, D; 1904 A.D.

0278 Ādityādinavagraha Stotra; *Kṛṣṇa Dvaipāyana Vyāsa*; B; 36, 6; SKT, D.

0279 Maṇimañjarī; *Nārāyaṇa Paṇḍita Ācārya*; B; 36, 7; SKT, D; 1925.

0280 Sat-Tattva-Ratna-Mālā; *Madhva/Ānandatīrtha*; B; 36, 8; SKT, D.

0281 Prātaḥ Saṅkalpa Gadya; *Rāghavendra Tīrtha*; B; 36, 9; SKT, D; 1971 A.D.

0282 Laghu Kāśīmāhātmyam from Bṛhannāradīyapurāṇa and Padma Purāṇa; B; 36, 10; SKT, D; 1900 A.D.

0283 Brahmasūtra Anuvyākhyāna; *Madhva/Ānandatīrtha*; B; 36, 11; SKT, D.

0283B Rāmarakṣāstotram; *Budhakauśika*; B; 36, 12; 1870 A.D.

0284 Madhva Vijaya Bhāvaprakāśikā Ṭīkā; *Nārāyaṇa Paṇḍita Ācārya*; B; 36, 13; SKT, D; 1925 A.D.

0285 Upādhi Khaṇḍana Mandāra Mañjarī; *Vyāsa Tīrtha*; B; 36, 14; SKT, D; 1896 A.D.

0286 Brahma Sūtra; *Kṛṣṇa Dvaipāyana Vyāsa*; B; 36, 15; SKT, D; 1881 A.D.

0287 Śrī Nārāyaṇahṛdaya and Lakṣmīhṛdaya; B; 36, 16; SKT, D; 1881 A.D.

0288 Māyāvāda Khaṇḍana Ṭīkā; *Jayatīrtha Bhikṣu*; PM; 36, 17; SKT, D.

0289 Dvādaśa Stotra; *Madhva*; B; 36, 18; SKT, D.

0290 Narasiṁha Stuti with Vyākhyā; *Trivikrama Paṇḍita Ācārya*; B; 36, 19; SKT, D; 1882 A.D.

0291 Rājarājeśvarī Lalitā Sahasranāma Stotra from Brahmāṇḍa Purāṇa; *Kṛṣṇa Dvaipāyana Vyāsa;* PM; 36, 20; SKT, D.

0292 Vāyu Stuti with Anvaya Samāsa; *Śrīnivāsa Tīrtha*; PM; 36, 21; SKT, D.

0293 Nyāya Vivaraṇa with Bhāva Bodha; *Ānandatīrtha*; B; 36, 22; SKT, D.

0294 Nṛsiṁha Stuti; *Trivikrama Paṇḍitācārya*; B; 36, 23; SKT, D; 1902 A.D.

0295 Antyeṣṭi Saṁskāra Vidhiḥ (Part of Saṁskāra Pradīpa); *Lakṣmaṇa*; B; 35, 24; SKT, D.

0296 Īśāvāsyādyupaniṣad Saptaka; PM; 36, 25; SKT, D.

0297 Śivagītā with Ṭīkā from Padmapurāṇa; B; 36, 26; SKT, D.

0298 Devī Sahasra Nāmāvalī Stotram; B; 36, 27; SKT, D.

0299 Vaiṣṇavānām Ṛgvedīya Śrāddhaprayoga; B; 36, 28; SKT, D; 1925 A.D.

0300 Nṛsiṁha Stuti with Vyākhyā by Nārāyaṇa; *Trivikrama Paṇḍitācārya*; B; 36, 29; SKT, D; 1904 A.D.

0301 Āśvalāyana Sandhyā Vandana; B; 36, 30; SKT, D.

0302 Tapta Cakra Bhūṣaṇa; B; 36, 31; SKT, D; 1891 A.D.

0303 Prapañca Mithyātvānumāna Khaṇḍana Ṭīkā; *Jayatīrtha Bhikṣu*; B; 36, 32; SKT, D; 1896 A.D.

0304 Sampradāya Paddhati with Aṇumadhvacarita and Granthamālikāstotra; *Hṛṣīkeśa Tīrtha*; B; 36, 33; SKT, D; 1914 A.D.

0305 Laghu Kāśī Māhātmya from Padmapurāṇa Pātālakhaṇḍa; *Kṛṣṇa Dvaipāyana Vyāsa*; B; 36, 34; SKT, D; 1911 A.D.

0306 Brahmasūtra Aṇubhāṣya; *Vallabhācārya* with *Gosvāmī Puruṣottama's Bhāṣyaprakāśa* and *Gosvāmī Gopeśvara's Bhāṣyaprakāśaraśmi*; B; 37, 1; SKT, D; 1941 A.D.

0307 Saviśeṣanirviśeṣa Śrī Kṛṣṇastava; *Nimbārka* with *Bhāvaprakāśikā Ṭīkā* by Śītaladās; 37, 2.

0308 Saviśeṣanirviśeṣa Kṛṣṇastavarāja with Ṭīkā; *Nimbārkācārya*; PM; 37, 3; SKT, D; c. 1973.

0309 Śrīmadbhāgavata Bhāṣā; *Rasajānī*; PM; 37, 4; H, D.

0310 Viṣṇusahasranāma with Ṭīkā; *Kṛṣṇadvaipāyana Vyāsa*; PM; 37, 5; SKT, D.

0311 Daśaślokī with Ṭīkā; *Nimbārkācārya*; PM; 37, 6; SKT H, D; c. 1874.

0312 Vaijayantī Guruparamparāvandanastotra; PM; 37, 7; SKT, D.

0313 Laghustavarāja; *Śrīnivāsācārya*; PM; 37, 8; SKT, D.

0314 Laghustavarāja; *Śrīnivāsācārya*; PM; 37, 9; SKT, D.

0315 Laghustavarāja; *Gopālabhṛtyācārya*; PM; 37, 10; SKT, D; c. 1896

0316 Laghustavarāja; *Gopālabhṛtyācārya*; PM; 37, 11; SKT, D.

0317 Guruparamparā (Nimbārka) Stotra with Ṭīkā; PM; 37, 12; SKT, D.

0318 Brajavilāsa; *Brajavāsīdāsa*; PM; 37, 13; H, D; c. 1830.

0319 Śrīmadbhāgavata; *Kṛṣṇa Dvaipāyana Vyāsa*; PM; 37, 14; SKT, D.

0320 Śrīmadbhāgavata; *Kṛṣṇa Dvaipāyana Vyāsa*; PM; 38, 1; SKT, D; (continuation of 37, 14)

0321 Catuḥsūtrīvyākhyā (Siddhāntajāhnavī); *Devācārya*; PM; 38, 2; SKT, D; c. 1881.

0322 Vedānta Siddhāntaratna Padyamālā with Ṭīkā; *Anantarāma*; PM; 38, 3; SKT H, D.

0323 Vedāntasiddhāntaratnapadyamālā with Ṭīkā; *Anantarāma*; PM; 38, 4; SKT H, D.

0324 Catuḥsūtrīvyākhyā (Siddhāntajāhnavī); *Devācārya*; PM; 38, 5; SKT, D; c. 1891.

0325 Vedāntaratnamālā; *Anantarāma*; PM; 38, 6; SKT, D.

0326 Vedāntasārapadyamālā; *Anantarāma*; PM; 38, 7; SKT, D; c. 1848.

0327 Tattvasiddhāntabindu; *Anantarāma*; PM; 38, 8; SKT, D; c. 1848.

0328 Pañca Saṁskāra Pramāṇa; *ascribed to Nimbārka*; PM; 38, 9; SKT, D.

0329 Pañca Saṁskāra Vidhi; *follower of Nimbārka*; PM; 38, 10; SKT, D.

0330 Pañca Saṁskāra; *Nikhila Mahīmaṇḍala*; PM; 38, 11; SKT, D.

0331 Vedāntatattvabodha; *Anantarāma*; PM; 38, 12; SKT, D.

0332 Vedāntatattvabodha; *Anantarāma*; PM; 38, 13; SKT, D; c. 1893 A.D.

0333 Vedāntatattvabodha; *Anantarāma*; PM; 38, 14; SKT, D; c. 1830 A.D.

0334 Vedāntatattvabodha; *Anantarāma*; PM; 38, 15; SKT, D; c. 1833 A.D.

0335 Vedānta Pārijāta; *Nimbārka*; PM; 38, 16; SKT, D.

0336 Vedānta Ratna Mañjūṣā; *Puruṣottamācārya*; PM; 38, 17; SKT, D; c. 1809 A.D.

0337 Daśaślokībhāṣya (Tattvasāraprakāśinī); *Nimbārka*; PM; 38, 18; SKT, D; c. 1889 A.D.

0338 Adhyātmakārikāvalī (with commentary Adhyātmasudhātaraṅgiṇī); *Niyamānanda*; PM; 38, 19; SKT, D; c. 1891 A.D.

0339 Śrīmadbhāgavata (with Ṭīkā Bhāvārthadīpikā); *Kṛṣṇa Dvaipāyana Vyāsa*; PM; 38, 20; SKT, D; c. 1834 A.D.

0340 Śrīmadbhāgavata (with Ṭīkā Bhāvārthadīpikā); *Kṛṣṇa Dvaipāyana Vyāsa*; PM; 39, 1; SKT, D; c. 1834 A.D.

0341 Lalit Kiśorī Devajī kī Vāṇī; *Lalit Kiśorī Dev*; PM; 39, 2; H, D; c. 1854 A.D.

0342 Jugalaśatapada Bhūṣaṇa; *Śyāmadāsa*; PM; 39, 3; H, D; c. 1854 A.D.

0343 Nimbārkācāryoṁ kī Badhāī; PM; 39, 4; H, D.

0344 Śrī Brahma Sūtra Govinda Bhāṣya; *Baladeva Vidyābhūṣaṇa*; B; 39, 5; SKT H, D; 1954.

0345 Braja Bhakti Vilāsam; *Nārāyaṇa Bhaṭṭa Gosvāmī*; B; 39, 6; SKT H, D.

0346 Caitanya Caritāmṛta in Braj Bhāṣā; *Subalaśyāmajī*; B; 39, 7; H, D; 1949 A.D.

0347 Sādhana Dīpikā; *Nārāyaṇa Bhaṭṭa*; B; 39, 8; SKT H, D; 1965 A.D.

0348 Brajotsava Candrikā; *Nārāyaṇa Bhaṭṭa Gosvāmī*; B; 39, 9; SKT, D; 1960 A.D.

0349 Rāsa-Pañcādhyāyī (from Bhāgavata with Rasikāhlādinī Ṭīkā); B; 39, 10; SKT, D; 1964 A.D.

0350 Bhakta Bhūṣaṇa Sandarbha (with Translation); *Nārāyaṇa Bhaṭṭa*; B; 39, 11; SKT H, D; 1964 A.D.

0351 Bhakti Tattva Prakāśikā; *Caitanya Dās*; B; 39, 12; SKT, D; 1963 A.D.

0352 Gīti Viṁśa Ṭīkā; *Gopīlāla Gosvāmī*; B; 39, 13; SKT, D; 1963 A.D.

0353 Bhakti Viveka; *Nārāyaṇa Bhaṭṭa*; B; 39, 14; SKT, D; 1963 A.D.

0354 Anarpitacarīṁ Cirād iti Ślokasya Vyākhyā; *Jīva Gosvāmī*; B; 39, 15; SKT, D; 1963 A.D.

0355 Siddhānta Ratnam or Govinda Bhāṣya Pīṭhakam (with Ṭippaṇī); *Baladeva Vidyābhūṣaṇa*; B; 39, 16; SKT, D; 1965 A.D.

0356 Commentaries on Kṛṣṇa-Śatāṣṭottara-Stotra (from Brahmāṇḍa Purāṇa), Gopāla Stava Rāja (from Gautamīya Tantra) with Mūla; *Vṛndāvana Dās*; B; 39, 17; SKT, D; 1960 A.D.

0357 Laḍileyāṣṭaka (from Grantha Ratnatraya); *Nārāyaṇa Bhaṭṭa*; B; 39, 18; SKT, D; 1960 A.D.

0358 Īśopaniṣad with Bhāṣya; B; 39, 19; SKT H, D; 1965 A.D.

0359 Svapnavilāsāmṛta with Ṭīkā and Padāvalī, and Kapila Tantra; B; 39, 20; SKT H BL, D; 1968 A.D.

0360 Svakīyātva Nirāsa Vicāra tathā Parakīyātva Nirūpaṇa; *Viśvanātha Cakravartī*; B; 39, 21; SKT, D; 1963 A.D.

0361 Jagannātha Vallabha Nāṭaka with Translation; *Rāmānanda Rāy*; B; 39, 22; SKT H, D; 1964 A.D.

0362 Premāmṛta Rasāyana Stotra; *Kṛṣṇacaitanyadeva*; B; 39, 23; SKT H, D; 1967 A.D.

0363 Grantha Ratna Pañcaka (Śrī Rādhā Kṛṣṇa Gaṇoddeśa Dīpikā: I Part); *Rūpa Gosvāmī*; B; 39, 24; SKT H, D; 1954 A.D.

0364 Grantha Ratna Pañcaka (Śrī Kṛṣṇa Līlā Stava: II Part); *Sanātana Gosvāmī*; B; 39, 25; SKT, H, D; 1954 A.D.

0365 Grantha Ratna Pañcaka (Śrī Gaura Gaṇoddeśa Dīpikā: III Part); *Kavikarṇapūra*; B; 39, 26; SKT H, D; 1954 A.D.

0366 Grantha Ratna Pañcaka (Śrī Saṅkalpa Kalpadruma: V Part); *Viśvanātha Cakravarti*; B; 39, 27; SKT H, D; 1954 A.D.

0367 Grantha Ratna Pañcaka (Braja Vilāsa Stava: V Part); *Raghunātha Dās Gosvāmī*; B; 39, 28; SKT H, D; 1954 A.D.

0368 Dānakeli Kaumudī (with Mahatī Ṭīkā and Hindi Translation); *Rūpa Gosvāmī*; B; 39, 29; SKT H, D; 1967 A.D.

0369 Caitanya Candrāmṛta Tathā Saṅgīta Mādhava (with Translation); *Prabodhānanda Sarasvatī*; B; 39, 30; SKT, H, D; 1951 A.D.

0370 Haṁsa-Dūta with Ṭīkā and Translation; *Rūpa Gosvāmī*; B; 39, 31; SKT H, D; 1957 A.D.

0371 Sarvasaṁvādinī; *Jīva Gosvāmī*; B; 39, 32; SKT, D; 1965 A.D.

0372 Sarvasaṁvādinī; *Jīva Gosvāmī*; B; 40, 1; SKT, D; 1965 A.D; (continues 0371).

0373 Bhagavad Gītā (with Sārārtha Varṣiṇī Ṭīkā and Gītā Bhūṣaṇa Bhāṣya and Svayambhagavatvāṣṭakam from Stavāmṛtalaharī); *Viśvanātha Cakravartī* and *Baladeva Vidyābhūṣaṇa*; B; 40, 2; SKT, D; 1966 A.D.

0374 Braja Maṇḍala Darśana (Parikramā); *Kṛṣṇa Dās Bābā*; B; 40, 3; H, D; 1967 A.D.

0375 Bhāṣā Bhāgavata (with Māhātmya of Skandha-s I and II); *Rasajānī Vaiṣṇavadās*; B; 40, 4; H, D; 1960 A.D.

0376 Govinda Līlāmṛta (Dvitīya Khaṇḍa); *Kṛṣṇa Dāsa Kavirāja Gosvāmī*; B; 40, 5; SKT H, D; 1965 A.D.

0377 Mādhava Dās Jī kī Vāṇī tathā Ādarśa jīvanī; B; 40, 6; H, D; 1963 A.D.

0378 Śrī Bhāgavata Bhāṣā (Dūsarā Khaṇḍa, 10th, 11th, 12th Cantos); *Rasajānī Vaiṣṇava Dās*; B; 40, 7; H, D; 1953 A.D.

0379 Rādhā Ramaṇa Rasa Sāgara; *Mandhara Dās*; B; 40, 8; H, D; 1951 A.D.

0380 Mādhurī Vāṇī (Braja Bhāṣā); *Mādhurī* (Disciple of *Rūpa Gosvāmī*); B; 40, 9; H, D; 1965 A.D.

0381 Kiśorī Dās Kī Vāṇī; *Kiśorī Dās*; B; 40, 10; H, D; 1960 A.D.

0382 Sampradāya Bodhinī; *Manohar Dās*; B; 40, 11; SKT H, D; 1959 A.D.

0383 Govinda Līlāmṛta and Padyāvalī Bhāṣā; *Śītala Dāsa* and *Śivapada*; B; 40, 12; H, D; 1963 A.D.

0384 Padyāvalī Bhāṣā; *Śivapada*; B; H, D; 40, 13; (Continues 0383).

0385 Gauranāma Rasa Campū tathā Laghu Gopāla Campū Bhāṣā; *Kṛṣṇa Kavi*; B; 40, 14; H, D; 1960 A.D.

0386 Rasacandrikā; *Hara Deva*; B; 40, 15; H, D; 1965 A.D.

0387 Vilāpa Kusumāñjalī (Braj Bhāṣā translation by Vṛndāvana Dās); *Raghunātha Dās Gosvāmī (Mūla)*; B; 40, 16; H, D; 1950 A.D.

0388 Prema Bhakti Candrikā; *Vṛndāvan Dās*; B; 40, 17; H, D; 1950 A.D.

0389 Rāma Hari Granthāvalī; *Buddhivilāsa, Satahaṁsī, Bodhabāvanī, Rasapacīsī, Laghunāmāvalī, Laghuśabdāvalī, Premapatrī, Dhyānarahasi; Rāma Hari*; B; 40, 18; H, D; 1951 A.D.

0390 Śrī Hari Līlā; *Brahma Gopāla Gosvāmī*; B; 40, 19; H, D; 1948 A.D.

0390a Vidagdhamādhavavārtā; B; 40, 20; SKT, H, D; 1959 A.D.

0391 Kṣaṇadā Gīti Cintāmaṇi; *Manohar Dās*; B; 40, 21; H, D; 1960 A.D.

0392 Vallabha Rasika Jī kī Vāṇī; *Vallabha Rasika*; B; 40, 22; H, D; 1948 A.D.

0393 Gīta Govinda (Braj Bhāṣā); *Rasajānī Vaiṣṇava Dāsa*; B; 40, 23; H, D.

0394 Smaraṇa maṅgala Bhāṣā; *Guṇa mañjarī*; B; 40, 24; H, D; 1962 A.D.

0395 Rasika Jīvanī; *Manohar Dās* (Compiler); B; 40, 25; H, D; 1962 A.D.

0396 Śobhana Padāvalī; *Śobhana Gosvāmī*; B; 40, 26; H, D.

0397 Gaurāṅga Bhūṣaṇa Mañjāvalī; B; 40, 27; H, D; 1950 A.D.

0398 Prabodhasudhākara (with Braj Bhāṣā Ṭīkā); *Śaṅkarācārya*; B; 40, 28; SKT H, D.

0399 Daśaślokī with Vedānta Rasāmṛta Ṭīkā (by Gopāla Dās); *Nimbārkācārya*; B; 40, 29; SKT H, D; 1924 A.D.

0400 Śrī Vaiṣṇava Matābja Bhāskara (Śrī Rāmārcana Paddhati Sahitaś ca); *Rāmānanda Svāmī*; B; 40, 30; H, D; 1927 A.D.

0401 Ṣoḍaśa Grantha; *Vallabhācārya*; B; 40, 31; SKT GUJ, GUJ; 1925 A.D.

0402 Śrī Rādhā Janmāṣṭamī Vrata Mahotsava kī Prācīnatā, Mahimā aur Pūjā-Vidhi; B; 40, 32; SKT H, D; 1968 A.D.

0403 Catuś Ślokī and Stotra Ratnam (with Hindi Chāyāpadya by Lakṣmīprasāda Śarmā); *Yāmunācārya*; B; 40, 33; SKT H, D; 1961 A.D.

0404 Vṛtrāsura Catuś Ślokī (from Bhāgavata with Subodhinī Vyākhyā); *Kṛṣṇa Dvaipāyana Vyāsa*; B; 40, 34; SKT, D; 1880 A.D.

0405 Śrīmad Vaiṣṇava Siddhānta Ratna Saṅgraha; *Śyāmlāl Hakīm* (Compiler); B; 40, 35; SKT H, D; 1953 A.D.

0406 Śrī Mahā Mantra Mīmāṁsā; *Gopāla Dās Kavi* (Compiler); B; 40, 36; SKT BL, BL; 1746 Baṅgābda.

0407 Divyonmāda Bā Bāī Unmādinī; *Kṛṣṇa Kamala Gosvāmī*; B; 40, 37; SKT BL, BL; 1968 A.D.

0408 Bhagavad Gītā (Mūla with Subodhinī Ṭīkā and Bengali Translation); *Śrīdhara Śvāmī*; B; 40, 38; SKT BL, BL.

0409 Īśāvāsyopaniṣat (with Vyākhyā and Hindi Translation); B; 40, 39; SKT H, D; 1953 A.D.

0410 Ṛg Veda Saṁhitā; B; 40, 40; SKT, D; 1900 A.D.

0411 Ṛg Veda Saṁhitā; B; 41, 1; SKT, D; 1900 A.D.; (Continues 40, 40).

0412 Atharva Veda Saṁhitā; B; 41, 2; SKT, D; 1900 A.D.

0413 Yajur Veda Saṁhitā; B; 41, 3; SKT, D; 1910 A.D.

0414 Sāmaveda Saṁhitā; B; 41, 4; SKT, D; 1910 A.D.

0415 Kalki Purāṇa, (with Hindi translation by Baladev Prasad Mishra); B; 41, 5; SKT H, D; 1906 A.D.

0416 Śrī Bhakta Māla (with Bhakti Rasa Bodhinī Ṭīkā); *Śrī Nārāyaṇa Dās (Nābhā Dās)*; B; 41, 6; H, D; 1910 A.D.

0417 Ekādaśī māhātmyaṁ with Dīpikā; *Kṛṣṇa Dvaipāyana Vyāsa*; B; 41, 7; SKT H, D; 1903 A.D.

0418 Sanat Kumāra Kārttika Māhātmya with Bhāṣāṭīkā; B; 41, 8; SKT H, D; 1911 A.D.

0419 Bhagavad Gītā with Subodhinī Commentary; *Vyāsa*; B; 41, 9; SKT, D; 1912 A.D.; (Some Bengali Ms. pages attached).

0420 Caitanya Caritāmṛta; *Kṛṣṇa Dās Kavirāja*; B; 41, 10; BL, BL; 1840 A.D.

0421 Caitanya Bhāgavatam; *Vṛndāvana Das*; B; 41, 11; BL, BL.

0422 Narottama Vilāsa; *Narottama Dās*; B; 41, 12; BL, BL; 1816 A.D.

0423 Rāmapaṭalam (Laghu Rāma Paddhatiḥ); *Rāmānujācārya* (Edited by *Rāma Nārāyaṇa Dāsa*); B; 41, 13; SKT, D.

0424 Rāma Candra Stava Rāja Stotram (from *Sanat Kumāra Saṁhitā*); *Kṛṣṇa Dvaipāyana Vyāsa*; B; 41, 14; SKT, D.

0425 Caitanya Caritāmṛta (with Ānanda Candrikā Ṭīkā); *Kṛṣṇa Dāsa Kavirāja*; B; 41, 15; BL, BL.

0426 Phala Prakaraṇa Subodhinī (Commentary on Bhāgavata, Skandha X with Rāsa Pañcādhyāyī); *Vallabhācārya*; B; 41, 16; SKT, D; 1914 A.D.

0427 Śrī Rāma Tāpanīyopaniṣad with Bhāṣāṭīkā; B; 41, 17; SKT H, D; 1907 A.D.

0428 Śeṣa Upaniṣad; B; 41, 18; SKT, D; (Continues 41, 17).

0429 Rāmopaniṣad with Subodhinī Ṭīkā; B; 41, 19; SKT, D; (Continues 41, 17).

0430 Puṣṭimārgīya Siddhānta or Śuddhādvaita Mūlatattva; *Paṭavārī Raṇachoḍa Dāsa Vandrāvana Dāsa*; B; 41, 20; GUJ, GUJ; 1853 A.D.

0431 Śrī Nāthajīnī Prākaṭya Vārtā; *Govardhana Lāljī Mahārāj*; B; 41, 21; GUJ SKT, GUJ D; 1920 A.D.

0432 Śuddha Puṣṭi Mārga Siddhānta; *Seṭh Caraṇa Dāsa Jī Adhikārī*; B; 41, 22; GUJ SKT H, GUJ D; 1899 A.D.

0433 Ṣoḍaśa Grantha; *Vallabhācārya*; B; 41, 23; SKT GUJ, D GUJ; 1924 A.D.

0434 Sarvopaniṣat Sāra Saṅgrahaḥ; *Govindānanda Svāmī* (Compiler); B; 41, 24; SKT, D; 1929 A.D.

0435 Sarvopaniṣat Sārasaṅgrahaḥ; *Govindānanda Svāmī*; B; 42, 1; SKT, D; 1929 A.D.; (Continues 0434)

0436 Śrī Śrī Vṛndāvana Mahimāmṛta and Saṅgraha with Anuvāda by Śrī Bhagavant Mudit; *Vaṁśī Dāsa Prabodhānanda Sarasvatīpāda* (Compiler); B; 42, 2; H, D.

0437 Gīta Govinda with Commentary; *Jayadeva Gosvāmī*; B; 42, 3; BL, BL.

0438 Rāsa Pañcādhyāya (with a Bengali commentary); *Dvija Pītāṁbara*; B; 42, 4; SKT BL, BL.

0439 Gopī Gītā with Ṭīkā (Bhāgavata Purāṇa); *Kṛṣṇa Dvaipāyana Vyāsa*; B; 42, 5; SKT, BL; 1858 A.D.

0440 Uddhava Saṁvāda; B; 42, 6; BL, BL.

0441 Praśna Muṇḍaka Māṇḍūkya: three Upaniṣads and Ṭīkā and Translation, with Anvaya Mukha Vyākhyā and Bengali Translation; B; 42, 7; SKT BL, BL.

0442 Premānanda Varṣiṇī; *Bāṅke Bihārīlāla* (Bāṅke Piyā); B; 42, 8; H, D; 1932 A.D.

0443 Bhagavat Sevāvidhi; *Bāṅke Bihārī Lāla* (Bāṅke Piyā); B; 42, 9; H, D; 1923 A.D.

0444 Śrī Vallabha Maṇimālā (Śrī Vallabhācāryajī kā Jīvana Caritra); (Paṇḍit) Kajjūlāla Śāstrī Kaviratna; B; 42, 10; SKT H, D; 1947 A.D.

0445 Cetana Dhārā; *Jīvana Kṛṣṇa Dās*; B; 42, 11; BL, BL.

0446 Bhakti Guccha; B; 42, 12; BL, BL.

0447 Gauḍīya Vaiṣṇava Sāhitya; *Haridās Dās*; B; 42, 13; SKT BL, BL.

0448 Prema Bhakti Candrikā; *Narottama Dās Ṭhākur*; B; 42, 14; BL, BL; Baṅgābda 1281.

0449 Vinaya Patrikā; *Tulasī Dās Gosvāmī*; B; 42, 15; H, D; 1887 A.D.

0450 Śrī Rāma Svabhāva; *Paṇḍit Rāma Kumāra Dās*; B; 42, 16; H, D; 1964 A.D.

0451 Śrī Tiruppāvaisvāpadeśaḥ (with Commentary in Sanskrit); *Godāmbājī*; B; 42, 17; SKT, D; 1950 A.D.

0452 Śrī Vṛndāvan (A Purāṇic and Itihāsic Description of Vṛndāvana, Past and Present); *Kiśorī Lāl Gosvāmī*; B; 42, 18; SKT H, D; 1914 A.D.

0453 Brahma Saṁhitā (with Anvaya in Sanskrit and Hindi Translation); *Virañci*; B; 42, 19; SKT H, D; 1950 A.D.

0454 Narottama Vilāsa; *Narahari Dās Cakravarti Ṭhākur*; B; 42, 20; BL, BL; Caitanyābda 407.

0455 Śrī Caitanya Candrāmṛta (with Rasikāsvādinī Ṭīkā and Bengali Translation); *Prabodhānanda Sarasvatī*; B; 42, 21; SKT BL, BL; Baṅgābda 1319.

0456 Dānakeli Kaumudī Bhāṇikā (with Poetic Translation); *Rūpa Gosvāmī*; B; 42, 22; BL, BL; Baṅgābda 1325.

0457 Govinda Līlāmṛta (Sanskrit) (with Bengali Versification); *Kṛṣṇa Dās Kavirāja Gosvāmī*; B; 42, 23; SKT BL, BL; Baṅgābda 1303.

0458 Vṛndāvana Śatakam (with Ṭīkā and Bengali Versification); B; 42, 24; BL, BL.

0459 Vidagdha Mukhamaṇḍanam (with Ṭīkā and Translation); *Dharma Dās Kavi*; B; 42, 25; SKT BL, BL; 1904 A.D.

0460 Śrī Śrī Rāsalīlā Tattva; *Śrīśacandra Rāya Caudhurī* (Compiler); B; 42, 26; SKT BL, BL; Baṅgābda 1343.

0461 Rādhāvallabha Aṣṭayāma; B; 42, 27; H, D; 1928 A.D.

0462 Gauḍīya Vaiṣṇava Tīrtha; *Haridās Dās*; B; 42, 28; BL, BL; Caitanyābda 465.

0463 Samāja Gāyana Śṛṅkhalā (Anthology of Haridāsī Songs); B; 42, 29; H, D; 1974 A.D.

0464 Bhakti Ratnāvalī with Commentary; *Viṣṇu Purī Gosvāmī*; B; 42, 30; SKT BL, BL; Caitanyābda 419.

0465 Kṛṣṇa Karṇāmṛta Stotram; *Bilva Maṅgala Ṭhākur*; B;42, 31; BL, BL; Caitanyābda 415.

0466 Hari Bhakti Vilāsa Rasāmṛta; B; 42, 32; SKT BL, BL; Baṅgābda 1297.

0467 Narottama Vilāsa; *Narahari Dās*; B; 42, 33; BL, BL; Baṅgābda 1328.

0468 Kalki Purāṇam (Sanskrit Mūla with Bengali Translation); *Kṛṣṇa Dvaipāyana Vyāsa*; B; 42, 34; SKT BL; BL; Baṅgābda 1315.

0469 Jagannātha Ballabha Nāṭakaṃ with Translation; *Rāmānanda Rāya*; B; 42, 35; SKT BL, BL; Baṅgābda 1282.

0470 Madhva Gauḍeśvara Sampradāya; *Dr. Priyācaraṇ Śaraṇ Dās*; B; 42, 36; H, D; 1961 A.D.

0471 Śrī Kṛṣṇārcana Paddhati; *Muralīmohan Gosvāmī* (*Advaita Vaṁśya*); B; 42, 37; BL, BL; Baṅgābda 1300.

0472 Gīta Govinda (Bengali Translation); *Giridhar Dās*; B; 42, 38; BL, BL; Baṅgābda 1339.

0473 Gīta Govinda with Ṭīkā; *Jayadeva Gosvāmī*; B; 42, 39; SKT BL, BL; Baṅgābda 1304.

0474 Dīkṣā Praṇālī; *Harilāl Caṭṭopādhyāya*; B; 42, 40; SKT BL, BL; Baṅgābda 1328.

0475 Braja Caurāśī Krośa Vana-Bhramaṇa and Brajavārtā Tan Māhātmya; *Pārvatīcaraṇa Mukhopādhyāya*; B; 42, 41; BL, BL; Baṅgābda 1359.

0476 Śrī Śrī Navadvīpa Darpaṇa Grantha Pariśiṣṭa (Dvitīya Khaṇḍa); *Vraja Mohan Dās;* B; 42, 42; BL, BL; Baṅgābda 1327.

0477 Saṅkalpa Kalpadruma; *Jīva Gosvāmī*; B; 42, 43; SKT BL; BL.

0478 Nikuñja Rahasya Stava (with Ṭīkā and Bengali Versification); *Rūpa Gosvāmī;* B; 42, 44; SKT BL, BL; 1902 A.D.

0479 Manośikṣā; *Premānanda Dās Mahānubhāva*; B; 43, 1; BL, BL; Baṅgābda 1304.

0480 Rūpa Sanātana Stotra with Bengali Versification; *Govardhana Bhaṭṭa*; B; 43, 2; SKT BL, BL; Caitanyābda 442.

0481 Śrī Rāma Sahasranāma with Bhāṣā Ṭīkā; *Jayarāmadeva*; B; 43, 3; SKT H, D; 1968 A.D.

0482 Vilāpa Kusumāñjalī; *Vṛndāvanavāsa Jī* and *Raghunāthadāsa Gosvāmī*; B;43, 4; SKT H, D; 1950 A.D.

0483 Gaura Premollāsa Kāvyam with Introductory Biography of Author; *Nandakiśora Candra Gosvāmī*; B; 43, 5; SKT H, D; 1925 A.D.

0484 Uddhava Sandeśa (with Ṭīkā in Sanskrit and Hindi Translation); *Rūpa Gosvāmī*; B; 43, 6; SKT H, D; 1957 A.D.

0485 Lalita Mādhava; *Śrī Yukta Svarūp Caraṇ Gosvāmī*; B; 43, 7; BL, BL.

0486 Nāgarī Dās Vāṇī Aṅka (Śrī Sarveśvara kā Viśeṣāṅka); B; 43, 8; H, D; 1965 A.D.

0487 Siddhānta Ratnākara; B; 43, 9; H, D; 1956 A.D.

0488 Bhakti Rasa-Phuṭakara Prasaṅga; *Bābā Viśeśvara Śaraṇa* (Compiler); B; 43, 10; H, D; 1962 A.D.

0489 Śrī Govinda Śaraṇa Devācāryajī kī Vāṇī; *Govinda Śaraṇa Devācārya*; B; 43, 11; H, D; 1970 A.D.

0490 Kṛṣṇa Stava Rāja (with Anvayārtha and Bhāṣānuvāda); B; 43, 12; SKT H, D; 1965 A.D.

0491 Ṣaṭsandarbhanāmaka Bhāgavata Sandarbha; *Jīva Gosvāmī*; B; 43, 13; SKT, D.

0492 Parapakṣa Girivajra (Fourth Part); *Mādhava Mukunda*; B; 43, 14; SKT, D.

0493 Ṣaḍa Gosvāmī Sūcaka; B; 43, 15; SKT BL, BL.

0494 Vraja Vinoda; *Lāl Balabīr and Prema Sakhī* (Brothers); B; 43, 16; H, D; 1969 A.D.

0495 Śuka Sampradāya Prakāśa; *Rūpa Mādhurī Śaraṇa*; B; 43, 17; SKT H ENG, D ROM.

0496 Siddhānta Darpaṇa and Ṭīkā with Bengali Translation; *Baladeva Vidyābhūṣaṇa*; B; 43, 18; SKT BL, D BL.

0497 Vaiṣṇava Vaibhava (Bhāga 2); B; 43, 19; SKT H, D; 1924 A.D.

0498 Sevā Sukha; *Harivyāsadevācārya*; B; 43, 20; H, D; 1965 A.D.

0499 Ṣoḍaśa Grantha (with Yamunāṣṭakam with Artha and Vivecana); *Vallabhācārya*; PM; 43, 21; H, D; c. 1928 A.D.

0500 Svāmī Haridāsa Jī kī Vāṇī; *Svāmī Haridāsa*; PM; 43, 22; H, D; c. 1781 A.D.

0501 Viṭhal Bipul Dev Jī kī Vāṇī; *Svāmī Viṭhalbipuladeva*; PM; 43, 23; H, D; c. 1781 A.D.

0502 Svāmī Bihārin Dās Jī kī Vāṇī; *Bihārin Dās*; PM; 43, 24; H, D; c. 1781 A.D.

0503 Mahāvāṇī Pañcaratna; *Hari Vyāsa Devācārya*; PM; 43, 25; H, D; c. 1928 A.D.

0504 Bihārin Dās Svāmī kī Vāṇī; *Bihārin Dās Svāmī*; PM; 43, 26; H, D.

0505 Padyāvalī with Hindi Bhāṣāṭīkā—Padyāvalī Prakāśikā; *Rūpa Gosvāmī*; B; 43, 27; SKT H, D; 1959 A.D.

0506 Ṣaṭ Sandarbha Nāmakabhāgavata Sandarbha; *Jīva Gosvāmī*; B; 44, 1; SKT, D.

0507 Bhagavad Gītā Mālā Mantra, Viṣṇu Sahasra Nāma, Bhīṣma Stava Rāja, Anusmṛti, Gajendra Mokṣaṇa, etc., *Kṛṣṇa Dvaipāyana Vyāsa*; PM; 44, 2; SKT, D; c. 1823 A.D.

0508 Bṛhad Bhāgavatāmṛtam with Ṭīkā; *Sanātana Gosvāmī*; B; 44, 3; SKT, D; Caitanyābda 419.

0509 Brahma Vaivarta Purāṇa; *Rāmalocana Dās*; B; 44, 4; BL, BL; Baṅgābda 1337.

0510 Viṣṇu Sahasra Nāma (from Mahābhārata); *Kṛṣṇa Dvaipāyana Vyāsa*; PM; 44, 5; SKT, D.

0511 Rāsa Pañcādhyāyī (A Portion of the Bhāgavata Purāṇa); *Kṛṣṇa Dvaipāyana Vyāsa*; PM; 44, 6; SKT, D.

0512 Bhagavad Gītā from Mahābhārata (Also Contains Bhagavad Gītāmālāmantra); *Kṛṣṇa Dvaipāyana Vyāsa*; PM; 44, 7; SKT, D.

0513 Gīta Govinda; *Jayadeva*; PM; 44, 8; SKT, D.

0514 Kṛṣṇa Karṇāmṛta; *Bilva Maṅgala Līlā Śuka*; PM; 44, 9; SKT, D.

0515 Vaiṣṇava Dharma Suradruma Mañjarī with Hindi Ṭīkā; *Saṅkarṣaṇa Śaraṇa Deva*; B; 44, 10; SKT H, D; 1929 A.D.

0516 Nityānanda Caritāmṛta; *Vṛndāvan Dās Ṭhākur*; B; 44, 11; BL, BL; Baṅgābda 1309.

0517 Nimbārkāvataraṇa (Nāṭaka); *Dānabihārīlāl Śarmā*; B; 44, 12; H, D; 1928 A.D.

0518 Kṛṣṇa Karṇāmṛta (with Three Commentaries); *Līlāśuka Bilva Maṅgala*; B; 44, 13; SKT, D.

0519 Rādhā Ramaṇa Prākaṭya; *Madhusūdana Gosvāmī*; B; 44, 14; H, D; 1969 A.D.

0520 Rādhā Ramaṇa Pada Puṣpāñjalī; *Puṣpādevī Gosvāmī*; B; 44, 15; H, D; 1969 A.D.

0521 Caitanya Candrāmṛtam; *Prabodhānanda Sarasvatī*; B; 44, 16; SKT, D; 1910 A.D.

0522 Praśnopaniṣad (with Vaiṣṇava Bhāṣya and Bhāṣābhāṣya); B; 44, 17; SKT H, D; 1942 A.D.

0523 Bhakta Nāmāvalī; *Vṛndāvana Dās*; B; 44, 18; H, D; 1950 A.D.

0524 Śrī Guru Paramparā; B; 44, 19; SKT H, D.

0525 Śrīmad Bhāgavata Purāṇa with Bhāvārthadīpikā; *Kṛṣṇa Dvaipāyana Vyāsa*; B; 44, 20; SKT, D; 1861 A.D.

0526 Bhagavad Gītā (with Ṭīkā Gūḍhārthadīpikā); *Kṛṣṇa Dvaipāyana Vyāsa*; B; 47, 1; SKT, D; 1880 A.D.

0527 Mantra Bhāgavata; B; 47, 2; SKT, D; 1903 A.D.

0528 Nṛsiṁha Campū; *Keśava Bhaṭṭa*; B; 47, 3; SKT, D; 1764 A.D.

0529 Ānanda Vṛndāvana Campū (with Ṭīkā Sukhavartanī); *Kavi Karṇapūra*; B; 47, 4; SKT, D.

0530 Śrīmad Bhāgavata (with Bhāṣā Ṭīkā, Five Commentaries); *Kṛṣṇa Dvaipāyana Vyāsa*; B; 47, 5; SKT H, D; 1966 A.D.

0531 Śrīmad Bhāgavata with Bhāṣā Ṭīkā; *Kṛṣṇa Dvaipāyana Vyāsa*; B; 48, 1; SKT, D; 1966 A.D; (Continues 0530).

0532 Kārttika Māhātmya (From Padma Purāṇa with Hindi Ṭīkā Bhāṣāśabda Prakāśikā); *Kṛṣṇa Dvaipāyana Vyāsa*; B; 48, 2; SKT H, D; 1885 A.D.

0533 Gaurāṅga Campū with Ṭīkā; *Raghunandana Gosvāmī*; B; 48, 3; SKT BL, BL; Caitanyābda 472.

0534 Abhilāṣa Mādhurī; *Lalita Kiśorī*; B; 48, 4; H, D; 1931 A.D.

0535 Caitanya Caritāmṛta (Paraphrase in Braj Poetry); *Rādhā Caraṇa Dās Gosvāmī*; B; 48, 5; H, D; 1924 A.D.

0536 Kelimālā (with Life History of Svāmī Haridās by Sudarśana Siṁha); *Svāmī Haridās*; B; 48, 6; H, D; 1952 A.D.

0537 Smaraṇa Maṅgala Stotram; *Rūpa Gosvāmī*; B;48, 7; SKT H, D; 1952 A.D.

0538 Dān Līlā, Naukā Līlā, and Kṣīr Nahar Līlā; *Lalitakiśorī*; B; 48, 8; H, D; 1938 A.D.

0539 Adbhuta Rasa Sāgara; *Viṭṭhal Bipul Devjī*; B; 48, 9; H, D; 1939 A.D.

0540 Yugala Saneha Patrikā; *Vṛndāvan Dās*; B; 48, 10; H, D; 1928 A.D.

0541 Ananya Modinī Tathā Cāha Velī; *Priyā Dās*; B; 48, 11; H, D; 1934 A.D.

0542 Rahasya Siddhānta Grantha Mālā (First Part); B; 48, 12; SKT, D; 1920 A.D.

0543 Śrī Nimbārka Sampradāya kī Sādhana Praṇālī; *Kiśora Dās*; B;48, 13; H, D; 1937 A.D.

0544 Śrī Guru Śaraṇāgati (with Translation in Hindi); *Kiśora Dās*; B; 48, 14; SKT H, D; 1934 A.D.

0545 Prameya Ratnāvalī; *Baladeva Vidyābhūṣaṇa*; B; 48, 15; SKT BL, D; 1927 A.D.

0546 Gaura Tattva; *Rādhā Govinda Nāth*; B; 48, 16; SKT BL, BL; Baṅgābda 1360.

0547 Caitanya Caritāmṛta; *Kṛṣṇa Dās Kavirāj*; B; 48, 17; BL, BL; Baṅgābda 1347.

0548 Rahasya Mīmāṁsā with Ṭīkā, Prapanna-Sura-Taru Mañjarī; B; 48, 18; SKT D.

0549 Nimbārkāṣṭottaraśatanāma Stotram with Ṭīkā; *Sadānanda Bhaṭṭācārya*; B; 48, 19; SKT D; 1925 A.D.

0550 Gopāla Pūjana Paddhati (with Hindi Comments); *Govinda Śaraṇa Deva*; B; 48, 20; SKT H, D; 1937 A.D.

0551 Aṇubhāṣyam (with Tattva Mañjarī Ṭīkā and Bengali Translation); *Madhvācārya*; B; 48, 21; SKT BL, BL.

0552 Preyobhakti Rasārṇava; *Nayanānanda Ṭhākur*; B; 48, 22; BL, BL; Caintanyābdą 463.

0553 Śyāma Candrodaya; *Jagadānanda Ṭhākur*; B; 48, 23; H, BL; Caitanyābda 463.

0554 Prameya Ratnāvalī with Kānti-Mālā Ṭīkā; *Baladeva Vidyābhūṣaṇa*; B; 48, 24; SKT H, D; Caitanyābda 455.

0555 Gauḍīya Anthology; B; 48, 25; SKT H, D.

0556 Vidagdha Mādhava; *Rūpa Gosvāmī*; B; 48, 26; SKT, D; 1937 A.D.

0557 Śrī Brajadhāma and Ācāryagaṇa (Caturtha Khaṇḍa); *Govardhana Dās*; B; 48, 27; BL, BL; Gaurābda 479.

0558 Madhu Keli Vallī, Śrī Rādhā-Kunda Stava, Śrī Rūpa-Sanātana Stotram; *Govardhana Bhaṭṭa*; B; 48, 28; SKT, D; 1955 A.D.

0559 Bhakti Rasa Taraṅgiṇī; *Nārāyaṇa Bhaṭṭācārya*; B; 48, 29; SKT H, D; 1947 A.D.

0560 Siddhānta Darpaṇa with Ṭippaṇī by Nanda Miśra; *Baladeva Vidyābhūṣaṇa*; B; 48, 30; SKT BL, D; Gaurābda 457.

0561 Siddhānta Darpaṇa; *Baladeva Vidyābhūṣaṇa*; B; 49, 1; SKT BL, D BL; Gaurābda 457.

0562 Vallabha Rasikajī kī Vāṇī; *Vallabha Rasikajī*; B; 49, 2; H, D; 1948 A.D.

0563 Mantra Rahasya Ṣoḍaśī with Vyākhyā; *Nimbārka*; B; 49, 3; SKT, D; 1937 A.D.

0564 Bhakti Ratnākara; *Narahari Cakravartī*; B; 49, 4; BL, BL; Gaurābda 402.

0565 Bhakti Sandarbha Vyākhyā; *Pūrī Dās Gosvāmī*; B; 49, 5; BL, BL.

0566 Rahasya Prakāśikā; *Haṁsa Dās*; B; 49, 6; H, D; 1913 A.D.

0567 Chadma Sāñjhī Līlā; *Mahant Kundana Dās Nirmohī*; B; 49, 7; H, D; 1940 A.D.

0568 Mañjarī Svarūpa Nirūpaṇa; *Kuñjabihārī Dās Bābājī*; B; 49, 8; BL, BL; Gaurābda 478.

0569 Vedānta Darśanam (with Vedānta Padārtha Prakāśa by Madhvācārya); *Bādarāyaṇa*; B; 49, 9; SKT H, D; 1930 A.D.

0570 Vañjārauvelī and Vāraha Māsa Vinoda Velī; *Cācā Vṛndāvan Dās*; B; 49, 10; H, D; 1931 A.D.

0571 Śrī Hita-Vṛndāvana Vilāsa; *Yugala Ballabha 'Nirmohī'*; B; 49, 11; H, D; 1940 A.D.

0572 Nārada Pāñcarātra; *Nārada Muni*; B; 49, 12; SKT, D; 1906 A.D.

0573 Nimbārka Sampradāya Prakāśa; *Śrī Haripriyā Das* (ed.); B; 49, 13; H, D.

0574 Vaiṣṇava Nitya Karma; *Hīrālāl Durgāśaṅkara* (ed.); B; 49, 14; SKT GUJ, D GUJ.

0575 Śrī Karuṇā Velī; *Cācā Vṛndāvana Dās*; B; 49, 15; H, D.

0576 Śrī Godā Raṅgeśvara Kṛṣṇa-aṣṭayāma Sevā; *Madhusūdana Dās*; B; 49, 16; SKT H, D; 1940 A.D.

0577 Rahasya Prakāśikā and Godanā Līlā; *Haṁsa Dās*; B; 49, 17; H, D; 1941 A.D.

0578 Namranivedana and Kucch Samıkṣā; *Kṛṣṇadās Bābā* (Kusumasarovar); B; 49, 18; H, D; 1946 A.D.

0579 Rāsa Līlānukaraṇa and Śrī Śrī Nārāyaṇa Bhaṭṭa; *Kṛṣṇadās* (Kusumasarovar); B; 49, 19; H, D; 1946 A.D.

0580 Vedānta Kāmadhenu with Daśaślokī Bhāṣā Ṭīkā; *Nimbārkācārya*; B; 49, 20; SKT H, D; 1925 A.D.

0581 Śrī Bhakta Nāmāvalī; *Śrī Hita Dhruvadāsa*; B; 49, 21; H, D.

0582 Bhagavad Gītā (with Tattva Prakāśikā Bhāṣya and Hindi Translation); *Kṛṣṇa Dvaipāyana Vyāsa*; B; 49, 22; 1935 A.D.

0583 Vedānta Kāmadhenu, (Contains Siddhānta Ratnāñjali, Part I, with Bhāṣā Kānti Prakāśikā); *Nimbārkācārya*; B; 49, 23; SKT H, D; 1926 A.D.

0584 Śrī Harivyāsa Yaśāmṛta; *Rūpa Rasika Deva*; B; 49, 24; H, D; 1925 A.D.

0585 Śrī Vyālīsa Līlā; *Dhruvadās*; B; 49, 25; H, D.

0586 Gulazār Caman, Ānanda Caman, Bihār Caman; *Mahant Śītaldās*; B; 49, 26; H UR; D; 1912 A.D.

0587 Śrī Paccīsī, Nakha Śikha Dhyāna, Ācāryoṁ kī Paramparā; *Kiśor Dās, Sakhī Śaraṇa*; B; 49, 27; H, D; 1912 A.D.

0588 Śrī Nikuñja Prema Mādhurī; *Mādhava Dās* (Upanāma: *Alīmādhurī*); B; 49, 28; H, D; 1934 A.D.

0589 Rādhā Sudhā Śataka; *Haṭhī*; B; 49, 29; H, D.

0590 Aṣṭādaśa Siddhānta ke Padoṁ with Ṭīkā; *Haridās Svāmī*; B; 49, 30; SKT H, D; 1928 A.D.

0591 Śrī Rasika Bhaktamālā; *Yamunā Vallabha*; B; 49, 31; H, D; 1929 A.D.

0592 Līlā-s: Gaunekī Līlā, Jog Līlā, Mālin Līlā, etc. (with Line Drawings); B; 49, 32; H, D.

0593 Hari Bhakti Vilāsa with Bhāṣā-Ṭīkā; *Gopāla Bhaṭṭa Gosvāmī*; B; 49, 33; SKT H, D; 1908 A.D.

0594 Hari Bhakti Vilāsa with Bhāṣā-Ṭīkā; *Gopāla Bhaṭṭa*; B; 50A, 1; SKT H, D; 1908 A.D.

0595 Śrī Nikuñja keli Mādhurī; *Mādhavā Dās* (Upanāma Alimādhurī); B; 50A, 2: H, D; 1926 A.D.

0596 Śrī Braja Premānanda Sāgara; *Cācā Vṛndāvana Dās*; B; 50A, 3; H, D; 1958 A.D.

0597 Subodhinī Ṭīkā on Rāsa Pañcādhyāya of Śrīmad Bhāgavatam; *Kṛṣṇa Dvaipāyana Vyāsa*; B; 50A, 4; SKT, D; 1923 A.D

0598 Rādhāballabha Bhaktamālā; *Priyādās Śukla*; B; 50A, 5; H, D; 1929 A.D.

0599 Ānanda Vanamālā; *Keśava Śaraṇadeva*; B; 50A, 6; SKT, D; 1859 A.D.

0600 Brahma Vaivarta Purāṇa (Kṛṣṇa Janma Khaṇḍa); *Kṛṣṇa Dvaipāyana Vyāsa*; PM; 50A, 7; SKT, D.

0601 Bhakta Mālā (with Ṭīkā Bhaktirasabodhinī); *Nava Dās*; PM; 50A, 8; SKT, D.

0602 Viṣṇu Purāṇam (with Commentary); *Kṛṣṇa Dvaipāyana Vyāsa*; B; 50A, 9; SKT, D; 1754 A.D.

0603 Mantrārtha Rahasya Ṭīkā; PM; 50A, 10; SKT, D; c. 1846 A.D.

0604 Vaiṣṇava Dharma Mīmāṁsā (Saṅkṣepa); *Ananta Rāma*; PM; 50A, 11; SKT, D.

0605 Sāra Saṅgraha; PM; 50A, 12; SKT, D; c. 1944 A.D.

0606 Vraja Siddhānta Jyotsnā; *Dhanīrāma*; PM; 50A, 13; SKT, D; c. 1893.

0607 Satya Nārāyaṇa Vrata Kathā (Extracted from Skanda Purāṇa); *Kṛṣṇa Dvaipāyana Vyāsa*; PM; 50A, 14; SKT, D.

0608 Bhāgavata Māhātmya (from Skanda Purāṇa with Commentary); *Kṛṣṇa Dvaipāyana Vyāsa*; PM; 50A, 15; SKT, D.

0609 Gopāla Sahasranāma Stotra with Ṭīkā (from Sammohana tantra); B; 50A, 16; SKT, D; 1900 A.D.

0610 Atharvaśikhāvilāsa; *Kauśika Rāmānujācārya*; PM; 50B, 1; SKT, GR.

0611 Advaita Kālānalaḥ; PM; 50B, 2; SKT, GR.

0612 Advaita Kālānalaḥ; PM; 50B, 3; SKT, D.

0613 Kāvyadīpikā; PM; 50B, 4; SKT, D.

0614 Advaitabahiṣkāraḥ; *Raṅgarāja*; PM; 50B, 5; SKT, D.

0615 Advaitavidyāvijayaḥ; *Mahācārya*; PM; 50B, 6; TE, TE.

0616 Adhikaraṇayuktivilāsaḥ; *Mahācārya*; PM; 50B, 7; SKT, D.

0617 Adhikaraṇasārārtha Dīpikā; *Maṅgācārya Śrīnivāsasūri*; PM; 50B, 8; SKT, D.

0618 Adhikaraṇasārāvalī; *Veṅkaṭanātha*; PM; 50B, 9; SKT, GR.

0619 Candrikākhaṇḍanam; *Rāmānujadāsa* (Upanāma, Rāmānujamātṛmuni); PM; 50B, 10; SKT, GR.

0620 Aruṇādhikaraṇa Saraṇi Vivaraṇī; *Śrīnivāsa*; PM; 50B, 11; SKT, D.

0621 Vyāvahārikasatyatvakhaṇḍanam; *Varadācārya*; PM; 50B, 12; SKT, GR.

0622 Prapañcamithyātvakhaṇḍanam; PM; 50B, 12; SKT, GR.

0623 Āśrayānupapattiḥ; PM; 50B, 12; SKT, GR.

0624 Tirodhānānupapattiḥ; PM; 50B, 12; SKT, GR.

0625 Svarūpānupattiḥ; PM; 50B, 12; SKT, GR.

0625B Lakṣaṇānupapattiḥ; PM; 50B, 12; SKT, GR.

0626 Pramāṇānupapattiḥ; PM; 50B, 12; SKT, GR.

0627 Avidyākhaṇḍanam; PM; 50B, 12; SKT, GR.

0628 Bhedasamarthanam; PM; 50B, 12; SKT, GR.

0629 Paratattvanirṇayaḥ; PM; 50B, 12; SKT, GR.

0630 Abhedakhaṇḍanam; PM; 50B, 12; SKT, GR.

0631 Ahaṁbrahmetiśrutivicāraḥ; *Vigraham Désika*; PM; 50B, 13; SKT, D.

0632 Ānandatāratamyakhaṇḍanam; *Śrīnivāsācārya*; PM; 50B, 14; SKT, D.

0633 Chāndogyopaniṣadvyākhyā; *Narasiṁhācārya*; PM; 50B, 15; SKT, TE.

0634 Chāndogyopaniṣadvyākhyā; *Narasiṁhācārya*; PM; 50B, 16; SKT, TE.

0635 Adhyātmacintā (with Commentary); *Saumyajāmātṛmuni*; PM; 50B, 17; SKT, GR.

0636 Aruṇādhikaraṇamañjarī; *Śrīnivāsa*; PM; 50B, 18; SKT, GR.

0637 Ānandatāratamyakhaṇḍanam; *Aṇṇayācārya*; PM; 50B, 19; SKT, GR.

0638 Īkṣatyadhikaraṇavicāraḥ; *Anantārya*; PM; 50B, 20; SKT, D.

0639 Upaniṣanmaṅgalābharaṇam (Twenty-four Upaniṣads); PM; 50B, 21; SKT, D.

0640 Kaivalyasthānanirṇayaḥ; *Varadasudarśana*; PM; 50B, 22; SKT, GR.

0641 Kudṛṣṭibhaṅga; *Appagoṇḍācārya*; PM; 50B, 23; SKT, D.

0642 Upaniṣanmaṅgalābharaṇam; *Mādhavayogin*; PM; 50B, 24; SKT, D.

0643 Aitareyopaniṣadvyākhyā; *Narasiṁhācārya*; PM; 50B, 25; SKT, TE.

0644 Jñānayāthārthyavādaḥ; *Anantācārya*; PM; 51A, 1; SKT, D.

0645 Jijñāsādarpaṇaḥ; *Śrīnivāsa*; PM; 51A, 2; SKT, TE.

0646 Gurubhāvaprakāśikā with Vyākhyā; *Lakṣmaṇārya*; PM; 51A, 3; SKT, D.

0647 Tattvanirṇayaḥ; *Appagoṇḍācārya*; PM; 51A, 4; SKT, D.

0648 Tattvasaṅgrahaḥ; *Śrīraṅgarājayajvan*; PM; 51A, 5; SKT, GR.

0649 Tattvanirṇayaḥ; *Varadācārya*; PM; 51A, 6 SKT, GR.

0650 Taittirīyopaniṣadbhāṣyavṛtti-Mitākṣarā; *Govindarāja*; PM; 51A, 7; SKT, D.

0651 Tattvatrayaculukārtha Saṁgraha; *Varadanātha*; PM; 51A, 8; SKT, D.

0652 Tattvamuktākalāpaḥ; *Veṅkaṭanātha*; PM; 51A, 9; SKT, GR.

0653 Tattvamuktākalāpavyākhyā-Sarvārthasiddhi; *Vedāntadeśika*; PM; 51A, 10; SKT, GR.

0654 Taittirīyopaniṣadbhāṣyam; *Kūranārāyaṇadāsa*; PM; 51A, 11; SKT, D.

0655 Nayamayūkhamālikā; *Appayyadīkṣita* ; PM; 51A, 12; SKT, GR.

0656 Taittirīyopaniṣadvyākhyā; *Narasiṁhācārya*; PM; 51A, 13; SKT, TE.

0657 Nayadyumaṇi; *Meghanādāri*; PM; 51A, 14; SKT, D.

0658 Dṛśyatvavicāraḥ; PM; 51A, 15; SKT, D.

0659 Nayamaṇikalikā; PM; *Śrīnivāsācārya*; 51A, 16; SKT, GR.

0660 Nayadyumaṇīdīpikā; *Śrīnivāsācārya*; PM; 51A, 17; SKT, D.

0661 Nyāyakuliśam; *Rāmānujācārya*; PM; 51A, 18; SKT, D.

0662 Nyāyapariśuddhivyākhyā-Nyāyasāra; *Śrīnivāsadāsa*; PM; 51A, 19; SKT, TE GR.

0663 Nirviśeṣavastupramāṇanirāsavicāraḥ; *Anantācārya*; PM; 51A, 20; SKT, D.

0664 Navakoṭiḥ with Daśakoṭi Ratnamālikā; *Kuṇiṅgala Rāmāśāstrī Aṇṇaṅgarārya*; PM; 51A, 21; SKT, GR.

0665 Tirodhānānupapatti with part of Prapañcamithyātvakhaṇḍanam, Āśrayānupapatti and Svarūpānupapatti; PM; 51A, 22; SKT, GR.

0666 Tattvāmṛtam; *Appagoṇḍācārya*; PM; 51A, 23; SKT, D.

0667 Nyāyapariśuddhivyākhyā-Nikaṣā; *Śrīnivāsaśaṭhakopa*; PM; 51A, 24; SKT, GR.

0668 Nītimālā; *Nārāyaṇārya*; PM; 51A, 25; SKT, D.

0669 Gopāla Sahasranāma Stotra (from Sammohanatantra) with Durgārthapradīpam; PM; 51B, 1; SKT, D.

0670 Aṣṭayāmanikuñjadarpaṇa; PM; 51B, 2; H, D.

0671 Priyājī kī Nāmāvalī; PM; 51B, 3; H, D.

0672 Phuṭakara Vāṇī; *Hita Hari Vaṁśa*; PM; 51B, 4; H, D.

0673 Yugala Rasa Mādhurī; *Rasika Govinda*; PM; 51B, 5; H, D.

0674 Kārttika Māhātmya; *Kṛṣṇa Dvaipāyana Vyāsa*; PM; 51B, 6; SKT, D.

0675 Pada Muktāvalī; *Vraja Nidhi Dās*; PM; 51B, 7; H, D.

0676 Pada Saṅgraha; PM; 51B, 8; H, D.

0677 Stava Mālā with commentary; *Rūpa Gosvāmī*; PM; 51B, 9; SKT, BL.

0678 Mantra Mahodadhi; *Mahīdhara*; PM; 51B, 10; SKT, D.

0679 Śrī Mahāprabhujī ke Śrī Gusāījī ke Sevya Svarūpa; PM; 51B, 11; H, D.

0680 Nāmatraya kalpa (Extract from Sanatkumāra Saṁhitā); PM; 51B, 12; SKT, D.

0681 Gauḍīya Paddhati; PM; 51B, 13; SKT, D.

0682 Mahāvākya Nirṇaya; *Śaṅkarācārya*; PM; 51B, 14; SKT, D.

0683 Śrī Kṛṣṇa-Stavarāja (from Brahmavaivarta Purāṇa); *Kṛṣṇa Dvaipāyana Vyāsa*; PM; 51B, 15; SKT, D.

0684 Rādhā Trailokyavikramakavacam (from Sammohana Tantra); PM; 51B, 15; SKT, D.

0685 Trailokya Vijayam Kavacam (from Kāmākṣā Tantra, Seventh Paṭala); PM; 51B, 15; SKT, D.

0686 Kabīr Sāhab kī Sākhī; *Kabīr Dās*; PM; 51B, 16; H, D.

0687 Sāra Candrikā; *Kiśorī Ali*; PM; 51B, 17; H, D.

0688 Amṛta Dhārā; *Bhagavān Dās*; PM; 51B, 18; H, D.

0689 Acha Roṭi; PM; 51B, 19; H, D.

0690 Sat Nāma (Pṛthī Khaṇḍa); *Dharma Dās*; PM; 51B, 20; H, D.

0691 Rāma Stava Rāja (Extract from Sanat Kumāra Saṁhitā); PM; 51B, 21; SKT?, D.

0692 Viṣṇu Sahasranāma; *Kṛṣṇa Dvaipāyana Vyāsa*; PM; 51B, 22; SKT, D.

0693 Savaiyā Sundara Dāsjī ke; *Sundara Dās*; PM; 51B, 23; H, D.

0694 Mahāvāṇī; *Harivyāsadevācārya*; PM; 51B, 24; H, D.

0695 Nimbārkācārya-Vṛndabadhāi or Ācārya Utsava Mālikā; PM 51B, 25; H, D.

0696 Muṇḍakopaniṣat with Commentary; PM; 51B, 26; SKT, D.

0697 Padyāvalī; compilation from *Jayadeva* and *Bilvamaṅgala*; PM; 51B, 27; SKT, D.

0698 Kandarpārka Prakāśaṃ; *Rāmacandra*; PM; 51B, 28; SKT, D.

0699 Praśnottara Ratna-Mālā; *Śuka Yatendriya*; PM; 51B, 29; SKT, D.

0700 (Atharvaṇī) Kali Santaraṇopaniṣat; PM; 51B, 30; SKT, D.

0701 Saṅkṣepa Paddhati; *Devācārya*; PM; 51B, 31; SKT, D.

0702 Vrata Nirṇaya (Also contains Rādhājanmakathā from Harilīlāmṛtatantra) *Gopāla Kṛṣṇa*; PM; 51B, 32; SKT, D.

0703 Gopāla Tāpinī Upaniṣat; PM; 51B, 33; SKT, D.

0704 Rūpa Cintāmaṇi; *Viśvanātha Cakravarti*; PM; 51B, 34; SKT, D.

0705 Śaraṇāgata mantra Vidhi; PM; 51B, 35; SKT, D.

0706 Saṅkṣepa Paddhati; *Devācārya*; PM; 51B, 36; SKT, D.

0707 Gopāla Tāpinī Upaniṣat; PM; 51B, 37; SKT, D.

0708 Bṛhad Gautamīya Tantra (Chapter 6, *Govinda Vṛndāvana*); PM; 51B, 38; SKT, D.

0709 Yamunāṣṭakam and Yamunāstotram; PM; 51B, 39; SKT, D.

0710 Vrata Nirṇaya with Śakunāvalī; PM; 51B, 40; SKT, D.

0711 Kṛṣṇa Stavarāja with Śruti Siddhānta Mañjarī Ṭīkā; PM; 51B, 41; SKT, D.

0712 Catuḥ Sūtrī Vyākhyā-Siddhāntajāhnavī; *Devācārya*; PM; 51B, 42; SKT, D.

0713 Rādhā Rasa Sudhānidhi with Ṭīkā; *Hitaharivaṁśa*; PM; 51B, 43; SKT H, D.

0714 Laghu Stavarāja with Ṭīkā; *Śrīnivāsācārya*; PM; 51B, 44; SKT, D.

0715 Bhakti Rahasya; *Somanātha*; PM; 51B, 45; SKT, D.

0716 Mantrārtha Rahasya with Ṭīkā; PM; 51B, 46; SKT, D.

0717 Bhakti Haṁsa Vivṛti; *Raghunātha Gosvāmī*; PM; 51B, 47; SKT, D.

0718 Smaraṇa Maṅgala (From Govindalīlāmṛta); *Rūpa Gosvāmī*; PM; 51B, 48; SKT, D.

0719 Bhakti Rasa Pañcakāmṛta Bindu; PM; 51B, 49; SKT, D.

0720 Gopāla Kavaca (Extracted from *Sanat Kumāra Saṁhitā*); PM; 51B, 50; SKT, D.

0721 Laghu Stavarāja (With Commentary Gurubhakti-Mandākinī by *Puruṣottama Prasāda*); *Śrīnivāsācārya*; PM; 51B, 51; SKT, D.

0722 Śrī Kṛṣṇa Stavarāja (With Ṭīkā-Śrutisiddhāntamañjarī); *Nimbārkācārya*; PM; 51B, 52; SKT, D.

0723 Praśnottara Mālā; *Śukadeva*; PM; 51B, 53; SKT, D.

0724 (Atharvaṇa) Netropaniṣatsūtra; PM; 51B, 54; SKT, D.

0725 Kṛṣṇāṣṭakam; PM; 51B, 55; H, D.

0726 Praśnottara Ratna Mālā; *Tulasī Dās*; PM; 51B, 56; SKT H, D.

0727 Gopāla Durgā Mantra (Extracted from Atharva Veda); PM; 51B, 57; SKT, D.

0728 Aṣṭa Sakhī Rūpa Sevādi; PM; 51B, 58; SKT H, D.

0729 Yugala Stavarāja from Maheśvara Gaurī Tantra; PM; 51B, 59, SKT, D.

0730 Śrī Kṛṣṇa Sahasranāma Stotram from Sarvottama Māhātmya Tantra; PM; 51B, 60; SKT, D.

0731 Ālamandāra-Stotram with Vyākhyā; *Yāmunācārya*; PM; 51B, 61; SKT, D.

0732 Sata Pañcāśikā; *Rāma Caraṇa*; PM; 51B, 62; H, D.

0733 Nānārthakalpavallī; *Veṅkaṭabhaṭṭar*; PM; 52, 1; SKT, GR.

0734 Nyāyaratnāvalī; *Vedāntācārya*; PM; 52, 2; SKT, D.

0735 Nyāyaratnāvalī; *Vedāntācārya*; PM; 52, 3; SKT, D.

0736 Praṇavadarpaṇaḥ; *Śrīnivāsācārya*; PM; 52, 4; SKT, TE.

0737 Pañcamānāyasāraḥ; *Samarapuṅgava*; PM; 52, 5; SKT, TE.

0738 Prapañca Mithyātvakhaṇḍanam; *Varadanātha*; PM; 52, 6; SKT, GR.

0739 Pramāṇānupapatti; PM; 52, 7; SKT, GR.

0740 Pradhāna Pratitantradarpaṇam; *Śrīnivāsa*; PM; 52, 8; SKT, GR.

0741 Praṇavadīpikā; *Gopālasudhī*; PM; 52, 9; SKT, D.

0742 Pūrvottaramīmāṁsaikakaṇṭhyam; PM; 52, 10; SKT, D.

0743 Puruṣasūktacaramārthaniṣkarṣa; *Rāmānujācārya*; PM; 52, 11; SKT, D.

0744 Parikaravijayaḥ; *Doḍḍayyācārya*; PM; 52, 12; SKT, D.

0745 Paramukhacapeṭikā; *Śrīkṛṣṇatātācārya*; PM; 52, 13; SKT, GR.

0746 Paratattvaprakāśikā; *Śrīnivāsadāsa*; PM; 52, 14; SKT, GR.

0747 Padārthasaṅgraha; *Śaṭhakopa*; PM; 52, 15; SKT, D.

0748 Nyāya Pariśuddhi Vyākhyā-Sannyāyadīpikā; *Kṛṣṇatātācārya*; PM; 52, 16; SKT, D.

0749 Bhagavadgītā with Vyākhyā-Gītārtha Saṅgraha; *Nārāyaṇamuni*; PM; 53, 1; SKT, D.

0750 Bimbatattvaprakāśikā; *Devarāja*; PM; 53, 2; SKT, GR.

0751 Brahmavidyāvijaya; *Rāmānujadāsa*; PM; 53, 3; SKT, GR.

0752 Bhagavadgītābhāṣyavyākhyā-Tātparyacandrikā; *Vedāntadeśika*; PM; 53, 4; SKT, GR.

0753 Bṛhadāraṇyakopaniṣad Vyākhyā; *Narasiṁhācārya (Mudumbai)*; PM; 53, 5; SKT, TE.

0754 Brahmalakṣaṇavākyārthaḥ; PM; 53, 6; SKT, D.

0755 Praśnopaniṣadvyākhyā; *Narasiṁhācārya (Mudumbai)*; PM; 53, 7; SKT, TE.

0756 Prameyamālā; *Varadasūri*; PM; 53, 8; SKT, GR.

0757 Brahmasūtrabhāṣyavyākhyā-Vākyārthadīpikā; *Parāṅkuśayati*; PM; 53, 9; SKT, D.

0758 Brahmasūtravṛtti; PM; 53, 10; SKT, D.

0759 Brahmasūtraśrībhāṣyavyākhyā-Mitaprakāśikā; PM; 53, 11; SKT, D.

0760 Bhedadhikkāranyakkāra; *Nṛsiṁhadeva*; PM; 53, 12; SKT, GR.

0761 Brahmasūtrārthaṭippaṇī; *Varadārya*; PM; 53, 13; SKT, D.

0762 Bhedadarpaṇaḥ; *Śrīnivāsācārya*; PM; 53, 14; SKT, TE.

0763 Māyibhaṅga with Telugu Ṭīkā; *Appagoṇḍācārya*; PM; 53, 15; SKT, D.

0764 Brahmasūtrabhāṣyavyākhyā-Śrutapradīpikā; *Sudarśana Sūri*; PM; 53, 16; SKT, GR.

0765 Brahmasūtrabhāṣyavyākhyā-Laghubhāvaprakāśikā; *Govardhana*; PM; 53, 17; SKT, GR.

0766 Brahmasūtrabhāṣyavyākhyā-Mūlabhāvaprakāśikā; *Raṅgarāmānuja*; PM; 53, 18; SKT, D.

0767 Brahmasūtrabhāṣyavyākhyā-Nayaprakāśikā; *Meghanādārī*; PM; 53, 19; SKT, D.

0768 Brahmasūtrabhāṣyavyākhyā-Nayaprakāśikā; *Meghanādāri*; PM; 54, 1; Continuation of 53, 19; SKT, D.

0769 Brahmasūtrabhāṣyavyākhyā-Tattvamārtaṇḍa; *Śrīnivāsa*; PM; 54, 2; SKT, TE.

0770 Brahmasūtrabhāṣyasaṅgrahavivaraṇam; PM; 54, 3; SKT, TE.

0771 Brahmasūtravyākhyātattvamārtaṇḍa; *Śrīnivāsa*; PM; 54, 4; SKT, D.

0772 Śārīrikamīmāṁsābhāṣyasaṅgrahaḥ; *Nṛsiṁhārya*; PM; 54, 5; SKT, GR.

0773 Śatadūṣaṇīvyākhyā-Sahasrakiraṇī; *Śrīnivāsācārya*; PM; 54, 6; SKT, D.

0774 Śatadūṣaṇīvyākhyā-Sahasrakiraṇī; *Śrīnivāsācārya*; PM; 54, 7; SKT, GR.

0775 Śatadūṣaṇī; *Veṅkaṭadeśika*; PM; 54, 8; SKT, GR.

0776 Śatadūṣaṇīvyākhyā-Sahasrakiraṇī; PM; 54, 9; SKT, TE.

0777 Śatadūṣaṇīvyākhyā Caṇḍamāruta; *Rāmānujadāsa*; PM; 54, 10; SKT, GR.

0778 Śatadūṣaṇīvyākhyā-Caṇḍamāruta; *Mahācārya*; PM; 54, 11; SKT, GR.

0779 Śatadūṣaṇīvyākhyā-Caṇḍamāruta; *Mahācārya*; PM; 55, 1; Continuation of 54, 11; SKT, GR.

0780 Śārīrikaśāstrārthasaṅgrahaḥ; *Raṅgarāmānujasvāmin*; PM; 55, 2; SKT, D.

0781 Śārīrikaśāstradīpikā; *Raṅgarāmānujasvāmin*; PM; 55, 3; SKT, TE.

0782 Siddhitrayam; *Yāmunācārya*; PM; 55, 4; SKT, D.

0783 Śrutaprakāśikāvyākhyā; *Campakeśācārya*; PM; 55, 5; SKT, GR.

0784 Śrutaprakāśikāvyākhyā-Gurubhāvaprakāśikā; *Lakṣmaṇārya*; PM; 55, 6; SKT, D.

0785 Śrutaprakāśikāsaṅgrahaḥ; *Śrīnivāsasūri Śrīśailapūrṇa*; PM; 55, 7; SKT, GR.

0786 Sarvārthasiddhivyākhyā; *Saumyavaradarāmānujamuni*; PM; 55, 8; SKT, GR.

0787 Sajjanāmṛtam; *Appagoṇḍācārya*; PM; 55, 9; SKT, D.

0788 Sarvārthasiddhivyākhyā; *Nṛsiṁhadeva*; PM; 55, 10; SKT, GR.

0789 Sadvidyāvijayaḥ; *Mahācārya*; PM; 55, 11; SKT, D.

0790 Śrutaprakāśikāvivaraṇam-Tātparyadīpikā; PM; 56, 1; SKT, GR.

0791 Triṁśacclokī; PM; 56, 2; SKT, TE.

0792 Upendrasaṁhitā; PM; 56, 3; SKT, D.

0793 Sarvārthasiddhivyākhyā; *Śrīnivāsācārya*; PM; 56, 4; SKT, GR.

0794 Śrutaprakāśikāsaṅgraha; *Śrīnivāsasūri Śrīśailapūrṇa*; PM; 56, 5; SKT, GR.

0795 Śrutaprakāśikāsārasaṅgraha; PM; 56, 6; SKT, GR.

0796 Ārādhanotsava Saṅgraha; PM; 56, 7; SKT, D.

0797 Vedāntasiddhāntakaumudī; PM; 56, 8; SKT, GR.

0798 Brahmalakṣaṇavākyārthaḥ; PM; 56, 9; SKT, D.

0799 Vedāntakārikāvali; *Bucciveṅkaṭācārya*; PM; 56, 10; SKT, TE.

0800 Prapañcamithyātvakhaṇḍanam; PM; 56, 11; SKT, D.

0801 Praṇavadīpikā; *Gopālasudhī*; PM; 56, 12; SKT, D.

0802 Pūrvottaramīmāṁsaikakaṇṭhyam; PM; 56, 13; SKT, D.

0803 Nītimālā; *Nārāyaṇārya*; PM; 56, 14; SKT, D.

0804 Nyāyamandāraḥ; *Vīrarāghava*; PM; 56, 15; SKT, D.

0805 Bimbatattvaprakāśikā; *Devarāja*; PM; 56, 16; SKT, GR.

0806 Prapannāmṛtam; *Pillailokācārya*; PM; 56, 17; SKT, GR.

0807 Pañcamāmnāyasāraḥ; *Samarapuṅgava*; PM; 56, 18; SKT, TE.

0808 Nikṣepacintāmaṇiḥ; *Gopāladeśika*; PM; 56, 19; SKT, GR.

0809 Arcanākhaṇḍaḥ; PM; 56, 20; SKT, TE.

0810 Agastyasaṁhitā; PM; 56, 21; SKT, D.

0811 Aṣṭākṣaradīpikā; PM; 56, 22; SKT, GR.

0812 Arcanākhaṇḍavyākhyā; PM; 56, 23; SKT, TE.

0813 Arcanākhaṇḍaḥ; PM; 56, 24; SKT, TE.

0814 Aṣṭādaśabhedanirṇayaḥ; *Raṅganāthasūri*; PM; 56, 25; SKT, D.

0815 Arcanānavanītam; *Keśavācārya*; PM; 56, 26; SKT, D.

0816 Avaiṣṇavagurumantratyāgavicāraḥ; *Gārgyaveṅkaṭācārya*; PM; 56, 27; SKT, D.

0817 Aṣṭākṣaradīpikā; PM; 56, 28; SKT, GR.

0818 Vedāntaratnamālā; *Śrīnivāsa*; PM; 56, 29; SKT, D.

0819 Vedāntakārikāvali; *Bucciveṅkaṭācārya*; PM; 56, 30; SKT, D.

0820 Vādārthamālā; *Campakeśācārya*; PM; 56, 31; SKT, D.

0821 Rahasyatrayasārādhikārasaṁgraha with Vyākhyā; *Śrīnivāsācārya*; PM; 56, 32; SKT, TE.

0822 Āgamapradīpaḥ; *Sundaravīrarāghava*; PM; 57, 1; SKT, GR.

0823 Ahirbudhnyasaṁhitā; PM; 57, 2; SKT, GR.

0824 Āgamapradīpaḥ; *Sundaravīrarāghava*; PM; 57, 3; SKT, GR TA.

0825 Aṣṭādaśarahasyārthavivaraṇam; *Rāmānuja*; PM; 57, 4; SKT, D.

0826 Aṣṭādaśabhedasaṁvāda; PM; 57, 5; SKT, GR.

0827 Ahirbudhnyasaṁhitā; PM; 57, 6; SKT, GR.

0828 Īśvarasaṁhitā; PM; 57, 7; SKT, GR.

0829 Ucitāpāyanirṇayaḥ; PM; 57, 8; SKT, GR.

0830 Utsavasaṁgraha; PM; 57, 9; SKT, TE.

0831 Kapiñjala Saṁhitā; PM; 57, 10; SKT, GR.

0832 Utsavasaṁgraha with Telugu Ṭīkā; PM; 57, 11; SKT, TE.

0833 Ūrdhvāmnāya Saṁhitā; PM; 57, 12; SKT, D.

0834 Kapiñjalasaṁhitā; PM; 57, 13; SKT, GR.

0835 Upayuktāṁśasaṁgrahaḥ; PM; 57, 14; SKT, GR.

0836 Kurukeśagāthānukaraṇam; PM; 57, 15; SKT, TE.

0837 Kṛṣṇāmṛtamahārṇavaḥ Savyākhyā; *Kṛṣṇācārya*; PM; 57, 16; SKT, D.

0838 Kriyākairavacandrikā; *Varāhadeśika*; PM; 57, 17; SKT, TE.

0839 Kārikādarpaṇaḥ; *Varadakavi*; PM; 57, 18; SKT, GR.

0840 Kārpaṇyadarpaṇam; *Śaṭhakopācārya*; PM; 57, 19; SKT, D.

0841 Kārikādarpaṇaḥ; *Varadakavi*; PM; 57, 20; SKT, GR.

0842 Taptamudrāvilāsa; *Nṛsiṁha*; PM; 57, 21; SKT, GR.

0843 Tulasimālādhāraṇanirṇayaḥ; PM; 57, 22; SKT, D.

0844 Tattvadīpikā; *Śrīnivāsācārya*; PM; 57, 23; SKT, GR.

0845 Taptamudrādhāraṇapramāṇa Vacanāni; PM; 57, 24; SKT, D.

0846 Ṇatvadarpaṇaḥ; *Śrīnivāsācārya*; PM; 57, 25; SKT, GR.

0847 Tattvanirṇaya; *Varadācārya*; PM; 57, 26; SKT, GR.

0848 Ṇatvopapattibhaṅgavādaḥ; *Tirumalācārya*; PM; 57, 27; SKT, GR.

0849 Paratattvanirṇayaḥ; PM; 57, 28; SKT, GR.

0850 Nikṣeparakṣāvyākhyā; *Nṛsiṁhārya*; PM; 57, 29; SKT, GR.

0851 Nityārcanavidhiḥ; PM; 58, 1; SKT, GR.

0852 Ṇatvatattvaparitrāṇam; *Śrīnivāsadāsa*; PM; 58, 2; SKT, GR.

0853 Divyaprabandhanigamanavacanāni; PM; 58, 3; SKT, GR.

0854 Paramukhacapeṭikā; *Śrīśailakṛṣṇatātācārya*; PM; 58, 4; SKT, GR.

0855 Pāñcarātravacanasāgaraḥ; PM; 58, 5; SKT, GR.

0856 Pāñcarātram; PM; 58, 6; SKT, GR.

0857 Parikaravijayaḥ; *Mahācārya*; PM; 58, 7; SKT, D.

0858 Parārthayajanādhikāranirvāhaḥ; *Sundaravīrarāghava*; PM; 58, 8; SKT, GR.

0859 Pāñcarātrakaṇṭakoddhāraḥ; *Varadācārya*; PM; 58, 9; SKT, D.

0860 Paramasaṁhitā; PM; 58, 10; SKT, D.

0861 Pāñcarātrasaṁhitā; PM; 58, 11; SKT, D.

0862 Pādmatantram; PM; 58, 12; SKT, D.

0863 Pāñcarātrāgamaḥ; PM; 58, 13; SKT, TE.

0864 Pāñcarātrāgamaḥ; PM; 58, 14; SKT, TE.

0865 Pāñcarātrasārasaṅgraha; PM; 58, 15; SKT, GR.

0866 Parameśvaravivṛti; *Nṛsiṁhayajvan*; PM; 58, 16; SKT, GR.

0867 Pādmasaṁhitātantram; PM; 58, 17; SKT, D.

0868 Pādmatantram; PM; 58, 18; SKT, GR.

0869 Pādmatantram; 59, 1; PM; SKT, GR.

0870 Parameśvarasaṁhitā; PM; 59, 2; SKT, GR.

0871 Brahmasampradāyapaddhati; PM; 59, 3; SKT, D.

0872 Prapannavijayaḥ; *Raṅgācārya*;; PM; 59, 4; SKT, GR.

0873 Pramāṇasaṅgraha; *Saumyajāmātṛmuni*; PM; 59, 5; SKT, GR.

0874 Pramāṇasāra Prakāśikā; *Govindaguru*; PM; 59, 6; SKT TA, GR.

0875 Pramāṇasaṅgraha; *Lakṣmaṇa*; PM; 59, 7; SKT, D.

0876 Prapatyadhikāri Viśeṣaṇatva Niṣkarṣaḥ; PM; 59, 8; SKT, GR.

0877 Pratiṣṭhātantram; PM; 59, 9; SKT, GR.

0878 Pratiṣṭhāpradīpaḥ; *Narasiṁhavājapeyin*; PM; 59, 10; SKT, GR.

0879 Prāyaścittasaṅgraha; PM; 59, 11; SKT GR.

0880 Prāyaścittapaṭalam; PM; 59, 12; SKT, GR.

0881 Bṛhadbrahmasaṁhitā; PM; 59, 13; SKT, GR.

0882 Brahmasaṁhitā; PM; 59, 14; SKT, GR.

0883 Bhārgavatantra Prayogaḥ; PM; 59, 15; SKT, GR.

0884 Bharadvājasaṁhitā; PM; 59, 16; SKT, GR.

0885 Bhṛgusaṁhitā; PM; 59, 17; SKT, GR.

0886 Mantrārthakaṭhinapada Dīpikā; PM; 59, 18; SKT TA, GR.

0887 Bhagavadviṣayaḥ; *Govardhanam Raṅgācārya*; PM; 59, 19; SKT, D.

0888 Mārkaṇḍeyasaṁhitā; PM; 60, 1; SKT, TE.

0889 Rahasyatrayakārikā Savyākhyā; PM; 60, 2; SKT TA, GR TA.

0890 Rahasyacaramaślokacandrikā; *Pelapūrdīkṣita* and *Śuddha Sattvadāsa*; PM; 60, 3; SKT, GR.

0891 Rahasyatrayamīmāṁsābhāṣyam; *Rāmānujadāsa*; PM; 60, 4; SKT, TE.

0892 Rahasyatrayakārikādarpaṇam; PM; 60, 5; SKT, TE.

0893 Rahasyatrayamīmāṁsābhāṣya Kaṭhina Padadīpikā; PM; 60, 6; SKT TA, GR.

0894 Rahasyatrayasārapramāṇa Saṁgrahaḥ; *Śrīnivāsācārya*; PM; 60, 7; SKT, D.

0895 Rahasyatrayavyākhyātātparyadīpikā; *Vīrarāghava*; PM; 60, 8; SKT TA, GR.

0896 Rahasyarakṣā; *Veṅkaṭadeśika*; PM; 60, 9; SKT, D.

0897 Rahasyarakṣā; *Vedāntadeśika*; PM; 60 10; SKT, D.

0898 Vārtāmālā; PM; 60, 11; SKT, D.

0899 Lakṣmītantram; PM; 60, 12; SKT, GR.

0900 Rahasyatrayavyākhyā-Tātparyadīpikā; *Vīrarāghava*; PM; 60, 13; SKT TA, GR.

0901 Tattvasaṅgrahaḥ; PM; 60, 14; SKT, D.

0902 Tattvatrayaculukārthasaṅgrahaḥ; *Varadanātha*; PM; 60, 15; SKT, D.

0903 Triṁśaccloki; PM; 60, 16; SKT, TE.

0904 Tattvadīpaprakāśaḥ; *Saumyajāmātṛmuni*; PM; 60, 17; SKT, GR.

0905 Tattvaniṣkarṣaḥ; *Kandādai Appagoṇḍācārya*; PM; 60, 18; SKT, D.

0906 Tattvabhāskaraḥ; *Pelapūrdīkṣita*; PM; 60, 19; SKT, D.

0907 Tattva Nirṇayaḥ; *Kandādai Appagoṇḍācārya*; PM; 60, 20; SKT, D.

0908 Siddhāntasāraḥ; *Appagoṇḍācārya*; PM; 60, 21; SKT, D.

0909 Seśvaramīmāṁsā; *Vedāntācārya*; PM; 60, 22; SKT, GR.

0910 Nyāyaratnāvalī; *Vedāntācārya*; PM; 60, 23; SKT, D.

0911 Viṣṇusaṁhitā; *Nārāyaṇamuni*; PM; 60, 24; SKT, GR.

0912 Viṣvaksena Saṁhitā; PM; 60, 25; SKT, GR.

0913 Vaikhānasāgamaḥ (Bhṛgusaṁhitā); PM; 61, 1; SKT, GR.

0914 Vaikhānasasūtravyākhyā-Tattvaprakāśikā; *Narasiṁhācārya*; PM; 61, 2; SKT, TE.

0915 Vaikhānasaviṣayaślokaḥ; PM; 61, 3; SKT, TE.

0916 Vaikhānasasakalāgamasaṅgrahaḥ; PM; 61, 4; SKT, GR.

0917 Vaikhānasasakalāgamasaṅgrahaḥ; PM; 61, 5; SKT, D.

0918 Vaikhānasāgamaḥ; *Marīci*; PM; 61, 6; SKT, TE.

0919 Vaibhaveṣṭi; *Bhṛgu*; PM; 61, 7; SKT, D.

0920 Vaikhānasāgamaḥ; *Marīci*; PM; 61, 8; SKT, TE.

0921 Vaikhānasāgamaḥ; *Marīci*; PM; 61, 9; SKT, GR.

0922 Vaikhānasasaṁhitā; PM; 61, 10; SKT, GR.

0923 Vaikhānasasaṅgraha Smṛti Mīmāṁsā; *Śiṅgarācārya*; PM; 61, 11; SKT, TE.

0924 Vaikhānasāgamaḥ (Kāśyapīya); *Kāśyapa*; PM; 61, 12; SKT, GR.

0925 Vaiṣṇavaprasādādipratiṣṭhāvidhiḥ; *Mohanarāyaguru*; PM; 61, 13; SKT, GR.

0926 Saṁhitāratnākaraḥ; PM; 61, 14; SKT, TE.

0927 Saṁhitāratnākaraḥ; PM; 61, 15; SKT, TE.

0928 Sampradāya Candrikā; *Veṅkaṭānandasūri*; PM; 61, 16; SKT, TE.

0929 Sampradāyacandrikā; *Veṅkaṭānandasūri*; PM; 61, 17; SKT, D.

0930 Sampradāyavicāraḥ; PM; 61, 18; SKT, D.

0931 Satvatantrabhāṣyam; *Alasiṅgabhaṭṭa*; PM; 61, 19; SKT, GR.

0932 Sātvatāmṛtam; *Yogānanda*; PM; 61, 20; SKT, GR.

0933 Kiraṇāgamaḥ; PM; 61, 21; SKT, GR.

0934 Sārasaṅgrahaḥ; PM; 61, 22; SKT, D.

0935 Sudarśanasaṁhitā; PM; 61, 23; SKT, TE.

0936 Sudarśanaprapattiḥ; PM; 61, 24; SKT, TE.

0937 Pañcaratnavyākhyā; (a) Tantrasāraprakāśikā, (b) Tārakadīpikā, (c) Śivatattvaprakāśikā, (d) Śrutyarthaprakāśikā, (e) Smaratattvaprakāśikā; Vīraṇārādhya; PM; 61, 25; SKT, D.

0938 Smaratattvaprakāśikā; *Revaṇārādhyayami*; PM; 61, 26; SKT, GR TE.

0939 Saṁhitāratnākara; PM; 61, 27; SKT, TE.

0940 Sudarśanasaṁhitā; PM; 61, 28; SKT, TE.

0941 Śrīvibhutvasamarthanam; *Raghunātha*; PM; 61, 29; SKT, GR.

0942 Śiṣṭabhūṣaṇam; *Rāmānujācārya*; PM; 61, 30; SKT, GR.

0943 Śaraṇāgatipañcaviṁśati-savyākhyā; PM; 61; 31; SKT, GR.

0944 Śrīyaḥśaraṇyatvavicāraḥ; PM; 62, 1; SKT TA, GR TA.

0945 Śrītattvaratnam; PM; 62, 2; SKT, D.

0946 Śaivadīkṣāvidhiḥ (with Commentary); PM; 62, 3; SKT, D.

0947 Vīraśaivāhnikam with Telugu Meaning; PM; 62, 4; SKT, TE.

0948 Śaivalakṣaṇam with Telugu Meaning; PM; 62, 5; SKT, TE.

0949 Satkriyākalpamañjarī; PM; 62, 6; SKT, TE.

0950 Śivajñānam; *Nandikeśvara*; PM; 62, 7; SKT, D.

0951 Vaidikācāranirṇayaḥ; *Saccidānanda*; PM; 62, 8; SKT, D.

0952 Vīraśaivāhnikam with Telugu Meaning; *Vīraśaivadīkṣāvidhānam*; PM; 62, 9; SKT, D.

0953 Śivādvaitam; PM; 62, 10; SKT, TE.

0954 Śivasūtrāṇi; PM; 62, 11; SKT, TE.

0955 Śivasūtravārtikam; *Devarāja*; PM; 62, 12; SKT, TE.

0956 Vīramāheśvarācārasaṅgrahaḥ; *Nīlakaṇṭhanāganāth*; PM; 62, 13; SKT, D.

0957 Sadanuṣṭhānadarpaṇaḥ; PM; 62, 14; SKT, GR.

0958 Saddarśanasudarśanam; PM; 62, 15; SKT, GR.

0959 Śivatattvopalabdhi; PM; 62, 16; SKT, D.

0960 Śivārcanacandrikā; *Appayyadīkṣita*; PM; 62, 17; SKT, D.

0961 Śaivaparibhāṣā; *Śivāgrayogin*; PM; 62, 18; SKT, D.

0962 Sadvidyākalpataruḥ; *Ramyajāmātṛmuni*; PM; 62, 19; SKT, TE.

0963 Vijayottarasaṁhitā; PM; 62, 20; SKT, GR.

0964 Brahmasūtravivaraṇam-śivadarśanam; PM; 62, 21; SKT, D.

0965 Mṛgendrāgamavṛtti; *Bhaṭṭa Nārāyaṇa*; PM; 62, 22; SKT, D.

0966 Mātaṅgaparameśvaram; PM; 62, 23; SKT, TE.

0967 Śrībhāṣyādyantabhāgaḥ; PM; 62, 24; SKT, GR.

0968 Siddhitrayam; *Yāmunācārya*; PM; 62, 25; SKT, GR.

0969 Śrutaprakāśikāsaṅgrahaḥ; PM; 62, 26; SKT, GR.

0970 Ṣatadūṣaṇī; *Vedāntadeśika*; PL; 62, 27; SKT, GR.

0971 Śrībhāṣyasaṅgraha; *Veṅkaṭācārya*; PL; 62, 28; SKT, GR.

0972 Siddhitrayam; *Yāmunācārya*; PL; 62, 29; SKT, GR.

0973 Siddhāntanyāyacandrikā; *Devarāja*; PL; 62, 30; SKT, GR.

0974 Śatadūṣaṇī; *Vedāntadeśika*; PL; 62, 31; SKT, GR.

0975 Śrutaprakāśikāvyākhyā-Bhāvaprakāśikā; *Raṅgarāmānuja*; PL; 62, 32; SKT, GR.

0976 Siddhāntaratnāvaliḥ; *Veṅkaṭācārya*; PL; 62, 33; SKT, GR.

0977 Śatadūṣaṇīvyākhyā; *Rāmānujadāsa*; PL; 62, 34; SKT, GR.

0978 Haripāramyacandrikā; PL; 63, 1; SKT, GR.

0979 Śrutaprakāśikāvyākhyā-Tūlikā; PL; 63, 2; SKT, GR.

0980 Śatadūṣaṇī; *Vedāntadeśika*; PL; 63, 3; SKT, TE.

0981 Śrutaprakāśikāvyākhyā; *Raṅgarāmānuja*; PL; 63, 4; SKT, GR.

0982 Sajjanāmṛtam; *Appagoṇḍārya*; PL; 63, 5; SKT, TE.

0983 Siddhāntasiddhāñjanam; *Anantācārya*; PL; 63, 6; SKT, GR.

0984 Upādānatvasamarthanam; *Śrīnivāsa*; PL; 63, 7; SKT, TE.

0985 Sāmānādhikaraṇyavādaṭippaṇī; *Anantācārya*; PL; 63, 8; SKT, GR.

0986 Kāśyapottarasaṁhitā; PL; 63, 9; SKT, GR.

0987 Ārādhanotsavasaṅgrahaḥ; PL; 63, 10; SKT, GR.

0988 Arcādījyāprabhāvaḥ; PL; 63, 11; SKT, GR.

0989 Ādhāraśaktitarpaṇam; PL; 63, 12; SKT, GR.

0990 Kāraṇamālāśatakakṣyā; PL; 63, 13; SKT, GR.

0991 Agastyasaṁhitā; PL; 63, 14; SKT, TE.

0992 Āgamaprāmāṇyam; *Yāmunācārya*; PL; 63, 15; SKT, GR.

0993 Āgamaprāmāṇyam; *Yāmunācārya*; PL; 63, 16; SKT, GR.

0994 Kapiñjalasaṁhitā; PL; 63, 17; SKT, GR.

0995 Kaśyapottarasaṁhitā; PL; 63, 18; SKT, GR.
0996 Kaśyapottarasaṁhitā; PL; 63, 19; SKT, GR.
0997 Kārikādarpaṇaḥ; *Varadakavi*; PL; 63, 20; SKT, GR.
0998 Ādhāraśaktidarpaṇam; PL; 63, 21; SKT, GR.
0999 Ārādhanakārikā; PL; 63, 22; SKT, GR.
1000 Ārādhanakramaḥ; PL; 63, 23; SKT, GR.
1001 Upendrasaṁhitā; PL; 63, 24; SKT, GR.
1002 Aṣṭādaśabhedanirṇayaḥ; *Raṅganāthasūri*; PL; 63, 25; SKT, TE.
1003 Aṣṭādaśabhedanirṇayaḥ; *Raṅganāthasūri*; PL; 63, 26; SKT, GR.
1004 Aṣṭādaśabhedanirṇayaḥ; *Raṅganāthasūri*; PL; 63, 27; SKT, GR.
1005 Aṣṭākṣarabrahmavidyā; *Nārada*; PL; 63, 28; SKT, GR.
1006 Arthapañcakam; *Gārgyaveṅkaṭācārya*; PL; 63, 29; SKT, TE.
1007 Tirupati-vaṇṇa-viruttam; PL; 63, 30; TA, TA.
1008 Irukāmyavilakkam; *Aritātar*; PL; 63, 31; TA, TA.
1009 Araṅganāyakar Mālai; *Muthukumārapaṇḍāram*; PL; 63, 32; TA, TA.
1010 Rāma Liṅga Tiruppugal; *Pālapārati*; PL; 63, 33; TA, TA.
1011 Yatīndramatadīpikā; *Śrīnivāsadāsa*; PL; 78, 1; SKT, TE.
1012 Vādādrikuliśam; *Śrīnivāsācārya*; PL; 78, 2; SKT, GR.
1013 Vijayīndraparājayaḥ; *Tātācārya*; PL; 78, 3; SKT, GR.
1014 Viṣayatāvādaḥ; *Anantācārya*; PL; 78, 4; SKT, GR.
1015 Siddhāntasārāvaliḥ; *Trilocanaśivācārya*; PL; 78, 5; SKT, TE.
1016 Siddhāntacintāmaṇiḥ; *Śrīnivāsācārya*; PL; 78, 6; SKT, TE.
1017 Sadvidyāvijayaḥ; *Rāmānujadāsa*; PL; 78, 7; SKT, GR.
1018 Sarvārthasiddhivyākhyā-Ānandavallarī; *Nṛsiṁhadeva*; PL; 78, 8; SKT, GR.

1019 Samāsavādaḥ; *Anantārya*; PL; 78, 9; SKT, GR.

1020 Śrutaprakāśikāvyākhyā; PL; 78, 10; SKT, GR.

1021 Sūtrabhāṣyavyākhyā; PL; 78, 11; SKT, GR.

1022 Śārīrakārthacintā; *Śrīśailayogirāja*; PL; 78, 12; SKT, GR.

1023 Sūtrabhāṣyavyākhyā; PL; 78, 13; SKT, TE.

*1024 Śruti Tātparya Nirṇayaḥ; PM; 91, 1; SKT, TE. (123.1)

1025 Śrutaprakāśikāvyākhyānam; *Lakṣmaṇamuni* (Embar Svāmī); PM; 91, 2; SKT, TE. (123.2)

1026 Śrutaprakāśikātūlikā; *Vādhūla Śrīnivāsācār*; PM; 91, 3; SKT, TE. (123.3)

1027 Gurubhāvaprakāśikā (Part I); *Śuddhasattvam Lakṣmaṇācār*; PM; 91, 4; SKT, TE. 1938 A.D. (123.4)

1028 Gurubhāvaprakāśikā (Part II); *Śuddhasattvam Lakṣmaṇācār*; PM; 91, 5; SKT, TE. 1938 A.D. (123.5)

1029 Gurubhāvaprakāśikā (Part III); *Śuddhasattvam Lakṣmaṇācār*; PM; 91, 6; SKT, TE. 1938 A.D. (123.6)

1030 Brahmavidyākaumudī; *Śrīnivāsācār*; PM; 91, 7; SKT, TE. 1938 A.D. (123.7)

1031 Śrutaprakāśikāsāra (I Pāda); *Añjanagrāmavāsī Varadācār*; PM; 91, 8; SKT, TE. 1938 A.D. (123.8)

1032 Caramaślokasiddhatātparyaṭippaṇī; *Śrīśailācārya Embar Tiruveṅkaṭācārya Jīyarsvāmi*; PM; 91, 9; SKT, TE. 1940 A.D. (123.9)

1033 Siddhopāyasudarśanam; PM; 91, 10; SKT, TE. 1940 A.D. (123.10)

1034 Kaivalyaśatadūṣaṇī; *Kurukaśrīśailayogīśa*; PM; 91, 11; SKT, TE. 1944 A.D. (123.11)

1035 Siddhadharmavijaya Maṅgaladīpikā; PM; 91, 12; SKT, TE. 1941 A.D. (123.12)

1036 Caramaśloka Ṭippaṇīvyākhyāna and Campaka; PM; 92, 1; SKT, TE. 1909 A.D. (124.1)

1037 Campakeśīya (I and II); *Kauśikaśrīnarasiṁha*; PM; 92, 2; SKT, TE. (124.2)

1038 Emberumānār Panniraṇḍu Vārtai; *Periyavāccān Pilla*; PL; 92, 3; TA, GR. (124.3)

1039 Tātparyadīpikā Rahasyatrayavyākhyāna; *Vīrarāghavasūri*; PL; 92, 4; SKT, GR. (No text in 124)

1040 Perumāltirumozhi Vyākhyāna and Tiruppāvaisaṅgati; *Periyavāccān Pillai*; PL; 92, 5; TA, GR. (124.4)

1041 Tattvatraya Vyākhyāna; *Śrīvaravaramuni*; PL; 92, 6; TA, GR. (124.5)

1042 Tātparyadīpikārahasyatraya Vyākhyāna; *Vīrarāghavasūri*; PL; 92, 7; SKT, GR. (No text in 124.6)

1043 Gītārthasaṅgraha; *Śrīvaravaramuni*; PL; 92, 8; SKT, GR. (124.7)

1044 Bhagavadviṣayavyākhyāna III Śataka; *Mudumbai Anantācār*; PL; 92, 9; TA, TA. (124.8)

1045 Bhagavadviṣayam 36000 Padi-4.5.6 Śataka; *Vadakku Tiruvīdi Pillai*; PL; 92, 10; TA, TA. (124.9)

1046 Bhagavadviṣaya III Śataka vyākhā-Adaivalanthan; *Attantiruveṅkaṭa Rāmānujajīyar*; PL; 92, 11; TA, TA. (124.10)

1047 Rāmānuja Nuttandādi Vyākhyāna; *Pillailokam Jīyar*; PL; 92, 12; TA, TA. (124.11)

1048 Divyadeśa Attavanai; *Vangipurattu Nambi*; PL; 99.1; TA, GR.

1049 Yatīndrapravaṇaprabhava; *Pillailokaṁ Jīyar*; PL; 99, 2; TA, GR.

1050 Kāraṇavyākhyānam-Śivaparatvakhaṇḍana; PL; 99, 3; SKT, GR.

1051 Bhagavadviṣaya 6000 Padi; *Tirukkurukai Pirānpillān*; PL; 99, 4; TA, GR.

1052 Campakāraṇya Dakṣiṇadvārakāmāhātmya; PL; 99, 5; SKT, GR.

1053 Śrībhāṣyādi Sūkti Sādhutva mālikā; PL; 99, 6; SKT, GR.

1054 Sudarśanaśatakam Vyākhyāna; *Nārāyaṇabhaṭṭa*; PL; 99, 7; SKT, GR.

1055 Tiruvāimoli Vyākhyā I; *Nammālvār, Tirukkurukai Pirān Pillan* and others; B; 99, 8; TA, TE.

1056 Tattvanirṇaya; *Vātsya Śrīvaradācārya*; B; 99, 9; SKT, D.

1057 Tattvamārtaṇḍa I; Śrīnivāsācārya (Sūrapuram); B; 99, 10; SKT, D.

1058 Tattvamārtaṇḍa II; Śrīnivāsācārya (Sūrapuram); B; 99, 11; SKT, D.

1059 Viṣṇupurāṇa with Commentary; *Parāśara*, (c) *Viṇṣucittārya*; B; 99, 12; SKT, D.

1060 Īśādidaśopaniṣad Bhāṣyam; *Gopālānandasvāmī*; B; 99, 13; SKT, D.

1061 Śrībhāṣya I with Śrutaprakāśikā; *Bhagavad Rāmānuja*, (c) *Sudarśanasūri*; B; 99, 14; SKT, D.

1062 Śrībhāṣya II with Śrutaprakāśikā; *Bhagavad Rāmānuja*, (c) *Sudarśanasūri*; B; 99, 15; SKT, D.

1063 Viṣṇusahasranāma Bhāṣya with Nirvacana and Nirukta; *Parāśara Bhaṭṭa*; B; 100, 1; SKT, D.

1064 Īśāvāsyopaniṣadbhāṣya; *Vedāntadeśika, (c) Kūranārāyaṇamuni* and *Śrīraṅgācārya*; B; 100, 2; SKT, D.

1065 Śatadūṣaṇī with Caṇḍamāruta and Nṛsiṁharājīya; *Vedānta Deśika, (c) Mahācārya and Nṛsiṁharāja*; B; 100, 3; SKT, TE.

1066 Viṣayavākyadīpikā; *Raṅgarāmānujamuni*; B; 100, 4; SKT, D.

1067 Vedārthasaṅgraha with Tātparyadīpikā; *Bhagavad Rāmānuja*; B; 100, 5; SKT, TE.

1068 Bhāvaprakāśikā; *Raṅgarāmānujamuni*; B; 100, 6; SKT, GR.

1069 Vilakṣaṇamokṣādhikārinirṇayam; *Erumbiyappa*; B; 100, 7; TA, TE.

1070 Bhāṣyārtha Saṅgraham; *Veṅkaṭa Rāghavācārya (Karakuruchi)*; B; 100, 8; Maṇipravala, TE.

1071 Kudṛṣṭidhvāntamārtaṇḍa I; *Raṅgācāryasvāmī*; B; 100, 9; SKT, D.

1072 Paramavaidikasiddhāntatattvaratnākara; *Rāmānujācārya* (Śrībhāṣyam); B; 100, 10; SKT, TE.

1073 Īśāvāsyopaniṣad, Kenopaniṣad, Kaṭhopaniṣad (c) Vedāntadeśika, *Kūranārāyaṇamuni* and *Raṅgarāmānuja*; 100, 11; B; SKT TA, D TA.

1074 Śrīguṇaratnakośa-savyākhyā; *Parāśara Bhaṭṭa* (c) *Vīrarāghava*; B; 100, 12; SKT, TE.

1075 Viśiṣṭādvaita Siddhāntamu; *Sampatkumāravarada Veṅkaṭa Raṅgācārya (Nallān Cakravarti)*; B; 100, 13; SKT, TE.

1076 Atharvaśikhāvilāsavistara; *Rāmānujācārya (Śuddhasatvam)*; B; 100, 14; SKT, TE.

1077 Mānameyarahasya Ślokavārttikam; *Śrīnivāsācārya (Lakṣmīpuram)*; B; 100, 15; SKT, D.

1078 Pārāśaryavijaya; *Mahācārya*; B; 100, 16; SKT, D.

1079 Yādavagirimāhātmya; B; 100, 17; SKT, TE.

1080 Ānandasaṁhitā III with commentary; *Marīcimaharṣi*; B; 100, 18; SKT, TE.

1081 Ānandasaṁhitā IV with commentary; *Marīcimaharṣi*; B; 100, 19; SKT, TE.

1082 Vaikhānasopākhyānam; B; 100, 20; SKT, TE.

1083 Daśopaniṣadvyākhyānam; *Rāmānujācārya (Śrī Bhāṣyam)*; B; 100, 21; SKT, TE.

1084 Sūtrānuguṇyasiddhivimarśaḥ; *Gopālācārya*; B; 100, 22; SKT, D.

1085 Nyāyasiddhāñjana with commentary Ratnapeṭikā; *Vedāntadeśika, (c) Kṛṣṇatātārya*; B; 100, 23; SKT, GR.

1086 Nikṣeparakṣā with Nikṣepacintāmaṇi-I; *Vedāntadeśika, (c) Gopālasūri*; B; 100, 24; SKT, GR.

1087 Ācāryahṛdayasāra Saṅgraham; *Gopālakṛṣṇapillai*; B; 100, 25; TA TE, TA TE.

1088 Daśopaniṣattukkalin Draviḍa Pratipada Bhāṣyam; B; 100, 26; SKT TA, GR TA TE.

1089 Vedāntakaustubha-I to XVII; *Rāmānujācārya (Śuddhasatvam)*; PM; 101, 1; SKT, D.

1090 Maudgalyapurāṇam; PM; 101, 2; SKT, D.

1091 Viṣvaksenasaṁhitā-II; PM; 101, 3; SKT, TE.

1092 Śatadūṣaṇīvyākhyā-Nṛsiṁharājīya; *Nṛsiṁharāja*; PM; 101, 4; SKT, TE.

1093 Śrībhāṣyam; *Bhagavadrāmānuja*; PL; 101, 5; SKT, GR.

1094 Rāmāyaṇasāram; PL; 101, 6; *Maṇipravālam*, GR.

1095 Śrīvacanabhūṣaṇa Rahasyajālam; *Pillai Lokācārya*; PL; 101, 7; Maṇipravālam, GR.

1096 Kriyākairavacandrikā; *Varāhaguru*; PL; 101, 8; SKT, GR.

1097 Vyāsaśikṣāvivaraṇam; PL; 101, 9; SKT, GR.

1098 Vedāntasāra and Vedānta Dīpa; *Bhagavad Rāmānuja*; PL; 101, 10; SKT, GR.

1099 Prapannadharmasārasamuccayaḥ; PL; 101, 11; SKT, GR.

1100 Trailokyamaṅgalakavaca (From Sanatkumāra Saṁhitā); PM; 103, 1; SKT, D.

1101 Adhyātmakārikāvalī with Adhyātmasudhātaraṅgiṇī; *Śrīnivāsācārya*; PM; 103, 2; SKT, D.

1102 Bhaktiratnāvalī; *Viṣṇupurī*; PM; 103, 3; SKT, D.

1103 Kṛṣṇastavarāja with Ṭīkā Śrutyantasuradruma; *Nimbārka, (c) Puruṣottama Prasāda*; PM; 103, 4; SKT, D.

1104 Bhagavadgītā with Nigūḍhārtha Candrikā Ṭīkā; *Vanamālī*; PM; 103, 5; SKT, D.

1105 Siddhāntasetuka (Commentary on Siddhānta Jāhnavī of Devācārya); *Sundara Bhaṭṭa*; PM; 103, 6; SKT, D.

1106 Siddhāntasetuka (Commentary on Siddhānta Jāhnavī of Devācārya); *Sundara Bhaṭṭa*; PM; 103, 7; SKT, D.

1107 Siddhānta Jāhnavī (Commentary on Pārijāta Saurabha, of Nimbārka) I Taraṅga; *Devācārya*; PM; 103, 8; SKT, D.

1108 Bhagavadgītā with Subodhinī Ṭīkā; *Śrīdharasvāmī*; PM; 103, 9; SKT, D.

1109 Vedānta Tattva Bodha; PM; 103, 10; SKT, D.

1110 Vedāntaratnamañjūṣā; *Puruṣottamācārya*; PM; 103, 11; SKT, D.

1111 Vedānta Tattva Sārasiddhānta; *Śītaladās*; PM; 103, 12; H, D.

1112 Paramayogarahasya (from Sanatkumāratantra); PM; 103, 13; SKT, D.

1113 Daśaślokī; *Nimbārka*; PM; 103, 14; SKT, D.

1114 Vidvanmaṇḍanam; *Viṭṭhala (Viṭṭhaleśvara)*; PM; 103, 15; SKT, D.

1115 Paramaguṇa Rahasya (from Sanatkumāra Saṁhitā); PM; 103, 16; SKT, D.

1116 Raghuvaṁśa; *Kālidāsa*; PM;103, 17; SKT, D.

1117 Bṛhadāraṇyakopaniṣad; PM; 103, 18; SKT, D.

1118 Mādhuryalaharī; *Kṛṣṇadāsa*; PM; 103, 19; H, D.

1119 Gopālasahasranāma (from Sammohanatantra) with Commentary; (c) *Keśava Kāśmīri Bhaṭṭācārya*; PM; 103, 20; SKT, D.

1120 Laghubhāgavatāmṛta; *Rūpagosvāmī*; PM; 103, 21; SKT, D.

1121 Bhagavadgītā with Ṭīkā; *Anantarāma*; PM; 103, 22; SKT, D.

1122 Śrīharivyāsajasāmṛtasāgara; *Rūpa*; PM; 103, 23; SKT, D.

1123 Sata Pañcāśikā; *Rāma Caraṇa*; PM; 104, 1; H, D.

1124 (a) Śrī Bhaṭṭa Stuti, (b) Rūpa Mañjarī Aṣṭaka Stotra, (c) Jugala Bhāvanā; *Rādhā Sarveśvara Śaraṇa Gosvāmī*; PM; 104, 2; SKT, D.

1125 Vedānta Pārijāta Saurabha; *Nimbārkācārya*; PM; 104, 3; SKT, D.

1126 Rādhā Kṛṣṇa Sagāratha Līlā; *Nanda Kavi*; PM; 104, 4; H, D.

1127 Pada Saṅgraha; PM; 104, 5; H, D.

1128 Śatadūṣaṇī; *Śrīnivāsa Dāsa*; PM; 104, 6; SKT, D.

1129 Prema Bhakti Candrikā; *Narottama Dās*; PM; 104, 7; BL, D.

1130 Sudarśana Kavaca; PM; 104, 8; SKT, D.

1131 Jānakī Stavarāja; PM; 104, 9; SKT, D.

1132 Hanumad Kavacam; *Kṛṣṇa Dvaipāyana Vyāsa*; PM; 104, 10; SKT, D.

1133 Hanumat Kavaca; *Kṛṣṇa Dvaipāyana Vyāsa*; PM; 104, 11; SKT, D.

1134 Bhakta Mālā; *Nābhā Dās*; PM; 104, 12; H, D.

1135 Pada Saṅgraha; PM; 104, 13; H, D.

1136 Nimbārkācārya Caritra; *Nārāyaṇa Devācārya*; PM; 104, 14; SKT, D.

1137 Svayambhūdevācārya Caritra; PM; 104, 15; SKT, D.

1138 Abhilāṣā Taraṅgiṇī; *Ali Kiśorī*; PM; 104, 16; H, D.

1139 Svayambhūdevācārya Caritra; PM; 104, 17; SKT, D.

1140 Mahāvāṇī; *Harivyāsadevācārya*; PM; 104, 18; H, D.

1141 Gajendra Mokṣa; *Kṛṣṇa Dvaipāyana Vyāsa*; PM; 104, 19; SKT, D.

1142 Vrata Nirṇaya, Pañca Saṁskāra; PM; 104, 20; SKT, D .

1143 Gopīcandanopaniṣat, etc.; PM; 104, 21; SKT, D.

1144 Nārāyaṇa Kavaca, etc.; PM; 104, 22; SKT, D.

1145 Guru Paraṁparā; PM; 104, 23; SKT, D.

1146 Guru Paraṁparā Stotra; PM; 104, 24; SKT, D.

1147 Rādhikāṣṭaka; 104, 25; PM; SKT, D.

1148 Gopāla Hṛdaya Stotra; PM; 104, 26; SKT, D.

1149 Gopāla Stavarāja; PM; 104, 27; SKT, D.

1150 Śrīmad Bhagavad Gītā Mālā Mantra, etc.; *Kṛṣṇa Dvaipāyana Vyāsa*; PM; 104, 28; SKT, D.

1151 Gītā Sāra, etc.; PM; 104, 29; SKT, D.

1152 Harināmamālā; *Śaṅkarācārya*; PM; 104, 30; SKT, D.

1153 Śrī Bhīṣma Stavarāja; *Kṛṣṇa Dvaipāyana Vyāsa*; PM; 104, 31; SKT, D.

1154 Saneha Sāgara Līlā; *Haṁsarāja Vakasī*; PM; 104, 32; H, D.

1155 Śrī Yugula Śatakam; *Śrī Bhaṭṭadevācārya*; PM; 104, 33; H, D.

1156 Vṛndāvana Rasāmṛta; *Prabodhānanda Sarasvatī*; PM; 104, 34; SKT, D.

1157 Vedānta Ratna Mañjūṣā; *Puruṣottamācārya*; PM; 104, 35; SKT, D.

1158 Kavitā Ratnamālikā; *Rāma Nārāyaṇa*; PM; 104, 36; H, D.

1159 Deva Pūjā Vidhi; PM;104, 37; SKT, D.

1160 Garga Saṁhitā; *Gargācārya*; PM; 104, 38; SKT, D.

1161 Garga Saṁhitā; *Gargācārya*; PM; 105, 1; SKT, D.

1162 Veṅkaṭeśa Stotra & Kṛṣṇāṣṭakam; *Śaṅkarācārya*; PM; 105, 2; SKT, D.

1163 Nīlakaṇṭha Stotra; PM; 105, 3; SKT, D.

1164 Sarvavidyā Mantrāgamotkīlanam; PM; 105, 4; SKT, D.

1165 Śāligrāma Stotra; *Kṛṣṇa Dvaipāyana Vyāsa*; PM; 105, 5; SKT; D.

1166 Rāsa Pañcādhyāyī; *Kṛṣṇa Dvaipāyana Vyāsa*; PM; 105, 6; SKT, D.

1167 Gopāla Sahasranāma; PM; 105, 7; SKT, D.

1168 Vyāsajī kī Sākhī; *Hari Rāma Vyāsa*; PM; 105, 8; H, D.

1169 Vyāsajī kī Vāṇī; *Hari Rāma Vyāsa Gosvāmī*; PM; 105, 9; H, D.

1170 Rāma Sahasranāma; PM; 105, 10; SKT, D.

1171 Āditya Hṛdaya Stotra; *Kṛṣṇa Dvaipāyana Vyāsa*; PM; 105, 11; SKT, D.

1172 Garga Saṁhitā; *Gargācārya*; PM; 105, 12; SKT, D.

1173 Girirāja Khaṇḍa; *Gargācārya*; PM; 105, 13; SKT, D.

1174 Girirāja Utpatti; *Gargācārya*; PM; 105, 14; SKT, D.

1175 Kramadīpikā with Ṭīkā; *Keśava Kaśmīrī Bhaṭṭācārya*; PM; 105, 15; SKT, D.

1176 Nārada Pañcarātra; *Nārada Muni*; PM; 105, 16; SKT, D.

1177 Nārada Pañcarātra; *Nārada Muni*; PM; 105, 17; SKT, D.

1178 Ujjvala Rasa Nirdeśa; *Rāmacandra*; PM; 105, 18; SKT, D.

1179 Svadharmādhvabodha; *Rāmacandra*; PM; 105, 19; SKT, D.

1180 Svadharmādhvabodha; *Rāmacandra*; PM; 106, 1; SKT, D.

1181 Haṁsadūta with commentary; *Śrī Rūpa Gosvāmī*; PM; 106, 2; SKT, D.

1182 Ujjvala Nīlamaṇi with Ṭīkā; *Śrī Rūpa Gosvāmī*; PM; 106, 3; SKT, D.

1183 Laghu Bhāgavatāmṛta with Ṭippaṇī; *Śrī Rūpa Gosvāmī*; PM; 106, 4; SKT, D.

1184 Laghu Bhāgavatāmṛta with Ṭippaṇī; *Śrī Rūpa Gosvāmī*; PM; 106, 5; SKT, D.

1185 Hari Bhakti Vilāsa with Ṭīkā; *Gopāla Bhaṭṭa Gosvāmī*; PM; 106, 6; SKT, D.

1186 Bhagavad Gītā; *Kṛṣṇa Dvaipāyana Vyāsa*; PM; 106, 7; SKT, D.

1187 Bhagavad Gītā with Ṭīkā; *Kṛṣṇa Dvaipāyana Vyāsa*; PM; 106, 8; SKT, D.

1188 Bhagavad Gītā with Braj translation; *Kṛṣṇa Dvaipāyana Vyāsa*; PM; 106, 9; SKT H; D.

1189 Bhagavad Gītā with Ṭīkā; *Kṛṣṇa Dvaipāyana Vyāsa*; PM; 106, 10; SKT, D.

1190 Bhagavad Gītā with Ṭīkā; *Kṛṣṇa Dvaipāyana Vyāsa*; PM; 106, 11; SKT, D.

1191 Rāma Gītā with Ṭīkā; *Kṛṣṇa Dvaipāyana Vyāsa*; PM; 106, 12; SKT, D.

1192 Gītā Sāra; *Kṛṣṇa Dvaipāyana Vyāsa*; PM; 106, 13; SKT, D.

1193 Aṣṭāvakra Gītā with Ṭīkā; *Kṛṣṇa Dvaipāyana Vyāsa*; PM; 106, 14; SKT, D.

1194 Padyāvalī; *Śrī Rūpa Gosvāmī*; PM; 106, 15; SKT, D.

1195 Haṁsadūta; *Śrī Rūpa Gosvāmī*; PM; 106, 16; SKT, D.

1196 Yugala Kiśora Sahasra Nāma; *Kṛṣṇa Dvaipāyana Vyāsa*; PM; 106, 17; SKT, D.

1197 Gaṅgā Sahasranāma; *Kṛṣṇa Dvaipāyana Vyāsa*; PM; 106, 18; SKT, D.

1198 Rādhā Stotra; *Kṛṣṇa Dvaipāyana Vyāsa*; PM; 106, 19; SKT, D.

1199 Rādhikāstavarāja; *Kṛṣṇa Dvaipāyana Vyāsa*; PM; 106, 20; SKT, D.

1200 Rādhā Kṛpā Kaṭākṣastotram; *Kṛṣṇa Dvaipāyana Vyāsa*; PM; 106, 21; SKT, D.

1201 Rādhā Sudhānidhi Stotra; *Kṛṣṇa Dvaipāyana Vyāsa*; PM; 106, 22; SKT, D.

1202 Nimbārka Kavaca; PM; 106, 23; SKT, D.

1203 Vairāgya Śatakam; *Bhartṛhari*; PM; 106, 24; SKT, D.

1204 Bhajanāṣṭaka; PM; 106, 25; H, D.

1205 Rāma Paṭala Vidhi; PM; 106, 26; SKT, D.

1206 Gopāla Stavarāja; PM; 106, 27; SKT, D.

1207 Varma Nārāyaṇa Kavaca; *Kṛṣṇa Dvaipāyana Vyāsa*; PM; 106, 28; SKT, D.

1208 Gopāla Kavaca; *Viriñci*; PM; 106, 29; SKT, D.

1209 Rādhā Stavarāja; PM; 106, 30; SKT, D.

1210 Nimbārka Śatanāma; *Kṛṣṇa Dvaipāyana Vyāsa*; PM; 106, 31; SKT, D.

1211 Nikuñja Darpaṇa; Anurāgamālā; Sudarśanāṣṭaka; Siddhāntadarpaṇa; Ācāryanāmāvalī; Aparādhakṣamāpaṇa; Ātmabodha; Chadmayoginīlīlā; Bhavaśveta Vedānta; Sudarśana Dās; PM; 106, 32; H SKT, D.

1212 Yugalabadhāi; PM; 106, 33; H, D.

1213 Yugalabadhāi; PM; 107, 1; H, D.

1214 Caubīs Gāyatrī; PM; 107, 2; SKT, D.

1215 Samāja Gāyan Śṛṅkhalā; PM; 107, 3; H, D.

1216 Vratārka; *Bhaṭṭaśaṅkara*; PM; 107, 4; SKT, D.

1217 Sandhyā Traya Kāla Vidhi; PM; 107, 5; SKT, D.

1218 Nārāyaṇa Cintāmaṇi Stotra; *Kṛṣṇa Dvaipāyana Vyāsa*; PM; 107, 6; SKT, D.

1219 Gopāla Tāpinī Upaniṣad; PM; 107, 7; SKT, D.

1220 Govindāṣṭakam; *Śaṅkarācārya*; PM; 107, 8; SKT, D.

1221 Viṣṇu Pañjara Stotra; *Kṛṣṇa Dvaipāyana Vyāsa*; PM; 107, 9; SKT, D.

1222 Gopāla Kavaca; PM; 107, 10; SKT, D.

1223 Gopāla Sundarī Mantra Saṁdhyā Vidhi; PM; 107, 11; SKT, D.

1224 Rādhā Kavacam; PM; 107, 12; SKT, D.

1225 Rādhikā Stava Rāja; PM; 107, 13; SKT, D.

1226 Nimbārkākhya Śatam; PM; 107, 14; SKT, D.

1227 Kṛṣṇa Stava Rāja; PM; 107, 15; SKT, D.

1228 Gopāla Kavacam; PM; 107, 16; SKT, D.

1229 Mudāṣṭakam; *Madhusūdana Dās*; PM; 107, 17; SKT, D.

1230 Rādhāgopālāṣṭakam; *Madhusūdana Dās*; PM; 107, 18; SKT, D.

1231 Kṛṣṇa Baladevāṣṭakam; *Madhusūdana Dās*; PM; 107, 19; SKT, D.

1232 Nārāyaṇa Līlā; *Mādhava Dās Gosvāmī*; PM; 107, 20; SKT, D.

1233 Hari Guru Caraṇa Dhyāna Tattvaprakāśī Stotra; PM; 107, 21; SKT, D.

1234 Caturdaśaślokī; *Hari Vyāsa Devācārya*; PM; 107, 22; SKT, D.

1235 Dvārakā māhātmyam; PM; 107, 23; SKT, D.

1236 Siddhānta Puṣpāñjalī Bhāṣya; PM; 107, 24; SKT, D.

1237 Rādhā Mādhavayor Aṣṭakāla Bhāvanā Prakāśa; PM; 107, 25; SKT, D.

1238 Gopāla Sahasranāmāvalī; PM; 107, 26; SKT, D.

1239 Vedānta Siddhānta Ratnāñjalī; PM; 107, 27; SKT, D.

1240 Khyāla Vilāsa, etc.; *Dhruva Dāsa*; PM; 107, 28; H, D.

1241 Rāmānugraha; *Viṣṇusiṁha*; PM; 107, 29; H, D.

1242 Caurāsī; *Hari Vaṁśa*; PM; 107, 30; H, D.

1243 Caubīs Autārajas; *Dharma Dāsa*; PM; 107, 31; H, D.

1244 Rāma Dhyāna Mañjarī; *Agra Dāsa*; PM; 107, 32; H, D.

1245 Hanumāna Bāhuka; *Tulasīdāsa*; PM; 107, 33; H, D.

1246 Puruṣa Sūkta; PM; 107, 34; SKT, D.

1247 Hari Tālikā Vratam; PM; 107, 35; SKT, D.

1248 Sandhyopāsanā Vidhi; PM; 107, 36; SKT, D.

1249 Siddhānta Paddhati; *Rāghavānandajī*; PM; 107, 37; SKT, D.

1250 Rāma Paddhati; *Rāmānujācārya*; PM; 107, 38; SKT, D.

1251 Rāma Stavarāja Stotra; PM; 107, 39; SKT, D.

1252 Guru Caritra; *Jagannātha Dāsa*; PM; 107, 40; SKT, D.

1253 Ālavandārastotram; *Yāmunācārya*; PM; 107, 41; SKT, D.

1254 Ujjvala Nīlamaṇi with Ānanda Candrikā Ṭīkā; *Rūpa Gosvāmī*; PM; 107, 42; SKT, D.

1255 Śaṅkha Cakrādi Dhāraṇāvāda; *Puruṣottama Gosvāmī*; PM; 107, 43; SKT, D.

1256 Rādhānāma Mādhurī; PM; 107, 44; H, D.

1257 Alaṅkāra Kaustubha with Ṭīkā; *Kavikarṇapūra*; PM; 107, 45; SKT, D.

1258 Nāsiketopākhyāna; *Caraṇa Dās*; PM; 107, 46; H, D.

1259 Audumbarī Saṁhitā; *Audumbararṣi*; PM; 107, 47; SKT, D.

1260 Audumbarī Saṁhitā; *Audumbararṣi*; PM; 107, 48; SKT, D.

1261 Audumbarī Saṁhitā; *Audumbararṣi*; PM; 108, 1; SKT, D.

1262 Svapna Vicāra; *Kṛṣṇa Dvaipāyana Vyāsa*; PM; 108, 2; SKT, D.

1263 Śakuntala Prākṛta Vivṛtti; PM; 108, 3; SKT, D.

1264 Gīta Govinda; *Jayadeva Gosvāmī*; PM; 108, 4; SKT, D.

1265 Gīta Govinda; *Jayadeva Gosvāmī*; PM; 108, 5; SKT, D.

1266 Rākṣasakāvyam with Ṭīkā by Premadhara; PM; 108, 6; SKT, D.

1267 Raghuvaṁśa; *Kālidāsa*; PM; 108, 7; SKT, D.

1268 Bhagavad Gītā; *Kṛṣṇa Dvaipāyana Vyāsa*; PM; 108, 8; SKT, D.

1269 Mantra Saṁskāra; PM; 108, 9; SKT, D.

1270 Caubīs Gāyatrī; PM; 108, 10; SKT, D. [108.11 Missing]

1271 Ācārya Paramparā; PM; 108, 12; H, D.

1272 Nimbārkācārya Prādurbhāva; *Kṛṣṇa Dvaipāyana Vyāsa*; PM; 108, 13; SKT, D.

1273 Mantra Saṅgraha; PM; 108, 14; SKT, D.

1274 Pañca Saṁskāra; PM; 108, 15; SKT, D.

1275 Garga Saṁhitā with Bhāṣāprakāśa; PM; 108, 16; H, D.

1276 Mantrārtha Rahasya; PM; 108, 17; SKT, D.

1277 Nimbārka Sahasranāma; *Kṛṣṇa Dvaipāyana Vyāsa*; PM; 108, 18; SKT, D.

1278 Sanat Kumāra Saṁhitā (IX Paṭala); PM; 108, 19; SKT, D.

1279 Mantrārtha Rahasya; PM; 108, 20; SKT, D.

1280 Nimbārka Kavaca; PM; 108, 21; SKT, D.

1281 Ācāryavaryāṣṭakam; *Madhusūdana Dāsa*; PM; 108, 22; SKT, D.

1282 Nimbārka Dhyāna Mañjarī Bhāṣā; PM; 108, 23; H, D.

1283 Nimbārka Paddhati Pramāṇa Dhāmakṣetrastava; PM; 108, 24; SKT, D.

1284 Gopāla Mantra Nyāsa Vidhi; PM; 108, 25; SKT, D.

1285 Krama Dīpikā; *Keśava Kaśmīrī Bhaṭṭa*; PM; 108, 26; SKT, D.

1286 Kavaca Stavārtha Saṁgraha; PM; 108, 27; SKT, D.

1287 Mantrārtha Rahasya Ṭīkā; PM; 108, 28; SKT, D.

1288 Gopāla Dhyānam; PM; 108, 29; SKT, D.

1289 Catur Yugācāryaitihyānusandhi; PM; 108, 30; SKT, D.

1290 Guru Paramparā; PM; 108, 31; SKT, D.

1291 Śrī Ghamaṇḍadevācāryacaritra; PM; 108, 32; SKT, D.

1292 Śaraṇāgata Mantra Vidhi; PM; 108, 33; SKT, D.

1293 Gurumantra Vidhi; PM; 108, 34; SKT, D.

1294 Ācārya Pañcakam; PM; 108, 35; SKT, D.

1295 Nimbārka Prādurbhāva; *Kṛṣṇa Dvaipāyana Vyāsa*; PM; 108, 36; SKT, D.

1296 Mantrārtha Rahasya; PM; 108, 37; SKT, D.

1297 Nimbārka Stotra; *Audumbarācārya*; PM; 108, 38; SKT, D.

1298 Mantrārtha Rahasya; PM; 108, 39; SKT, D.

1299 Sampradāya Paramparā Nirṇaya Vidhi; PM; 108, 40; SKT, D.

1300 Gopāla Stava Rāja; PM; 108, 41; SKT, D.

1301 Niyamānandapañcaratna; PM; 108, 42; SKT, D.

1302 Ātmabodha; *Sudarśana Dāsa*; PM; 108, 43; SKT, D.

1303 Ācārya Paramparā; PM; 108, 44; SKT, D.

1304 Guru Paramparā Vandana Stotra; PM; 108, 45; SKT, D.

1305 Karṇahara Stotra; *Keśava Śarman*; PM; 108, 46; SKT, D.

1306 Gurudeva Māhātmyam; PM; 108, 47; SKT, D.

1307 Vicāra Mālā; PM; 108, 48; H, D.

1308 Jñāna Svaroda; *Caraṇa Dāsa*; PM; 108, 49; H, D.

1309 Yoga Śāstra with Ṭīkā Rājamārtaṇḍa; *Patañjali*; PM; 108, 50; SKT, D.

1310 Yoga Sūtra with Ṭīkā Rājamārtaṇḍa; *Patañjali*; PM; 108, 51; SKT, D.

1311 Yoga Sūtra; *Patañjali*; PM; 108, 52; SKT, D.

1312 Yoga Śāstra; PM; 108, 53; SKT, D.

1313 Padamuktāvalī; *Nāgarī Dāsa*; PM; 108, 54; SKT, D.

1314 Pada Saṅgraha; PM; 108, 55; H, D.

1315 Pada Saṅgraha; PM; 108, 56; H, D.

1316 Samaya Prabandha; *Rasika Govinda*; PM; 108, 57; H, D.

1317 Samaya Vibhāga Evaṁ Utsava Vidhi; PM; 108, 58; H, D.

1318 Bana Bihār Līlā; PM; 108, 59; H, D.

1319 Pada Saṅgraha; PM; 108, 60; H, D.

1320 Saneha Līlā; *Rasika Rāya*; PM; 108, 61; H, D.

1321 Vaṁśīvaṭ Vilāsa Mādhurī; *Mādhurī Dās*; PM; 108, 62; H, D.

1322 Śrutyanta Kalpavallī; *Puruṣottama Prasāda*; PM; 108, 63; SKT, D.

1323 Nārada Niyamānanda Goṣṭhī Rahasya Ṭīkā; PM; 108, 64; SKT, D.

1324 Satsaṅga Mahimā; *Kiśorī Alī*; PM; 108, 65; SKT, D.

1325 Brahma Sūtra Vyākhyā; PM; 108, 66; SKT, D.

1326 Vedānta Kaustubha Prabhā; *Keśava Kāśmīrī*; PM; 108, 67; SKT, D.

1327 Varṣotsava ke Pada; PM; 108, 68; H, D.

1328 Bhakta Cālīsī Mālā; *Sudarśana Dās*; PM; 108, 69; H, D.

1329 Vinaya Patrikā; *Sudarśana Dās*; PM; 108, 70; H SKT, D.

1330 Pada Muktāvalī; *Nāgarī Dās*; PM; 108, 71; H, D.

1331 Śakunāvalī: Kṛṣṇa Kathā Dvādaśādhyāya; *Sudarśana Dās*; PM; 108, 72; H, D.

1332 Bhramara Gīta Uddhava Caritra; *Sudarśana Dās*; PM; 108, 73; H, D.

1333 Rasa Mañjarī; *Sudarśana Dās*; PM; 108, 74; SKT H, D.

1334 Rasa Mañjarī; *Sudarśana Dās*; PM; 109, 1; SKT H, D.

1335 Dharalīlā and Assorted Līlā-s; *Agradāsa*; *et al.* PM; 109, 2; SKT H, D.

1336 Eighty-four Vaiṣṇavācāryoṁ kī Vārtā; PM; 109, 3; H, D.

1337 Bhāgavata Purāṇa with Ṭīkā Bhāvārtha Dīpikā; *Kṛṣṇa Dvaipāyana Vyāsa*; PM; 109, 4; SKT, D.

1338 Gopāla Sahasranāma; *Kṛṣṇa Dvaipāyana Vyāsa*; PM; 109, 5; SKT, D.

1339 Vedānta Siddhānta Ratnāñjalī; *Hari Vyāsa Devācārya*; PM; 109, 6; SKT, D.

1340 Rādhā Tāpanī Upaniṣad; PM; 109, 7; SKT, D.

1341 Nārāyaṇopaniṣatsārasaṅgraha; PM; 109, 8; SKT, D.

1342 Vedāntaratnamālā; *Anantarāma*; PM; 109, 9; SKT, D.

1343 Prameyaratnāvalī; *Baladevavidyābhūṣaṇa*; PM; 109, 10; SKT, D.

1344 Gurubhaktimandākinī; *Puruṣottamācārya*; PM; 109, 11; SKT, D.

1345 Yogopāyakathanam; PM; 109, 12; SKT, D.

1346 Trailokya Maṅgala Kavaca (From Sanatkumāra Saṁhitā); PM; 109, 13; SKT, D.

1347 Trailokya Maṅgala Kavaca (From Sanatkumāra Saṁhitā); PM; 110, 1; SKT, D.

1348 Adhyātmakārikāvalī with Adhyātmasudhā Taraṅgiṇī; *Śrīnivāsācārya, (c) Puruṣottama Prasāda*; PM; 110, 2; SKT, D.

1349 Śrī Bhagavad Bhakti Ratnāvalī; *Viṣṇupurī*; PM; 110, 3; SKT, D.

1350 Kṛṣṇastavarāja with Śrutyantasuradruma Ṭīkā; *Nimbārka, (c) Puruṣottamaprasāda*; PM; 110, 4; SKT, D.

1351 Bhagavadgītā with Nigūḍhārtha Candrikā Ṭīkā; *Vanamālī*; PM; 110, 5; SKT, D.

1352 Siddhāntasetukā (Commentary of Siddhānta Jāhnavī of Devācārya); *Sundarabhaṭṭa*; PM; 110, 6; SKT, D.

1353 Siddhāntasetukā (Commentary on Siddhānta Jāhnavī of Devācārya); *Sundarabhaṭṭa*; PM; 110, 7; SKT, D.

1354 Siddhāntajāhnavī; *Devācārya*; PM; 110, 8; SKT, D.

1355 Bhagavadgītā with Subodhinīṭīkā; *Śrīdharasvāmī*; PM; 110, 9; SKT, D.

1356 Vedāntatattvabodha; PM; 110, 10; SKT, D.

1357 Vedāntaratna Mañjūṣā; *Puruṣottamācārya*; PM; 110, 11; SKT, D.

1358 Vedāntatattvasārasiddhānta; *Sītaladās*; PM; 110, 12; H, D.

1359 Paramaguṇarahasya; PM; 110, 13; SKT, D.

1360 Daśaślokī; *Nimbārka*; PM; 110, 14; SKT, D.

1361 Vidvanmaṇḍanam; *Viṭṭhaleśvara*; PM; 110, 15; SKT, D.

1362 Paramaguṇarahasya (From Sanatkumāra Saṁhitā); PM; 110, 16; SKT, D.

1363 Raghuvaṁśa Vyākhyā-Sañjīvanī; *Mallinātha*; PM; 110, 17; SKT, D.

1364 Bṛhadāraṇyakopaniṣad with Mitākṣarā; PM; 110, 18; SKT, D.

1365 Mādhuryalaharī; *Kṛṣṇadāsa*; PM; 110, 19; H, D.

1366 Gopālasahasranāma (From Sammohana Tantra) with Vivṛtti; (c) *Keśavakāśmīri Bhaṭṭācārya*; PM; 110, 20; SKT, D.

1367 Laghubhāgavatāmṛta; *Rūpa Gosvāmī*; PM; 110, 21; SKT, D.

1368 Vaiṣṇavadharma Suradrumamañjarī; *Saṅkarṣaṇa Śaraṇa*; PM; 110, 22; SKT, D.

1369 Bhagavadgītā with Padārthabodhinīṭīkā; *Anantarāma*; PM; 110, 23; SKT, D.

1370 Śrīharivyāsarasāmṛtasāgara; PM; 110, 24; H, D.

1371 Vṛndāvanamahimāmṛta; *Prabodhānanda Sarasvatī*; PM; 110, 25; SKT, D.

1372 Vṛndāvana Mahimāmṛta; *Prabodhānandasarasvatī*; PM; 111, 1; SKT, D.

1373 Bayālīsalīlā; *Hitadhruvadāsa*; PM; 111, 2; H, D.

1374 Versified Gītā in Hindi; *Harivallabha*; PM; 111, 3; H, D.

1375 Divyasūricarita; PM; 111, 4; SKT, D.

1376 Vivekatrayaratna; *Rāmānujācārya Dās*; PM; 111, 5; SKT, D.

1377 Gopālasahasranāma (From Sammohanatantra) with Vivṛtti; PM; 111, 6; SKT, D.

1378 Caitanyacaritāmṛta; *Kṛṣṇadās Kavirāj*; PM; 111, 7; SKT BL, D.

1379 Ātmavicāra with Ṭīkā; *Māṇikadās*; PM; 111, 8; H, D.

1380 Ekādaśīmāhātmya (From various Purāṇa-s); *Kṛṣṇa Dvaipāyana Vyāsa*; PM; 111, 9; SKT, D.

1381 Tātparyadīpikā; *Ānandatīrtha (Madhvācārya)*; PM; 111, 10; SKT, D.

1382 Mahābhārta; *Kṛṣṇa Dvaipāyana Vyāsa*; PM; 111, 11; SKT, D.

1383 Mahābhārata; *Kṛṣṇa Dvaipāyana Vyāsa*; PM; 112, 1; SKT, D.

1384 Mahābhārata; *Kṛṣṇa Dvaipāyana Vyāsa*; PM; 112, 2; SKT, D.

1385 Mahābhārata Śāntiparva with Bhārata Bhāvadīpa Ṭīkā; *Kṛṣṇa Dvaipāyana Vyāsa, (c) Nīlakaṇṭha*; PM; 112, 3; SKT, D.

1386 Mahābhārata Śāntiparva with Bhāratabhāvadīpa Ṭīkā; *Kṛṣṇa Dvaipāyana Vyāsa (c) Nīlakaṇṭha*; PM; 113, 1; SKT, D.

1387 Mahābhārata; *Kṛṣṇa Dvaipāyana Vyāsa*; PM; 113, 2; SKT, D.

1388 Śrīmadbhāgavatam (Skandha-s 1-9) with Bhāgavatasiddhānta Pradīpa Vyākhyā; *Kṛṣṇa Dvaipāyana Vyāsa*; (c) Śukasudhī; PM; 113, 3; SKT, D.

1389 Śrīmadbhāgavatam (Skandha-s 1-9) with Bhāgavatasiddhānta Pradīpa Vyākhyā; *Kṛṣṇa Dvaipāyana Vyāsa*; (c) Śukasudhī; PM; 114, 1; SKT, D.

1390 Yajurveda Trikālasandhyā; PM; 114, 2; SKT, D.

1391 Jamunājī ke Cālīsapada; *Paramānandadāsa, Kṛṣṇadāsa, Kumbhanadāsa, Biṭṭhala*, etc.; PM; 114, 3; SKT, D.

1392 Sarvottamastotra, Vallabhāṣṭaka Premāmṛta; *Agnikumāra (Viṭṭhaleśvara)*; PM; 114, 4; H, D.

1393 Nāmaratna; *Raghunāthagosvāmī*; PM; 114, 5; SKT, D.

1394 Yamunāṣṭaka, Bālabodha, Siddhānta Muktāvalī, Puṣṭipravāha; *Vallabhācārya*; PM; 114, 6; H, D.

1395 Rāmāyaṇa; *Vālmīki*; PM; 114, 7; SKT, D.

1396 Rāmāyaṇa; *Vālmīki*; 115, 1; SKT, D.

1397 Brajavilāsa; *Brajavāsīdāsa*; PM; 115, 2; H, D.

1398 Brahmasaṁhitā, (5th Chapter) with Digdarśanī Ṭīkā; (c) *Jīva Gosvāmī*; PM; 115, 3; SKT, D.

1399 Bhaktirasāmṛtasindhu with Durgamasaṅgamanīṭīkā; *Rūpa Gosvāmī*, (c) *Jīva Gosvāmī*; PM; 115, 4; SKT, D.

1400 Mahāvākya Ratnāvalī; *Rāmacandrendra*; PM; 115, 5; SKT, D.

1401 Mukundaśaraṇāpattistotra; *Anantarāma*; PM; 115, 6; SKT, D.

1402 Māṇḍūkyopaniṣad with Māṇḍūkyopaniṣadarthaprakāśa; PM; 115, 7; SKT, D.

1403 Laghumañjūṣā; *Giridhāridās*; PM; 115, 8; SKT, D.

1404 Vedāntasiddhānta Jāhnavī (Prathama Taraṅga); *Devācārya*; PM; 115, 9; SKT, D.

1405 Brahmavaivarta Purāṇa (Kṛṣṇajanma, Prakṛti, Gaṇeśa and Brahmakhaṇḍas); *Kṛṣṇa Dvaipāyana Vyāsa*; PM; 115, 10; SKT, D.

1406 Brahmavaivartapurāṇa (Kṛṣṇajanma, Prakṛti, Gaṇeśa and Brahmakhaṇḍas); *Kṛṣṇa Dvaipāyanavyāsa*; PM; 116, 1; SKT, D.

1407 Vedānta/Vedavyāsa Sūtrabhāṣya; *Nimbādityācārya/ Nimbabhāskara*; PM; 116, 2; SKT, D.

1408 Vedānta Kaustubhaprabhā (Commentary on Vedānta Kaustubha of Śrīnivāsācārya); *Keśava Kāśmīri Bhaṭṭācārya*; PM; 116, 3; SKT, D.

1409 Nṛsiṁhaparicaryā (Translated into Bengali by Vidyaratna Rāmanārāyaṇa); *Kṛṣṇadevācārya*; B; 116, 4; SKT BL, BL.

1410 Nṛsiṁhaparicaryā (Translated into Bengali by Vidyāratna Rāmanārāyaṇa); *Kṛṣṇadevācārya*; B; 117, 1; SKT BL, BL.

1411 Harivaṁśapurāṇa; *Kṛṣṇa Dvaipāyana Vyāsa*; PM; 117, 2; SKT, D.

1412 Bhagavad Bhakti Vilāsa/Hari Bhakti Vilāsa with Digdarśanī Ṭīkā; *Gopālabhaṭṭagosvāmī, (c) Sanātana Gosvāmī*; PM; 117, 3; SKT, D.

1413 Bhaktihaṁsa; *Viṭṭhaleśvara*; PM; 117, 4; SKT, D.

1414 Brahmasūtra Aṇubhāṣya (Ch. 1 & 4); *Vallabhācārya*; PM; 117, 5; SKT, D.

1415 Bhaktamālā with Bhakti Rasa Bodhinī; *Nābhādās, (c) Priyādās*; PM; 117, 6; H SKT, D.

1416 Bhaktamālā with Bhakti Rasa Bodhinī; *Nābhādās, (c) Priyādās*; PM; 118, 1; SKT H, D.

1417 Bhaktirasāmṛtasindhu with Durgamasaṅgamanī Ṭīkā; *Rūpagosvāmī, (c) Jīvagosvāmī*; PM; 118, 2; SKT, D.

1418 Bhaktirasāmṛtasindhu with Durgamasaṅgamanī Ṭīkā; *Rūpagosvāmī, (c) Jīvagosvāmī*; PM; 118, 3; SKT, D.

1419 Vedāntaratnamañjūṣā; *Puruṣottamācārya*; PM; 118, 4; SKT, D.

1420 Bhaktamālā with Ṭīkā; *Nābhādās, (c) Priyādās*; PM; 118, 5; H, D.

1421 Vṛndāvanamahimāmṛta; *Prabodhānanda Sarasvatī*; PM; 118, 6; SKT, D.

1422 Rūparasikajī kī Vāṇī; *Rūpa Rasika*; PM; 118, 7; H, D.

1423 Gītāmṛta Gaṅgā; *Vṛndāvana Deva*; PM; 118, 8, H, D.

1424 Brajavinodavelī; *Hita Vṛndāvanadās*; PM; 118, 9; H, D.

1425 Vyālīsalīlā; *Dhruva Dās*; PM; 118, 10; H, D.

1426 Hita Caurāsī (Caturāsī); *Hita Harivaṁśa*; PM; 118, 11; H, D.

1427 Śrīsvāmīharidāsjī kī Vāṇī; *Haridās Svāmī*; PM; 118, 12; H, D.

1428 Lalitamādhava with Ṭīkā; *Rūpagosvāmī*; PM; 118, 13; SKT, D.

1429 Ujjvalanīlamaṇi with Ānandacandrikā Ṭīkā; *Rūpagosvāmī,* (c) *Jīvagosvāmī*; PM; 118, 14A; SKT, D.

1430 Alaṅkārakaustubha with Ṭīkā; *Kavi Karṇapūra (Paramānanda Dāsa),* (c) *Sārvabhauma* (Kṛṣṇadeva); PM; 118, 14B; SKT, D.

1431 Ujjvalanīlamaṇi with Ānandacandrikā Ṭīkā; *Rūpa Gosvāmī,* (c) *Jīva Gosvāmī*; PM; 118, 15; SKT, D.

1432 Ujjvalanīlamaṇi with Ānandacandrikā Ṭīkā; *Rūpa Gosvāmī*, (c) *Jīva Gosvāmī*; PM; 119, 1; SKT, D.

1433 Govindalīlāmṛta; *Kṛṣṇadāsa Kavirāja*; PM; 119, 2; SKT, D.

1434 Padyāvalī with Ṭīkā; *Rūpa Gosvāmī*; PM; 119, 3; SKT, D.

1435 Caitanyacandrodaya Nāṭaka; *Kavikarṇapūra*; PM; 119, 4; SKT, D.

1436 Premasampuṭa; *Viśvanātha Cakravarti*; 119, 5; SKT, D.

1437 Bhāgavata Sandarbha I-Tattvasandarbha; *Jīva Gosvāmī*; PM; 119, 6; SKT, D.

1438 Bhāgavata Sandarbha II-Bhagavat Sandarbha; *Jīva Gosvāmī*; PM; 119, 7; SKT, D.

1439 Bhāgavata Sandarbha III-Paramātma Sandarbha; *Jīva Gosvāmī*; PM; 119, 8; SKT, D.

1440 Bhāgavata Sandarbha IV-Kṛṣṇa Sandarbha; *Jīva Gosvāmī*; PM; 119, 9; SKT, D.

1441 Bhāgavata Sandarbha V-Bhakti Sandarbha; *Jīva Gosvāmī*; PM; 119, 10; SKT, D.

1442 Bhāgavata Sandarbha VI-Prīti Sandarbha; *Jīva Gosvāmī*; PM; 119, 11; SKT, D.

1443 Tattvasandarbha Ṭippaṇī; *Baladeva Vidyābhūṣaṇa*; PM; 119, 12; SKT, D.

1444 Muktācarita (Braja Bāsī-Bhāva-Nirūpaṇa); *Nārāyaṇadāsa*; PM; 119, 13; BL, D.

1445 Govindalīlāmṛta with Ṭīkā; *Kṛṣṇadāsa Kavirāja*; PM; 119, 14; SKT, D.

1446 Caitanyacaritāmṛta; *Kṛṣṇadāsa Kavirāja*; PM; 119, 15; BL, D.

1447 Caitanyacaritāmṛta; *Kṛṣṇadāsa Kavirāja*; PM; 119, 16; BL, D.

1448 Vaiṣṇava Vandanā; *Vṛndāvana Dāsa*; PM; 119, 17; BL, D.

1449 Bhāgavatāmṛta with Digdarśanī Ṭīkā; *Sanātanagosvāmī*; PM; 119, 18; SKT, D.

1450 Bhāgavatāmṛta with Digdarśanī Ṭīkā; *Sanātanagosvāmī*; PM; 120, 1; SKT, D.

1451 Śrīmadbhāgavata Purāṇa with Bhāvārthadīpikā; *Kṛṣṇa Dvaipāyana Vyāsa,* (c) *Śrīdharasvāmin*; B; 120, 2; SKT, D.

1452 Nandamahotsava (From Bhāgavata); *Kṛṣṇa Dvaipāyana Vyāsa*; B; 120, 3; H, D.

1453 Śrīmadbhāgavata Līlākalpadruma; *Govindaśāstrī*; B; 120, 4; SKT, D.

1454 Mahāprabhugranthāvalī (Contains, (1) Śikṣāṣṭakam by Gauracandra, (2) Premāmṛta Rasāyana Stotram by Gauracandra, (3) Yugalaparihāra Stotram by Mahāprabhu, (4) Rādhārasa Mañjarī by Caitanyacandras, (5); Yugalāṣṭaka by Mādhavendra Purī); B; 120, 5; SKT, H, D.

1455 Yugalāṣṭakam (Hindi Bhāṣānuvāda); *Mādhavendra Purīcaraṇa*; B; 120, 6; H, D.

1456 Grantharatnatrikam (Contains, (1) Śṛṅgāracūḍāmaṇi Grantham, (2) Bhāgavatāmṛta Kaṇikā, (3) Rasasiddhānta Cintāmaṇī Grantha) with Hindi translation; *Viśvanātha Cakravarti*; B; 120, 7; H SKT, D.

1457 Guruparamparā Navaratnanirṇaya with Hindi translation; *Harirāmavyāsagosvāmī*; B; 120, 8; SKT H, D.

1458 Gītagovinda with Padāvalī (Versification in Braj); *Jayadeva,* (Versifier) *Rāmarāya Gosvāmī*; B; 120, 9; SKT H, D.

1459 Viṣṇupriyā Sahasranāma Stotram; *Haridās Gosvāmiprabhupāda*; B; 120, 10; SKT H, D.

1460 Gauralīlā with Hindi Translation; *Nityānanda Bhaṭṭa* (Compiler); B; 120, 11; SKT H, D.

1461 Vaiṣṇavāvadhāna (Extract from Bhāgavata); *Nityānanda Bhaṭṭa*; B; 120, 12; SKT H, D.

1462 Caitanyamatamañjūṣā (Bhāgavata Ṭippaṇī); *Śrīnātha Cakravartipāda*; B; 120, 13; BL, BL.

1463 Caitanyamata Mañjūṣā (Bhāgavata Ṭippaṇī) (continues previous); *Śrīnātha Cakravarti Pāda*; B; 121, 1; BL, BL.

1464 Bhaktirasāmṛtasindhu with three Ṭīkās and translated into Bengali verse; *Rūpa Gosvāmī*, (c) *Jīva Gosvāmī*, *Mukunda Dās Gosvāmī* and *Viśvanātha Cakravartī*; B; 121, 2; SKT BL, BL.

1465 Bhaktirasakallolinī (Purports of Bhakti Rasāmṛtasindhu); *Haridās Dās*; B; 121, 3; BL, BL.

1466 Śrīnāthajī kī Kathā; *Ananya Rasika Vaiṣṇava Dās*; B; 121, 4; H, D. 1966 A.D.

1467 Śrī Śrī Śruti Ratna Mālā (Twelve Upaniṣads—Īśa, Kena, Kaṭha, Praśna, Muṇḍaka, Māṇḍūkya, Taittirīya, Aitareya, Chāndogya, Bṛhadāraṇyaka, Śvetāśvatara and Kauṣītakī; Compiled by *Niśikānta Sannyāla*; B; 121, 5; SKT BL, BL.

1468 Āścarya Rasa Prabandha with Bengali translation; *Prabodhānanda Sarasvatī*; B; 121, 6; SKT BL, BL.

1469 Śrī Śrī Suratakathāmṛtam with Ṭīkā and Translation; *Viśvanātha Cakravartī Ṭhākur*; B; 121, 7; SKT BL, BL.

1470 Śrī Śrī Bhakti Rasāmṛta Śeṣa; *Jīva Gosvāmī*; B; 121, 8; SKT BL, BL.

1471 Śrīyogasārastotram (From Padma Purāṇa) with Ṭīkā and Anuvāda; *Jīva Gosvāmī*; B; 121, 9; SKT BL, BL.

1472 Bhajana Ratnāvalī; Compiler *Rāmanārāyaṇa Dās*; B; 121, 10; H, D.

1473 Anantakathā Śataka (From Bhaviṣyottara Purāṇa); *Kṛṣṇa Dvaipāyana Vyāsa*; B; 121, 11; SKT H, D.

1474 Kāśīmāhātmya (From Brahmavaivarta Purāṇa) with Ṭīkā; *Kṛṣṇa Dvaipāyana Vyāsa*; B; 121, 12; SKT, D.

1475 Ekādaśīmāhātmya (From various Purāṇas); *Kṛṣṇa Dvaipāyana Vyāsa*; B; 121, 13; SKT, D.

1476 Bhāgavata Purāṇa—Daśama Skandha (Pūrva and Uttara Khaṇḍa) with Hindi Ṭīkā; *Kṛṣṇa Dvaipāyana Vyāsa*; B; 121, 14; SKT H, D.

1477 Caitanyacaritāmṛta with Ṭīkā; *Kṛṣṇadās Kavirāj*; B; 121, 15; BL, BL.

1478 Vaiṣṇavadharma Mīmāṁsā; *Ananta Rāma*; B; 121, 16; SKT, D.

1479 Adbhutarāmāyaṇam; *Vālmīki*; B; 121, 17; SKT, D.

1480 Rāmacaritamānasa; *Tulsīdās*; B; 121, 18; H, D.

1481 Mahānāṭaka/Hanuman Nāṭakam with Dīpikā Ṭīkā; *Hanumatkavi,* (c) Miśramohanadāsa; B; 121, 19; SKT, D.

1482 Harivaṁśapurāṇa with Hindi Ṭīkā; *Kṛṣṇa Dvaipāyana Vyāsa,* (c) *Jvālāprasāda*; B; 121, 20; SKT H, D.

1483 Harivaṁśapurāṇa with Hindi Ṭīkā; *Kṛṣṇa Dvaipāyana Vyāsa,* (c) *Jvālāprasāda*; B; 122, 1; SKT H, D.

1484 Bhagavadgītā with Ṭīkā; *Kṛṣṇa Dvaipāyana Vyāsa,* (c) *Madhusūdana Sarasvatī*; B; 122, 2; SKT, D.

*1485 Śruti Tātparya Nirṇayaḥ; *Rāmānuja*; PM; 123, 1; SKT, TE. [91.1]

1486 Śrutaprakāśikā Vyākhyānam; *Lakṣmaṇa Muni* (Embar Svāmi); PM; 123, 2; SKT, TE. [91.2]

1487 Śrutaprakāśikā Tūlikā; *Vādhūla Śrīnivāsācārya*; PM; 123, 3; SKT, TE. [91.3]

1488 Gurubhāvaprakāśikā Part I; *Śuddhasatvam Lakṣmaṇācārya*; PM; 123, 4; SKT, TE. 1938 A.D. [91.4]

1489 Gurubhāvaprakāśikā Part II; *Śuddhasatvam Lakṣmaṇācārya*; PM; 123, 5; SKT, TE. 1938 A.D. [91.5]

1490 Gurubhāvaprakāśikā Part III; *Śuddhasatvam Lakṣmaṇācārya*; PM; 123, 6; SKT, TE. 1938 A.D. [91.6]

1491 Brahmavidyākaumudī; *Śrīnivāsācārya*; PM; 123, 7; SKT, TE. 1938 A.D. [91.7]

1492 Śrutaprakāśikāsāra Pāda-I; *Añjana Grāmavāsīvaradācārya*; PM; 123, 8; SKT, TE . 1938 A.D. [91.8]

1493 Caramaśloka Siddhatātparya Ṭippaṇī; *Śrī Śailācārya Embār Tiruveṅkaṭācārya Jīyar Svāmī*; PM; 123, 9; SKT, TE. 1940 A.D. [91.9]

1494 Siddhopāyasudarśanam; PM; 123, 10; SKT, TE. 1940 A.D. [91.10]

1495 Kaivalyaśatadūṣaṇī; *Kuruka Śrī Śailayogīśa*; PM; 123, 11; SKT, TE. 1944 A.D. [91.11]

1496 Siddhadharma Vijayamaṅgala Dīpikā; PM; 123, 12; SKT, TE. 1941; A.D. [91.12]

1497 Caramaślokaṭippaṇī Vyākhyāna and Campakeśīya; B; 124, 1; SKT, TE. 1909 A.D. [92.1]

1498 Campakeśīya I and II; *Kauśika Śrī Narasiṁha*; B; 124, 2; SKT, TE. [92.2]

1499 Emberumānār Panniraṇḍu Vārtai; *Periyavāccān Pillai*; PL; 124, 3; TA, GR. [92.3]

1500 Perumāl Tirumoli Vyākhyānam and tiruppāvai Sangati; *Periyavāccānpillai*; PL; 124, 4; TA, GR. [92.4 text missing] [92.5]

1501 Tattvatraya Vyākhyāna; *Śrīvaravaramuni*; PL; 124, 5; TA, GR. [92.6]

1502 Tātparyadīpikā Rahasyatraya Vyākhyāna; *Vīrarāghava Sūri*; PL; 124, 6; SKT, GR. [92.7]

1503 Gītārtha Saṅgraha; *Śrīvaravaramuni*; PL; 124, 7; SKT, GR. [92.8]

1504 Bhagavadviṣaya Vyākhyāna-III Śataka; *Mudumbai Anantācār*; PL; 124, 8; TA, TA. [92.9]

1505 Bhagavadviṣayam 36000 Padi—4, 5, 6 Śataka; *Vadakku Tiruvīdipillai*; PL; 124, 9; TA, TA. [92.10]

1506 Bhagavadviṣaya-III Śataka Vyākhyāna—Adaiyavaḷantan; Attantiruveṅgaḍar Erāmānujajīyar; PL; 124, 10; TA, TA. [92.11]

1507 Erāmānujanuttandādivyākhyāna; *Pillailokam Jīyar*; PL; 124, 11; TA, TA. [92.12]

1508 Erāmānujanuttandādivyākhyāna; *Pillailokam Jīyar*; PL; 125, 1; TA, TA.

1509 Guruparamparāprabhāva; *Alahiya Perumāljīyar*; PL; 125, 2; TA, GR.

1510 Tiruppāvai Svāpadeśavyākhyāna; PL; 125, 3; TA, TA.

1511 Mumukṣuppadivyākhyāna; *Śrīvaravaramuni*; PL; 125, 4; TA, TA.

1512 Tiruppallāṇḍu, Kaṇṇinum Siruttāmbu, Amalanadipirān Tiruppallielucci—Vyākhyāna; *Periyavāccānpillai*; PL; 125, 5; TA, TA.

1513 Bhagavadviṣaya Arumbada from II Śataka to V Śataka; *Anna*; PL; 125, 6; TA, GR.

1514 Rāmāyaṇa Taniślokī; *Periyavāccān Pillai*; PL; 125, 7; SKT, GR.

1515 Pārāśaryavijaya; *Doḍḍayācārya*; PL; 125, 8; SKT, GR.

1516 Āgamaprāmāṇya; *Śrī Yāmunācārya*; PL; 125, 9; SKT, TE.

1517 Pañcarahasyaṅgal; *Śrīlokācārya*; PL; 125, 10; TA, GR.

1518 Tirukkurundaṇḍakam Vyākhyāna; *Periyavāccānpillai*; PL; 125, 11; TA, TA.

1519 Íśāvāsyopaniṣad and Māṇḍūkyopaniṣad Bhāṣya, Varāhopaniṣad Mūla; *Vedāntācārya* and *Vādhūlavaradācārya*; PL; 125, 12; SKT, GR.

1520 Periyatiruvandādi; *Periyavāccān Pillai*; PL; 125, 13; TA, TA.

1521 Tiruppāvai Vyākhyānārumpada, 36000 Padi Vyākhyāna; *Annan Appa, Periyavāccānpillai*; PL; 125, 14; TA, TA.

1522 Prameyaśekhara, Tirumantra Vivaraṇa, Mumukṣuppadi, Tattvatraya, Prapannaparitrāṇa and Navaratnamālā; *Śrī Pillailokācārya*; PL; 126, 1; TA, TA.

1523 Periyatirumolivyākhyāna Arumbada; *Periyavāccān Pillai*; PL; 126, 2; TA, TA.

1524 Periyālvār Tirumolivyākhyāna; *Śrī Varavaramuni*; PL; 126, 3; TA, TA.

1525 Śrīvacana Bhūṣaṇa Vyākhyāna; *Śrī Varavaramuni*; PL; 126, 4; TA, TE.

1526 Abhayapradāna Sāra; *Periyavāccān Pillai*; PL; 126, 5; TA, TA.

1527 Tiruviruttam Vyākhyānam—Īdu; Nambillai; PL; 126, 6; TA, TA.

1528 Vedāntasāra; *Śrī Rāmānujācārya*; PL; 126, 7; SKT, GR.

1529 Tirumālai Vyākhyāna; *Periyavāccān Pillai*; PL; 126, 8; TA, TA.

1530 Bhagavadviṣayārumbada; *Appu Iyengar*; PL; 126, 9; TA, TA.

1531 Śrī Rāmāyaṇasārasaṅgraha; PL; 126, 10; SKT, GR.

1532 Aitihyamālai; PL; 126, 11; TA, GR.

1533 Viṣṇupurāṇa with Commentary Viṣṇucittīya; *Parāśaramuni*, (c) *Viṣṇucitta*; PL; 128, 1; SKT, TE.

1534 Bhagavadviṣaya Īdu 36000 Padi (From Seventh Śataka to Tenth Śataka); *Vaḍakkutiruvīdipillai*; PL; 128, 2; TA, TA.

1535 Śrī Yādavagirimāhātmya; *Nārada*; PL; 128, 3; SKT, TE.

1536 Śrī Viṣṇupurāṇa Vyākhyāna; *Śrī Viṣṇucitta*; PL; 128, 4; SKT, GR.

1537 Tulākāverī Māhātmya; PL; 128, 5; SKT, GR.

1538 Trayodaśa Vākyavivaraṇa; PL; 128, 6; TA, GR.

1539 Śrī Rāmāyaṇa Vyākhyāna—Bālakāṇḍa; *Govindarāja*; PL; 128, 7; SKT, GR.

1540 Śrī Raṅgamāhātmyādi; PL; 128, 8; SKT, GR.

1541 Śrī Bhāgavata Vyākhyāna (Twelve Adhyāyas); *Śrīdhara*; PL; 128, 9; SKT, GR.

1542 Śrīveṅkaṭagiri Māhātmya; PL; 128, 10; SKT, GR.

1543 Śrī Rāmāyaṇa Vyākhyāna; *Kandādai Rāmānujācārya*; PL; 128, 11; SKT, GR.

1544 Rukmāṅgadacaritra, 1-40 Adhyāyas; PL; 128, 12; SKT, GR.

1545 Rukmāṅgadacaritra, 1-40 Adhyāyas; PL; 129, 1; SKT, GR.

1546 Śrīvacanabhūṣaṇa Arumbada; PL; 129, 2; TA, GR.

1547 Śrī Rāmāyaṇa Vyākhyāna—Araṇya and Kiṣkindhā Kāṇḍa; *Govindarāja*; PL; 129, 3; SKT, GR.

1548 Ācāryahṛdayavyākhyāna—4 Prakaraṇas; *Śrīvaravaramuni*; PL; 129, 4; TA, TE GR.

1549 Rahasyatrayasāra; *Śrīvedāntācārya*; PL; 129, 5; SKT, TE.

1550 Dīpaprakāśa; *Vādi Kesari Alahiyamanavālajīyar*; PL; 129, 6; TA, TA.

1551 Periyatirumoli Vyākhyāna 1 to 5 Śataka; *Periyavāccān Pillai*; PL; 129, 7; TA, TA.

1552 Śrī Bhāgavata; PL; 130, 1; SKT, GR.

1553 Yadriccikappadi; *Śrī Pillai Lokācārya*; PL; 130, 2; TA, TE.

1554 Amalanadipiran Tiruviruttam Vyākhyāna; *Periyavāccān Pillai*; PL; 130, 3; TA, GR.

1555 Śrī Vaiṣṇava Samayācāraniṣkarṣa; *Śrī Pillailokam Jīyar*; PL; 130, 4; TA, GR.

1556 Harivaṁśa; *Śrīśuka*; PL; 130, 5; SKT, GR.

1557 Perumāltirumoli Tiruchandaviruttam, Tirumālai, Tiruppalielucci and Amalaṇadīpirān Arumpadam; PL; 130, 6; TA, TA.

1558 Periyālvār Tirumoli; *Periyavāccān Pillai*; PL; 130, 7; TA, GR.

1559 Bhagavadviṣaya, (Ninth Śataka) Īḍu; *Vadakku Tiruvedipillai*; PL; 130, 8; TA, TA.

1560 Nācciyār Tirumoli Vyākhyāna; *Parakālasvāmī*; PL; 130, 9; TA, GR.

1561 Upadeśaratnamālāvyākhyāna; *Pillai Lokam Jīyar*; PL; 130, 10; TA, GR.

1562 Pādma Saṁhitā; PL; 131, 9; SKT, TE. [Roll 131 currently unavailable]

1563 Pādma Saṁhitā (continues previous); PL; 132, 1; SKT, TE.

1564 Rahasyarakṣa-Stotrādhikāra; *Śrī Vedāntadeśika*; PL; 132, 2; SKT, GR.

1565 Parāśara Saṁhitā; PL; 132, 3; SKT, GR.

1566 Viṣṇudharmottara Purāṇa 1-27 Adhyāya-s; PL; 132, 4; SKT, GR.

1567 Śrī Rāmāyaṇa Vyākhyāna (Bāla, Ayodhyā and Uttara Kāṇḍa-s); *Govindarāja*; PL; 132, 5; SKT, GR.

1568 Bhagavadviṣaya Īḍu-3600 Padi (From eighth Śataka to ninth Śataka, eighth Daśaka); PL; 132, 6; TA, TA.

1569 Bhagavad Viṣaya Arumbada sixth Śataka—V to VI Daśaka; *Śuddhasattvam Aṇṇa*; PL; 132, 7; TA,TA.

1570 Tirumālai 6000 Padi; *Alahiya Maṇavāla Perumāl Nāyanār*; PL; 132, 8; TA, TE.

1571 Śrī Bhāgavata Vyākhyāna (tenth Skandha, 50th Adhyāya); *Śrīdhara*; PL; 132, 9; SKT, GR.

1572 Vilakṣaṇamokṣādhikāranirṇaya; PL; 132, 10; TA, GR.

1573 Śāligrāmalakṣaṇādi; PL; 132, 11; SKT, GR.

1574 Śāligrāmalakṣaṇādi (continues previous); PL; 133, 1; SKT, GR.

1575 Divyadeśa Aṭṭavaṇai; *Vangipurattu Nambi*; PL; 133, 2; TA, GR.

1576 Yatīndra Pravaṇa Prabhāva; *Pillai Lokam Jīyar*; PL; 133, 3; TA, GR.

1577 Karaṇavyākhyānam-Śiva-Paratvakhaṇḍana; PL; 133, 4; SKT, GR.

1578 Bhagavadviṣaya 6000 Padi; *Tirukkurukai Pirān Pillān*; PL; 133, 5; TA, GR.

1579 Campakāraṇyadakṣiṇadvārakā Māhātmya; PL; 133, 6; SKT, GR.

1580 Śrī Bhāṣyādisūkti Sādhutvamālikā; PL; 133, 7; SKT, GR.

1581 Sudarśanaśatakam Vyākhyāna; *Nārāyaṇabhaṭṭa*; PL; 133, 8; SKT, GR.

1582 Tiruvāimoli with Vākhyā-I; *Nammālvār,* (c) *Tirukkurukaipirān Pillan and others*; B; 133, 9; TA, TE.

1583 Tattvanirṇaya; *Vātsyaśrīvaradācārya*; B; 133, 10; SKT, D.

1584 Tattva Mārtaṇḍa-II; *Śrīnivāsācārya* (Surapuram); B; 133, 11; SKT, D.

1585 Tattva Mārtaṇḍa-II; *Śrīnivāsācārya* (Surapuram); B; 133, 12; SKT, D.

1586 Viṣṇupurāṇam with Commentary; *Parāśara* (c) *Viṣṇucittārya*; B; 133, 13; SKT, D.

1587 Īśādidaśopaniṣad Bhāṣyam; *Gopālānandasvāmī*; B; 133, 14; SKT, D.

1588 Śrī Bhāṣya with Śrutaprakāśikā; *Bhagavad Rāmānuja,* (c) *Sudarśana Sūri*; B; 133, 15; SKT, D.

1589 Śrī Bhāṣya-II with Śrutaprakāśikā; *Bhagavad Rāmānuja,* (c) *Sudarśana Sūri*; B; 133, 16; SKT, D.

1590 Śrībhāṣya with Śrutaprakāśikā (continues 133.15); *Bhagavad Rāmānuja*; (c) *Sudarśana Sūri*; B; 134, 1; SKT, D. 1967 A.D.

1591 Śatadūṣaṇī-I with Commentary Caṇḍmāruta; *Vedānta Deśika,* (c) *Mahācārya*; B; 134, 2; SKT, D.

1592 Śatadūṣaṇī-II with Commentary Caṇḍmāruta; *Vedānta Deśika,* (c) *Mahācārya*; B; 134, 3; SKT, D.

1593 Śatadūṣaṇī-III with Commentary Caṇḍmāruta; *Vedānta Deśika,* (c) *Mahācārya*; B; 134, 4; SKT, D.

1594 Śatadūṣaṇī-IV with Commentary Caṇḍmāruta; *Vedānta Deśika,* (c) *Mahācārya*; B; 134, 5; SKT, D.

1595 Śaraṇaśabdārtha Vicāraḥ Prapattyanupāyatva Vicāraśca; *Anantācārya* (Musharpakkam); B; 134, 6; SKT, TE.

1596 Vacassudhāvicāra; *Śrīnivāsa Narasiṁhācārya* (Kuppana Iyengar); B; 134, 7; SKT, TE.

1597 Darśanodaya; *Śrīnivāsācārya* (Lakṣmīpuram); B; 134, 8; SKT, D.

1598 Sadvidyāvijaya; *Mahācārya*; B; 134, 9; SKT, D.

1599 Śrī Bhāṣyam with Śrutapradīpikā and Viṣayavākyadīpikā; *Bhagavad Rāmānuja,* (c) *Sudarśana Sūri* and *Raṅga Rāmānuja*; B; 134, 10; SKT, TE.

1600 Śrī Raṅgarājastavaḥ with Commentary; *Parāśara Bhaṭṭāraka,* (c) *Veṅkaṭācārya*; B; 134, 11; SKT, TE.

1601 Ṇatva Tattvavibhūṣaṇam; *Anantācārya*; B; 134, 12; SKT, TE.

1602 Viṣṇudharma (Bhaviṣyatpurāṇāntargata); B; 134, 13; SKT, TE.

1603 Sampradāya Akarādi; B; 134, 14; TA, TE.

1604 Pañcastavaḥ with Commentary; *Kūreśa Miśra,* (c) *Śrīnivāsācārya*; B; 134, 15; SKT, TE.

1605 Śārīrakaśāstrārtha Dīpikā; *Raṅgarāmānujamuni*; B; 134, 16; SKT, D.

1606 Nayamayūkhamālikā; *Appayyadīkṣita*; B; 134, 17; SKT, D.

1607 Viṣṇusahasranāma Bhāṣya with Nirvacana and Nirukta; *Parāśarabhaṭṭa*; B; 134, 18; SKT, D.

1608 Viṣṇusahasranāma Bhāṣya with Nirvacana and Nirukta; *Parāśarabhaṭṭa*; B; 135, 1; SKT, D.

1609 Īśāvāsyopaniṣad with Three Bhāṣya-s; *Vedāntadeśika, Kūranārāyaṇamuni* and *Śrīraṅgācārya*; B; 135, 2; SKT, D.

1610 Śatadūṣaṇī with Caṇḍamāruta and Nṛsiṁha Rājīya; *Vedānta Deśika,* (c) *Mahācārya* and *Nṛsiṁharāja*; B; 135, 3; SKT, TE.

1611 Viṣayavākyadīpikā with Ṭippaṇī; *Raṅgarāmānujamuni,* (c) *Lakṣmaṇadāsa*; B; 135, 4; SKT, D.

1612 Vedārtha Saṅgraha with Tātparyadīpikā; *Bhagavad Rāmānuja,* (c) *Sudarśana Sūri*; B; 135, 5; SKT; TE.

1613 Bhāvaprakāśikā (Forming part of Śrutaprakāśikā); *Raṅgarāmānujamuni*; B; 135, 6; SKT, GR.

1614 Vilakṣaṇa Mokṣādhikārinirṇayam; *Erumbiyappa*; B; 135, 7; TA, TE.

1615 Bhāṣyārtha Saṅgraham; *Veṅkaṭarāghavācārya* (Karakkuruchi); B; 135, 8; TA, TE.

1616 Kudṛṣṭidhvāntamārtaṇḍa-I; *Raṅgācāryasvāmī*; B; 135, 9; SKT, D.

1617 Paramavaidikasiddhāntatattva Ratnākara; *Rāmānujācārya* (Śrī Bhāṣyam); B; 135, 10; SKT, TE.

1618 Īśāvāsyopaniṣat, Kenopaniṣat and Kaṭhopaniṣat with Commentary; *Vedāntadeśika, Kūranārāyaṇamuni* and *Ramānuja*; B; 135, 11; SKT, D.

1619 Śrīguṇaratnakośa—Savyākhyā; *Parāśara Bhaṭṭa,* (c) *Vīrarāghava*; B; 135, 12; SKT, TE.

1620 Viśiṣṭādvaita Siddhāntamu; *Sampatkumāra Varadaveṅkaṭa Raṅgācārya* (Nallān Cakravarti); B; 135, 13; TE, TE.

1621 Atharvaśikhāvilāsavistara; *Rāmānujācārya* (Śuddhasattvam); B; 135, 14; SKT, TE.

1622 Mānameya Rahasya Ślokavārttikam; *Śrīnivāsācārya* (Lakṣmīpuram); B; 135, 15; SKT, D.

1623 Pārāśaryavijaya; *Mahācārya/Rāmānujadāsa*; B; 135, 16; SKT, D.

1624 Yādavagirimāhātmya; B; 135, 17; SKT, TE.

1625 Ānandasaṁhitā-III with Commentary; *Marīci Maharṣi,* (c) *Pārthasārathikṛṣṇamācārya*; B; 135, 18; SKT, TE.

1626 Ānandasaṁhitā-IV with Commentary; *Marīci Maharṣi,* (c) *Pārthasārathikṛṣṇamācārya*; B; 135, 19; SKT, TE.

1627 Vaikhānasopākhyānam; B; 135, 20; SKT, TE.

1628 Dásopaniṣadvyākhyānam; *Rāmānujācārya* (Śrībhāṣyam); B; 135, 21; SKT, TE.

1629 Sūtrānuguṇyasiddhivimarśaḥ; *Gopālācārya*; B; 135, 22; SKT, D.

1630 Nyāyasiddhāñjana with Commentary Ratnapeṭikā; *Vedānta Deśika, Kṛṣṇatātārya*; B; 135, 23; SKT, GR.

1631 Nikṣeparakṣā with Nikṣepacintāmaṇi; *Vedāntadeśika*, (c) *Siṁhadeva*; B; 135, 24; SKT, GR.

1632 Ācāryahṛdayasārasaṅgraham; *Gopālakṛṣṇapillai*; B; 135, 25; TA, TA.

1633 Daśopaniṣattukkalin Drāvida Pratipada Bhāṣyam; B; 135, 26; TA, TA.

[Roll 136 currently unavailable]

1634 Vedāntakaustubha I to XVIII; *Rāmānujācārya* (Śuddhasattvam); PM; 137, 1; SKT, D.

1635 Maudgalyapurāṇa; PM; 137, 2; SKT, D.

1636 Viṣvaksenasaṁhitā-II; PM; 137, 3; SKT, TE.

1637 Śatadūṣaṇīvyākhyā-Nṛsiṁharājīya; *Nṛsiṁharāja*; PM; 137, 4; SKT, TE.

1638 Śrībhāṣyam; *Bhagavad Rāmānuja*; PL; 137, 5; SKT, GR.

1639 Rāmāyaṇasāram; PL; 137, 6; Maṇipravāla; GR.

1640 Śrīvacanabhūṣaṇarahasya Jālam; *Pillai Lokācārya*; PL; 137, 7; Manipravalam; GR, TA.

1641 Kriyākairavacandrikā; *Varāhaguru*; PL; 137, 8; SKT, GR.

1642 Vyāsaśikṣāvivaraṇam; PL; 137, 9; SKT, GR.

1643 Vedāntaśāra and Vedāntadīpa; *Bhagavad Rāmānuja*; PL; 137, 10; SKT, GR.

1644 Prapannadharmasārasamuccayaḥ; PL; 137, 11; SKT, GR.

1645 Padmatantram; PL; 138, 14; SKT, GR . [Currently unavailable]

1646 Padmatantram; PL; 139, 1; SKT, GR.

1647 Bhāgavatam; *Vedavyāsamaharṣi*; PL; 139, 2; SKT, GR.

1648 Śrī Vaiṣṇavasamayācāraniṣkarṣa; PL; 139, 3; TA, GR.

1649 Taittirīyopaniṣadbhāṣyam; *Raṅgarāmānujamuni*; PL; 139, 4; SKT, GR.

1650 Stotrakadambam; *Ālvārs* and *Ācāryas*; PL; 139, 5; SKT TA, TE GR.

1651 Bhagavadviṣayam (Tiruvāimoli Vyākhyā)-I; *Vadakkutiruvedipillai*; PL; 139, 6; TA, GR.

1652 Kṛṣṇakathāsāra (Kalyāṇa Kāṇḍa)-III; PL; 139, 7; KAN, KAN.

1653 Śrī Vaiṣṇava Dharma Pramāṇa Saṅgrahaḥ; PL; 139, 8; SKT, GR.

1654 Upaniṣaddīpikā; PL; 139, 9; SKT, NA.

1655 Tātparyadīpikā (Vedārthasaṅgraha Vyākhyā); *Sudarśanasūri*; PL; 139, 10; SKT, GR.

1656 Tātparyadīpikā (Vedārthasaṅgraha Vyākhyā) (continuation of 139, 10); *Sudarśanasūri*; PL; 140, 1; SKT, GR.

1657 Deśikarahasyangal (twenty-seven Rahasya-s); *Vedānta Deśika*; PL; 140, 2; TA, GR.

1658 Tiuppāvai and Tirumālaivyākhyā; *Periyavāccān Pillai*; PL; 140, 3; Maṇipravālam, GR.

1659 Atharvaśikhāvilāsaḥ-II; *Rāmānujācārya* (Śuddhasattvam); PL; 140, 4; SKT, GR.

1660 Sāttvika Brahmavidyāvilāsaḥ; PL; 140, 5; SKT, GR.

1661 Tiruvāimoli Nuttandādivyākhyā; PL; 140, 6; Maṇipravālam, GR.

1662 Padukāsahasra and others; *Vedāntadeśika*; PL; 140, 7; SKT, GR.

1663 Pāñcarātrasāram and others; PL; 140, 8; SKT, GR.

1664 Bhārgava Upapurāṇam and Others; PL; 140, 9; SKT, GR.

1665 Śrīraṅgamāhātmya and Others; PL; 140, 10; SKT, GR.

1666 Bhāgavatavyākhyā (Śukapakṣīya); *Sudarśana Sūri*; PL; 140, 11; SKT, GR.

1667 Tiruvāimoli; *Nammālvār*; PL; 140, 12; TA, GR.

1668 Tiruvāimoli; *Nammālvār*; PL; 141, 1; TA, GR.

1669 Gītā Bhāṣya; *Bhagavad Rāmānuja*; PL; 141, 2; SKT, TE.

1670 Padmapurāṇam; PL; 141, 3; SKT, GR.

1671 Caturdaśa Veṅkaṭeśa ṃāhātmya with Veṅkaṭeśa Tāpinyupaniṣad; B; 141, 4; SKT, D.

1672 Tiruppallāṇḍu, Vaiṣṇavasamayācāra niṣkarṣa and others; *Periyālvār*; B; 141, 5; TA, GR.

1673 Tattvadīpam with Dīpa Prakāśa; *Alahiya Maṇavāla Jīyar* (Vādi Keśari); B; 141, 6; SKT, TE.

1674 Gñānasāram Vyākhyāna and Prameyasāram; *Aruḷālaperumāl Emberumānār Maṇavālamāmuni*; B; 141, 7; TA, TA.

1675 Śrī Bhāṣya with Śrutaprakāśikā (Jijñāsādhikaraṇa only); *Bhagavad Rāmānuja*; B; 141, 8; SKT TA, GR TA.

1676 Tātparyadīpikā and Carama Śloka Ṭippaṇī; *Bālasarasvatī and Rāmānujācārya* (Śuddhasattvam); B; 141, 9; Maṇipravālam SKT, TE.

1677 Tātparyadīpikā and Caramaśloka Ṭippaṇī; *Bālasarasvatī* and *Rāmānujācārya* (Śuddhasattvam); B; 142, 1; Maṇipravālam SKT, TE.

1678 Gītābhāṣyam with Tamil Translation; *Bhagavad Rāmānuja,* (Tr.) *Raṅgācārya* (Musharpakkam, Kidambi); B; 142, 2; TA SKT, TA, GR.

1679 Bhāgavata Ṭippaṇī; *Yadupati* (Yādavārya); B; 146, 1; SKT, D. [Currently unavailable]

*Please note that we have found there is a duplication between items 1024-1047 and 1485-1507. This came about in the copying and transfer of rolls from The American University Library Archives' master copy to the Adyar Library where the research necessary for the production of this Catalogue was carried out. Rather than renumber the whole collection it seemed more prudent to keep the duplicate copies in the collection for those exceptional occasions when use of both copies may be required. We believe that most other anomalies have been accounted for in the appropriate place.

A CATALOGUE OF VAIṢṆAVA LITERATURE*

ALPHABETICAL INDEX

---

* Please consult the note at the end of the preceding sequentially numbered catalogue.

0689 Acha Roṭi; PM; 51B, 19; H, D.

1479 Adbhutarāmāyaṇam; *Vālmīki*; B; 121, 17; SKT, D.

0539 Adbhuta Rasa Sāgara; *Viṭṭhal Bipul Devjī*; B; 48, 9; H, D; 1939 A.D.

0998 Ādhāraśaktidarpaṇaṃ; PL; 63, 21; SKT, GR.

0989 Ādhāraśaktitarpaṇam; PL; 63, 12; SKT, GR.

0617 Adhikaraṇasārārtha Dīpikā; *Maṅgācārya Śrīnivāsasūri*; PM; 50B, 8; SKT, D.

0618 Adhikaraṇasārāvalī; *Veṅkaṭanātha*; PM; 50B, 9; SKT, GR.

0616 Adhikaraṇayuktivilāsaḥ; *Mahācārya*; PM; 50B, 7; SKT, D.

0635 Adhyātmacintā (with Commentary); *Saumyajāmātṛmuni*; PM; 50B, 17; SKT, GR.

0338 Adhyātmakārikāvalī (with commentary Adhyātmasudhātaraṅgiṇi); *Niyamānanda*; PM; 38, 19; SKT, D; c. 1891 A.D.

1348 Adhyātmakārikāvalī with Adhyātmasudhā Taraṅgiṇī; *Śrīnivāsācārya,* (c) *Puruṣottama Prasāda*; PM; 110, 2; SKT, D.

1101 Adhyātmakārikāvalī with Adhyātmasudhātaraṅgiṇī; *Śrīnivāsācārya*; PM; 103, 2; SKT, D.

0277 Adhyātṃarasarañjanī; *Jayatīrtha*; B; 36, 5; SKT, D; 1904; A.D.

0278 Ādityādinavagraha Stotra; *Kṛṣṇa Dvaipāyana Vyāsa*; B; 36, 6; SKT, D.

0135 Ādityahṛdaya of Bhaviṣyottara Purāṇa; *Kṛṣṇadvaipāyana Vyāsa*; PM; 6, 8; SKT, D.

1171 Āditya Hṛdaya Stotra; *Kṛṣṇa Dvaipāyana Vyāsa*; PM; 105, 11; SKT, D.

0168 Āditya Hṛdaya Stotram of Bhaviṣyottara Purāṇa; *Kṛṣṇa Dvaipāyana Vyāsa*; PM; 6, 41; SKT, D.

0614 Advaitabahiṣkāraḥ; *Raṅgarāja*; PM; 50B, 5; SKT, D.

0612 Advaita Kālānalaḥ; PM; 50B, 3; SKT, D.

0731 Ālamandāra-Stotram with Vyākhyā; *Yāmunācārya*; PM; 51B, 61; SKT, D.

1257 Alaṅkāra Kaustubha with Ṭīkā; *Kavikarṇapūra*; PM; 107, 45; SKT, D.

1430 Alaṅkārakaustubha with Ṭīkā; *Kavi Karṇapūra* (Paramānanda Dāsa), (c) *Sārvabhauma* (Kṛṣṇadeva); PM; 118, 14B; SKT, D.

1253 Ālavandārastotram; *Yāmunācārya*; PM; 107, 41; SKT, D.

1554 Amalanadipiran Tiruviruttam Vyākhyāna; *Periyavāccān Pillai*; PL; 130, 3; TA, GR.

0174 Āmaśrāddha (Āśvalāyana Śrauta Sūtrokta Śrāddha Saṅkalpa Vidhi); PM; 6, 47; SKT, D.

0688 Amṛta Dhārā; *Bhagavan Dās*; PM; 51B, 18; H, D.

1080 Ānandasaṁhitā III with Commentary; *Marīcimaharṣi*; B; 100, 18; SKT, TE.

1625 Ānandasaṁhitā-III with Commentary; *Marīci Maharṣi*, (c) *Pārthasārathikṛṣṇamācārya*; B; 135, 18; SKT, TE.

1081 Ānandasaṁhitā IV with Commentary; *Marīcimaharṣi*; B; 100, 19; SKT, TE.

1626 Ānandasaṁhitā-IV with Commentary; *Marci Maharṣi*, (c) *Pārthasārathikṛṣṇamācārya*; B; 135, 19; SKT, TE.

0637 Ānandatāratamyakhaṇḍanam; *Aṇṇayācārya*; PM; 50B, 19; SKT, GR.

0632 Ānandatāratamyakhaṇḍanam; *Śrīnivāsācārya*; PM; 50B, 14; SKT, D.

0599 Ānanda Vanamālā; *Keśava Śaraṇadeva*; B; 50A, 6; SKT, D; 1859 A.D.

0529 Ānanda Vṛndāvana Campū (with Ṭīkā Sukhavartanī); *Kavi Karṇapūra*; B; 47, 4; SKT, D.

0167 Ananta Kathā of Bhaviṣyottara Purāṇa; *Kṛṣṇa Dvaipāyana Vyāsa*; PM; 6, 40; SKT, D.

0185 Ananta Kathā of Bhaviṣyottara Purāṇa; *Kṛṣṇa Dvaipāyana Vyāsa*; PM; 6, 58; SKT, D.

1473 Anantakathā Śataka (From Bhaviṣyottara Purāṇa); *Kṛṣṇa Dvaipāyana Vyāsa*; B; 121, 11; SKT H, D.

0541 Ananya Modinī Tathā Cāha Velī; *Priyā Dās*; B; 48, 11; H, D; 1934 A.D.

0354 Anarpitacarīṁ Cirād iti Ślokasya Vyākhyā; *Jīva Gosvāmī*; B; 39, 15; SKT, D; 1963 A.D.

0295 Antyeṣṭi Saṁskāra Vidhiḥ (Part of Saṁskāra Pradīpa); *Lakṣmaṇa*; B; 36, 24; SKT, D.

0551 Aṇubhāṣyam (with Tattva Mañjarī Ṭīkā and Bengali Translation); *Madhvācārya*; B; 48, 21; SKT BL, BL.

0253 Anumadhva Vijaya with Ṭīkā; *Nārāyaṇa Paṇḍitācārya*; PM; 35, 12; SKT, D.

0999 Ārādhanakārikā; PL; 63, 22; SKT, GR.

1000 Ārādhanakramaḥ; PL; 63, 23; SKT, GR.

0165 Ārādhanā Prayoga (Nāgara Khaṇḍa); PM; 6, 38; SKT, D.

0796 Ārādhanotsava Saṅgraha; PM; 56, 7; SKT, D.

0987 Ārādhanotsavasaṅgrahaḥ; PL; 63, 10; SKT, GR.

1009 Araṅganāyakar Mālai; *Muthukumārapaṇḍāram*; PL; 63, 32; TA, TA.

0988 Arcādījyāprabhāvaḥ; PL; 63, 11; SKT, GR.

0809 Arcanākhaṇḍaḥ; PM; 56, 20; SKT, TE.

0813 Arcanākhaṇḍaḥ; PM; 56, 24; SKT, TE.

0812 Arcanākhaṇḍavyākhyā; PM; 56, 23; SKT, TE.

0815 Arcanānavanītam; *Keśavācārya*; PL; 56, 26; SKT, D.

1006 Arthapañcakam; *Gārgyaveṅkaṭācārya*; PL; 63, 29; SKT, TE.

0636 Aruṇādhikaraṇamañjarī; *Śrīnivāsa*; PM; 50B, 18; SKT, GR.

0620 Aruṇādhikaraṇa Saraṇi Vivaraṇī; *Śrīnivāsa*; PM; 50B, 11; SKT, D.

1468 Āścarya Rasa Prabandha with Bengali translation; *Prabodhānanda Sarasvatī*; B; 121, 6; SKT BL, BL.

0623 Āśrayānupapattiḥ; PM; 50B, 12; SKT, GR.

1003 Aṣṭādaśabhedanirṇayaḥ; *Raṅganāthasūri*; PL; 63, 26; SKT, GR.

1002 Aṣṭādaśabhedanirṇayaḥ; *Raṅganāthasūri*; PL; 63, 25; SKT, TE.

1004 Aṣṭādaśabhedanirṇayaḥ; *Raṅganāthasūri*; PL; 63, 27; SKT, GR.

0814 Aṣṭādaśabhedanirṇayaḥ; *Raṅganāthasūri*; PL; 56, 25; SKT, D.

0826 Aṣṭādaśabhedasaṁvāda; PM; 57, 5; SKT, GR.

0825 Aṣṭādaśarahasyārthavivaraṇam; *Rāmānuja*; PM; 57, 4; SKT, D.

0590 Aṣṭādaśa Siddhānta ke Pada with Ṭīkā; *Haridās Svāmī*; B; 49, 30; SKT H, D; 1928 A.D.

1005 Aṣṭākṣarabrahmavidyā; *Nārada*; PL; 63, 28; SKT, GR.

0811 Aṣṭākṣaradīpikā; PM; 56, 22; SKT, GR.

0817 Aṣṭākṣaradīpikā; PM; 56, 28; SKT, GR.

0728 Aṣṭa Sakhī Rūpa Sevādi; PM; 51B, 58; SKT H, D.

1193 Aṣṭāvakra Gītā with Ṭīkā; *Kṛṣṇa Dvaipāyana Vyāsa*; PM; 106, 14; SKT, D.

0670 Aṣṭayāmanikuñjadarpaṇa; PM; 51B, 2; H, D.

0301 Āśvalāyana Sandhyā Vandana; B; 36, 30; SKT, D.

0145 Āśvalāyana Śrauta Sūtra (Pūrva Ṣaṭka); *Āśvalāyana*; PM; 6, 18; SKT, D.

0148 Āśvalāyana Śrauta Sūtra (Uttara Ṣaṭka); *Āśvalāyana*; PM; 6, 21; SKT, D.

0008 Ātharvaṇa Bhāṣya Ṭīkā; *Vyāsa Tīrtha Yati*; B; 1, 8; SKT, D; 1903.

0724 (Atharvaṇa) Netropaniṣatsūtra; PM; 51B, 54; SKT, D.

0014 Ātharvaṇa Upaniṣad Bhāṣya Vivaraṇam; (Umarji) *Kṛṣṇācāryasūri*; B; 1, 14; SKT, D; 1903; A.D.

0153 Bhagavad Gītā; *Kṛṣṇa Dvaipāyana Vyāsa*; PM; 6, 26; SKT, TU.

1186 Bhagavad Gītā; *Kṛṣṇa Dvaipāyana Vyāsa*; PM; 106, 7; SKT, D.

1268 Bhagavad Gītā; *Kṛṣṇa Dvaipāyana Vyāsa*; PM; 108, 8; SKT, D.

0526 Bhagavad Gītā (with Ṭīkā Gūḍhārthadīpikā); *Kṛṣṇa Dvaipāyana Vyāsa*; B; 47, 1; SKT, D; 1880 A.D.

0582 Bhagavad Gītā (with Tattva Prakāśikā Bhāṣya and Hindi Translation); *Kṛṣṇa Dvaipāyana Vyāsa*; B; 49, 22; 1935 A.D.

0373 Bhagavad Gītā (with Sārārtha Varṣiṇī Ṭīkā and Gītā Bhūṣaṇa Bhāṣya and Svayambhagavatvāṣṭakam from Stavāmṛtalaharī); *Viśvanātha Cakravartī* and *Baladeva Vidyābhūṣaṇa*; B; 40, 2; SKT, D; 1966 A.D.

0267 Bhagavad Gītā Bhāṣya; *Madhva/Ānanda Tīrtha*; PM; 35, 26; SKT, D.

0019 Bhagavad Gītā Bhāṣya with Prameya Dīpikā (or) (Gītā Bhāṣya Prameya Dīpikā); *Madhva*; B; 1, 19.

0018 Bhagavad Gītā Bhāṣya with Prameya Dīpikā (with two Ṭippaṇīs); *Madhva*; B; 1, 18; SKT, D; 1887 A.D.

0020 Bhagavad Gītā Bhāṣya Prameya Dīpikābhāvaratna Kośa; *Sumatīndra Tīrtha*; B; 1, 20; SKT, D.

0752 Bhagavadgītābhāṣyavyākhyā-Tātparyacandrikā; *Vedāntadeśika*; PM; 53, 4; SKT, GR.

0512 Bhagavad Gītā from Mahābhārata (Also Contains Bhagavad Gītāmālāmantra); *Kṛṣṇa Dvaipāyana Vyāsa*; PM; 44, 7; SKT, D.

0507 Bhagavad Gītā Mālā Mantra, Viṣṇu Sahasra Nāma, Bhīṣma Stava Rāja, Anusmṛti, Gajendra Mokṣaṇa, etc.; *Kṛṣṇa Dvaipāyana Vyāsa*; PM; 44, 2; SKT, D; c. 1823 A.D.

0150 Bhagavad Gītā Tātparya Nirṇaya Ṭīkā Nyāya Dīpikā; *Jayatīrtha*; PM; 6, 23; SKT, D.

1513 Bhagavadviṣaya Arumbada from II Śataka to V Śataka; *Anna*; PL; 125, 6; TA, GR.

1569 Bhagavad Viṣaya Arumbada sixth Śataka—V to VI Daśaka; *Śuddhasattvam Aṇṇa*; PL; 132, 7; TA, TA.

1568 Bhagavadviṣaya Īḍu-3600 Padi (From eighth Śataka to ninth Śataka, eighth Daśaka); PL; 132, 6; TA, TA.

1578 Bhagavadviṣaya 6000 Padi; *Tirukkurukai Pirān Pillān*; PL; 133, 5; TA, GR.

1051 Bhagavadviṣaya 6000 Padi; *Tirukkurukai Pirānpillān*; PL; 99, 4; TA, GR.

1534 Bhagavadviṣaya Īḍu 36000 Padi (From Seventh Śataka to Tenth Śataka); *Vaḍakkutiruvīdipillai*; PL; 128, 2; TA, TA.

1046 Bhagavadviṣaya III Śataka Vyākhyā-Advaivalanthan; *Attantiruveṅkaṭa Rāmānujajīyar*; PL; 92, 11; TA, TA.

1506 Bhagavadviṣaya-III Śataka Vyākhyāna—Adaiyavalantan; Attantiruveṅgaḍar Erāmānujajīyar; PL; 124, 10; TA, TA.

1504 Bhagavadviṣaya Vyākhyāna-III Śataka; *Mudumbai Anantācār*; PL; 124, 8; TA, TA.

0887 Bhagavadviṣayaḥ; *Govardhanam Raṅgācārya*; PM; 59, 19; SKT, D.

1651 Bhagavadviṣayam (Tiruvāmoli Vyākhyā)-I; *Vadakkutiruvedipillai*; PL; 139, 6; TA, GR.

1505 Bhagavadviṣayam 36000 Padi—4, 5, 6 Śataka; *Vadakku Tiruvīdipillai*; PL; 124, 9; TA, TA.

1045 Bhagavadviṣayam 36000 Padi—4, 5, 6 Śataka; *Vadakku Tiruvīdipillai*; PL; 92, 10; TA, TA.

1530 Bhagavadviṣayārumbada; *Appu Iyengar*; PL; 126, 9; TA, TA.

1044 Bhagavadviṣayavyākhyāna III Śataka; *Mudumbai Anantācār*; PL; 92, 9; TA, TA.

1647 Bhāgavatam; *Vedavyāsamaharṣi*; PL; 139, 2; SKT, GR.

1449 Bhāgavatāmṛta with Digdarśanī Ṭīkā; *Sanātanagosvāmī*; PM; 119, 18; SKT, D.

1450 Bhāgavatāmṛta with Digdarśanī Ṭīkā; *Sanātanagosvāmī*; PM; 120, 1; SKT, D.

0608 Bhāgavata Māhātmya (from Skanda Purāṇa with Commentary); *Kṛṣṇa Dvaipāyana Vyāsa*; B; 50A, 15; SKT, D.

0175 Bhāgavata Navama Skandha Ṭīkā (Pada Ratnāvalī); *Vijayadhvaja*; PM; 6, 48; SKT, D.

1476 Bhāgavata Purāna—Daśama Skandha (Pūrva and Uttara Khaṇḍa) with Hindi Ṭīkā; *Kṛṣṇa Dvaipāyana Vyāsa*; B; 121, 14; SKT H, D.

1337 Bhāgavata Purāṇa with Ṭīkā Bhāvārtha Dīpikā; *Kṛṣṇa Dvaipāyana Vyāsa*; PM; 109, 4; SKT, D.

1437 Bhāgavata Sandarbha I-Tattvasandarbha; *Jīvagosvāmī*; PM; 119, 6; SKT, D.

1438 Bhāgavata Sandarbha II-Bhagavat Sandarbha; *Jīvagosvāmī*; PM; 119, 7; SKT, D.

1439 Bhāgavata Sandarbha III-Paramātma Sandarbha; *Jīvagosvāmī*; PM; 119, 8; SKT, D.

1440 Bhāgavata Sandarbha IV-Kṛṣṇa Sandarbha; *Jīvagosvāmī*; PM; 119, 9; SKT, D.

1441 Bhāgavata Sandarbha V-Bhakti Sandarbha; *Jīvagosvāmī*; PM; 119, 10; SKT, D.

1442 Bhāgavata Sandarbha VI-Prīti Sandarbha; *Jīvagosvāmī*; PM; 119, 11; SKT, D.

0160 Bhāgavata Tātparya Nirṇaya; *Madhvācārya/ Ānandatīrtha*; PM; 6, 33; SKT, D.

0233 Bhāgavata Tātparya Nirṇaya with Ṭīkā (Dīpikā); *Madhvācārya*; B; 34, 1; SKT, D; 1890 A.D.; (Continues 33, 9).

0232 Bhāgavata Tātparya Nirṇaya with Ṭīkā (Dīpikā); *Madhvācārya*; B; 33, 9; SKT, D; 1890 A.D.

0149 Bhāgavata (Seventh Canto) Ṭīkā (Vijayadhavajīya); *Vijayadhvaja Tīrtha*; PM; 6, 22; SKT, D.

0029 Bhāgavata Ṭippaṇī (Sajjanahita); *Ceṭṭi Veṅkaṭādri*; B; 3, 4; SKT, D; Śaka 1850, 1928 A.D.

0025 Bhāgavata Ṭippaṇī; *Satyadharma Yati*; B; 2, 4; SKT, D.

1679 Bhāgavata Ṭippaṇī; *Yadupati* (Yādavārya); B; 146, 1; SKT, D.

0096 Bhāgavata Vyākhyā; *Sudhīndra Tīrtha*; PM; 5, 7; SKT, D; c. 1620 A.D.

0218 Bhāgavata-Ṭippaṇī; *Yadupati* (Yādavārya); B; 31, 5; SKT, D.

0219 Bhāgavata-Ṭippaṇī; *Yadupati* (Yādavārya); B; 32, 1; SKT, D.

1666 Bhāgavatavyākhyā (Śukapakṣīya); *Sudarśana Sūri*; PL; 140, 11; SKT, GR.

0024 Bhāgavata with Padaratnāvalīṭīkā; *Vyāsa*; B; 2, 3; SKT, D; Śaka 1790, 1868 A.D.

0443 Bhagavat Sevāvidhī; *Bāṅke Bihārī Lāla* (Bāṅke Piyā); B; 42, 9; H, D; 1923 A.D.

1472 Bhajana Ratnāvalī; Compiler *Rāmanārāyaṇ Dās*; B; 121, 10; H, D.

1204 Bhajanāṣṭaka; PM; 106, 25; H, D.

0350 Bhakta Bhūṣaṇa Sandarbha (with Translation); *Nārāyaṇa Bhaṭṭa*; B; 39, 11; SKT H, D; 1964 A.D.

1328 Bhakta Cālīsī Mālā; *Sudarśana Dās*; PM; 108, 69; H, D.

1134 Bhakta Mālā; *Nābhā Dās*; PM; 104, 12; H, D.

0601 Bhakta Mālā (with Ṭīkā Bhaktirasabodhinī); *Nava Dās*; PM; 50A, 8; SKT, D.

1415 Bhaktamālā with Bhakti Rasa Bodhinī; *Nābhādās,* (c) *Priyādās*; PM; 117, 6; H SKT, D.

1416 Bhaktamālā with Bhakti Rasa Bodhinī; *Nābhādās,* (c) *Priyādās*; PM; 118, 1; SKT H, D.

0351 Bhakti Tattva Prakāśikā; *Caitanya Dās*; B; 39, 12; SKT, D; 1963 A.D.

0353 Bhakti Viveka; *Nārāyaṇa Bhaṭṭa*; B; 39, 14; SKT, D; 1963 A.D.

0884 Bharadvājasaṁhitā; PM; 59, 16; SKT, GR.

0125 Bhārata Vyākhyā; *Vimala Bodha*; PM; 5, 36; SKT, TU.

0883 Bhārgavatantra Prayogaḥ; PM; 59, 15; SKT, GR.

1664 Bhārgava Upapurāṇam and Others; PL; 140, 9; SKT, GR.

0375 Bhāṣā Bhāgavata (with Māhātmya of Skandha-s I and II); *Rasajānī Vaiṣṇavadās*; B; 40, 4; H, D; 1960 A.D.

1070 Bhāṣyārtha Saṅgraham; *Veṅkaṭa Rāghavācārya* (Karakuruchi); B; 100, 8; Maṇipravala, TE.

1615 Bhāṣyārtha Saṅgraham; *Veṅkaṭarāghavācārya* (Karakkuruchi); B; 135, 8; TA, TE.

0105 Bhāva Dīpā on Tattva Prakāśikā of Jayatīrtha; PL; 5, 16; SKT, D.

1613 Bhāvaprakāśikā (Forming part of Śrutaprakāśikā); *Raṅgarāmānujamuni*; B; 135, 6; SKT, GR.

1068 Bhāvaprakāśikā; *Raṅgarāmānujamuni* ; B; 100, 6; SKT, GR.

0092 Bhāvaratnakośa on Bhaṭṭabhāṣyaṭīkā (First Part, Second Chapter Only); *Mudduveṅkaṭakṛṣṇa*; PM; 5, 3; SKT, D.

0091 Bhāvaratnakośa on Jayatīrtha's Prameyadīpikā *Sumatīndra Tīrtha*; PM; 5, 2; SKT, D; c. 1720 A.D.

0095 Bhāvavarṇana on Tattvasaṅkhyāna Vyākhyā; *Vijayīndra*; PM; 5, 6; SKT, D; c. 1500 A.D.

0762 Bhedadarpaṇaḥ; *Śrīnivāsācārya*; PM; 53, 14; SKT, TE.

0760 Bhedadhikkāranyakkāra; *Nṛsiṁhadeva*; PM; 53, 12; SKT,GR.

0628 Bhedasamarthanam; PM; 50B, 12; SKT, GR.

0083 Bheda Vidyā Vilāsa (Opposition to Narasiṁhāśrama

0765 Brahmasūtrabhāṣyavyākhyā-Laghubhāvaprakāśikā; *Govardhana*; PM; 53, 17; SKT, GR.

0766 Brahmasūtrabhāṣyavyākhyā-Mūlabhāvaprakāśikā; *Raṅgarāmānuja*; PM; 53, 18; SKT, D.

0768 Brahmasūtrabhāṣyavyākhyā-Nayaprakāśikā; *Meghanādāri*; PM; 54, 1; Continuation of 53, 19; SKT, D.

0767 Brahmasūtrabhāṣyavyākhyā-Nayaprakāśikā; *Meghanādārī*; PM; 53, 19; SKT, D.

0764 Brahmasūtrabhāṣyavyākhyā-Śrutapradīpikā; *Sudarśana Sūri*; PM; 53, 16; SKT, GR.

0769 Brahmasūtrabhāṣyavyākhyā-Tattvamārtaṇḍa; *Śrīnivāsa*; PM; 54, 2; SKT, TE.

0757 Brahmasūtrabhāṣyavyākhyā-Vākyārthadīpikā; *Parāṅkuśayati*; PM; 53, 9; SKT, D.

0761 Brahmasūtrārthaṭippaṇī; *Varadārya*; PM; 53, 13; SKT, D.

0759 Brahmasūtraśrībhāṣyavyākhyā-Mitaprakāśikā; PM; 53, 11; SKT, D.

0964 Brahmasūtravivaraṇam-Śivadarśanam; PM; 62, 21; SKT, D.

0758 Brahmasūtravṛtti; PM; 53, 10; SKT, D.

1325 Brahma Sūtra Vyākhyā; PM; 108, 66; SKT, D.

0771 Brahmasūtravyākhyātattvamārtaṇḍa; *Śrīnivāsa*; PM; 54, 4; SKT, D.

0231 Brahma-Vaivarta Mahāpurāṇa (Prakṛti Khaṇḍa and Śrī Kṛṣṇa-Janma Khaṇḍa); *Kṛṣṇa Dvaipāyana Vyāsa*; B; 33, 8; SKT, D; 1931.

0509 Brahma Vaivarta Purāṇa; *Rāmalocana Dās*; B; 44, 4; BL, BL; Baṅgābda 1337.

0600 Brahma Vaivarta Purāṇa (Kṛṣṇa Janma Khaṇḍa); *Kṛṣṇa Dvaipāyana Vyāsa*; PM; 50A, 7; SKT, D.

0204 Brahma Vaivarta Purāṇa Rahasya; *Kṛṣṇa Dvaipāyana Vyāsa*; PM; 7, 10; SKT, D.

1364 Bṛhadāraṇyakopaniṣad with Mitākṣarā; PM; 110, 18; SKT, D.

0508 Bṛhad Bhāgavatāmṛtam with Ṭīkā; *Sanātana Gosvāmī*; B; 44, 3; SKT, D; Caitanyābda; 419.

0881 Bṛhadbrahmasaṁhitā; PM; 59, 13; SKT, GR.

0708 Bṛhad Gautamīya Tantra (Chapter 6, Govinda Vṛndāvana); PM; 51B, 38; SKT, D.

1373 Byālīsalīlā; *Hitadhruvadāsa*; PM; 111, 2; H, D.

0421 Caitanya Bhāgavatam; *Vṛndāvana Das*; B; 41, 11; BL, BL.

0521 Caitanya Candrāmṛtam; *Prabodhānanda Sarasvatī*; B; 44, 16; SKT, D; 1910 A.D.

0369 Caitanya Candrāmṛta Tathā Saṅgīta Mādhava with Translation; *Prabodhānanda Sarasvatī*; B; 39, 30; SKT H, D; 1951 A.D.

1435 Caitanyacandrodaya Nāṭaka; *Kavikarṇapūra*; PM; 119, 4; SKT, D.

0535 Caitanya Caritāmṛta (Paraphrase in Braj Poetry); *Rādhā Caraṇa Dās Gosvāmī*; B; 48, 5; H, D; 1924; A.D.

0425 Caitanya Caritāmṛta (with Ānanda Candrikā Ṭīkā); *Kṛṣṇa Dāsa Kavirāja*; B; 41, 15; BL, BL.

0547 Caitanya Caritāmṛta; *Kṛṣṇa Dās Kavirāj*; B; 48, 17; BL, BL; Baṅgābda 1347.

0420 Caitanya Caritāmṛta; *Kṛṣṇa Dās Kavirāja*; B; 41, 10; BL, BL; 1840 A.D.

1477 Caitanyacaritāmṛta with Ṭīkā; *Kṛṣṇadās Kavirāj*; B; 121, 15; BL, BL.

1378 Caitanyacaritāmṛta; *Kṛṣṇadās Kavirāj*; PM; 111, 7; SKT BL, D.

1446 Caitanyacaritāmṛta; *Kṛṣṇadāsa Kavirāja*; PM; 119, 15; BL, D.

1447 Caitanyacaritāmṛta; *Kṛṣṇadāsa Kavirāja*; PM; 119, 16; BL, D.

1671 Caturdaśa Veṅkaṭeśa Māhātmya with Veṅkaṭeśa Tāpinyupaniṣad; B; 141, 4; SKT, D.

0155 Caturtha Skandha Tātparyanirṇaya Prakāśa Ṭīkā; *Śrīnivāsa*; PM; 6, 28; SKT, D.

1289 Catur Yugācāryaitihyānusandhi; PM; 108, 30; SKT, D.

0403 Catuś Ślokī and Stotra Ratnam (with Hindi Chāyāpadya by Lakṣmīprasāda Śarmā); *Yāmunācārya*; B; 40, 33; SKT H, D; 1961 A.D.

1243 Caubīs Autārajas; *Dharma Dāsa*; PM; 107, 31; H, D.

1270 Caubīs Gāyatrī; PM; 108, 10; SKT, D. (108.11 missing)

1214 Caubīs Gāyatrī; PM; 107, 2; SKT, D.

1242 Caurāsī; *Hari Vaṁśa*; PM; 107, 30; H, D.

0445 Cetana Dhārā; *Jīvana Kṛṣṇa Dāsa*; B; 42, 11; BL, BL.

0567 Chadma Sāṅjhī Līlā; *Mahant Kundana Dās Nirmohī*; B; 49, 7; H, D; 1940 A.D.

0633 Chāndogyopaniṣadvyākhyā; *Narasiṁhācārya*; PM; 50B, 15; SKT, TE.

0634 Chāndogyopaniṣadvyākhyā; *Narasiṁhācārya*; PM; 50B, 16; SKT, TE.

0005 Chāndogyopaniṣat Arthasaṅgraha (with text); *Rāghavendra Yati*; B; 1, 5; SKT, D.

0356 Commentaries on Kṛṣṇa-Śatāṣṭottara-Stotra (from Brahmāṇḍa Purāṇa), Gopāla Stava Rāja (from Gautamīya Tantra) with Mūla; *Vṛndāvana Dās*; B; 39, 17; SKT, D; 1960 A.D.

0245 Commentary on Madhva's Atharvanopaniṣad Bhāṣya (Vivaraṇa); *Vyāsa Tīrtha*; B; 35, 4; SKT, D; 1902 A.D.

0368 Dānakeli Kaumudī (with Mahatī Ṭīkā and Hindi Translation); *Rūpa Gosvāmī*; B; 39, 29; SKT H, D; 1967 A.D.

0456 Dānakeli Kaumudī Bhānikā (with Poetic Translation); *Rūpa Gosvāmī*; B; 42, 22; BL, BL; Baṅgābda 1325.

1575 Divyadeśa Aṭṭavaṇai; *Vangipurattu Nambi*; PL; 133, 2; TA, GR.

0853 Divyaprabandhanigamanavacanāni; PM; 58, 3; SKT, GR.

1375 Divyasūricarita; PM; 111, 4; SKT, D.

0407 Divyonmāda Bā Bāī Unmādinī; *Kṛṣṇa Kamala Gosvāmī*; B; 40, 37; SKT BL, BL; 1968 A.D.

0658 Dṛśyatvavicāraḥ; PM; 51A, 15; SKT, D.

0152 Dvādaśa Stotra; *Ānandatīrtha*; PM; 6, 25; SKT, D.

0289 Dvādaśa Stotra; *Madhva*; B; 36, 18; SKT, D.

0164 Dvādaśa Stotra; *Madhvācārya/Ānandatīrtha*; PM; 6, 37; SKT, D.

0181 Dvādaśa Stotra; *Madhvācārya/Ānandatīrtha*; PM; 6, 54; SKT, D.

0264 Dvādaśa Stotra with Ṭīkā; *Madhva*; B; 35, 23; SKT, D; 1890 A.D.

1235 Dvārakā māhātmyaṁ; PM; 107, 23; SKT, D.

1336 Eighty-four Vaiṣṇavācāryaṁ kī Vārtā; PM; 109, 3; H, D.

1475 Ekādaśīmāhātmya (from various Purāṇas); *Kṛṣṇa Dvaipāyana Vyāsa*; B; 121, 13; SKT, D.

1380 Ekādaśīmāhātmya (from various Purāṇa-s); *Kṛṣṇa Dvaipāyana Vyāsa*; PM; 111, 9; SKT, D.

0417 Ekādaśī māhātmyaṁ with Dīpikā; *Kṛṣṇa Dvaipāyana Vyāsa*; B; 41, 7; SKT H, D; 1903 A.D.

1499 Emberumānār Panniraṇḍu Vārtai; *Periyavāccān Pillai*; PL; 124, 3; TA, GR.

1038 Emberumānār Panniraṇḍu Vārtai; *Periyavāccān Pillai*; PL; 92, 3; TA, GR.

1507 Erāmānujanuttandādivyākhyāna; *Pillailokam Jīyar*; PL; 124, 11; TA, TA.

1508 Erāmānujanuttandādivyākhyāna; *Pillailokam Jīyar*;PL; 125, 1; TA, TA.

1141 Gajendra Mokṣa; *Kṛṣṇa Dvaipāyana Vyāsa*; PM; 104, 19; SKT, D.

1265 Gīta Govinda; *Jayadeva Gosvāmī*; PM; 108, 5; SKT, D.

1264 Gīta Govinda; *Jayadeva Gosvāmī*; PM; 108, 4; SKT, D.

0513 Gīta Govinda; *Jayadeva*; PM; 44, 8; SKT, D.

0472 Gīta Govinda (Bengali Translation); *Giridhar Dās*; B; 42, 38; BL, BL; Baṅgābda 1339.

0393 Gīta Govinda (Braj Bhāṣā); *Rasajāni Vaiṣṇava Dāsa*; B; 40, 23; H, D.

0437 Gīta Govinda with Commentary; *Jayadeva Gosvāmī*; B; 42, 3; BL, BL.

1458 Gītagovinda with Padāvalī (Versification in Braj); *Jayadeva,* (Versifier) *Rāmarāya Gosvāmī*; B; 120, 9; SKT H, D.

0473 Gīta Govinda with Ṭīkā; *Jayadeva Gosvāmī*; B; 42, 39; SKT BL, BL; Baṅgābda 1304.

1423 Gītāmṛta Gaṅgā; *Vṛndāvana Deva*; PM; 118, 8; H, D.

1503 Gītārtha Saṅgraha; *Śrīvaravaramuni*; PL; 124, 7; SKT, GR.

1043 Gītārthasaṅgraha; *Śrīvaravaramuni*; PL; 92, 8; SKT, GR.

1151 Gītā Sāra, etc.; PM; 104, 29; SKT, D.

1192 Gītā Sāra; *Kṛṣṇa Dvaipāyana Vyāsa*; PM; 106, 13; SKT, D.

0072 Gītā Tātparya Nirṇaya Nyāya Dīpakiraṇāvalī Ṭippaṇī; *Śrīnivāsa Tīrtha*; B; 4, 6; SKT, D; 1905 A.D.

0240 Gītā Tātparya Nirṇaya with Nyāya Dīpikā Ṭippaṇī and Nyāyadīpikākiraṇāvalī; *Madhvācārya*; B; 34, 9; SKT, D; 1905 A.D.

0208 Gītā Vivaraṇam; PL; 7, 14; SKT, TU.

0021 Gītātātparya Pañcikā with Nyāya Dīpa (with a Ṭippaṇī); *Madhva*; B; 1, 21; SKT, D; 1905 A.D.

0022 Gītātātparya Pañcikā with Nyāya Dīpa (with Ṭippaṇī); *Madhva*; B; 2, 1; SKT, D; 1905 A.D.; (Continuation of 0021).

0352 Gīti Viṁśa Ṭīkā; *Gopīlāla Gosvāmī*; B; 39, 13; SKT, D; 1963 A.D.

1674 Gñānasāram Vyākhyāna and Prameyasāram; *Arulālaperumāl Emberumānār Maṇavālamāmuni*; B; 141, 7; TA, TA.

1288 Gopāla Dhyānam; PM; 108, 29; SKT, D.

0727 Gopāla Durgā Mantra (Extracted from Atharva Veda); PM; 51B, 57; SKT, D.

1148 Gopāla Hṛdaya Stotra; PM; 104, 26; SKT, D.

0720 Gopāla Kavaca (Extracted from Sanat Kumāra Saṁhitā); PM; 51B, 50; SKT, D.

1222 Gopāla Kavaca; PM; 107, 10; SKT, D.

1208 Gopāla Kavaca; *Viriñci*; PM; 106, 29; SKT, D.

1228 Gopāla Kavacam; PM; 107, 16; SKT, D.

1284 Gopāla Mantra Nyāsa Vidhi; PM; 108, 25; SKT, D.

0550 Gopāla Pūjana Paddhati (with Hindi Comments); *Govinda Śaraṇa Deva*; B; 48, 20; SKT H, D; 1937 A.D.

1338 Gopāla Sahasranāma; *Kṛṣṇa Dvaipāyana Vyāsa*; PM; 109, 5; SKT, D.

1167 Gopāla Sahasranāma; PM; 105, 7; SKT, D.

1119 Gopālasahasranāma (from Sammohanatantra) with Commentary; (c) *Keśava Kāśmīri Bhaṭṭācārya*; PM; 103, 20; SKT, D.

1366 Gopālasahasranāma (From Sammohanatantra) with Vivṛtti; (c) *Keśavakāśmīri Bhaṭṭācārya*; PM; 110, 20; SKT, D.

1377 Gopālasahasranāma (From Sammohanatantra) with Vivṛti; PM; 111, 6; SKT, D.

0180 Gopālasahasranāma of Saṁmohana Tantra; PM; 6, 53; SKT, D.

0669 Gopāla Sahasranāma Stotra (from Sammohanatantra) with Durgārthapradīpam; PM; 51B, 1; SKT, D.

0609 Gopāla Sahasranāma Stotra with Ṭīkā (from Sammohana Tantra); B; 50A, 16; SKT, D; 1900 A.D.

1238 Gopāla Sahasranāmāvalī; PM; 107, 26; SKT, D.

1300 Gopāla Stava Rāja; PM; 108, 41; SKT, D.

1206 Gopāla Stavarāja; PM; 106, 27; SKT, D.

1149 Gopāla Stavarāja; PM; 104, 27; SKT, D.

1223 Gopāla Sundarī Mantra Saṁdhyā Vidhi; PM; 107, 11; SKT, D.

1219 Gopāla Tāpinī Upaniṣad; PM; 107, 7; SKT, D.

0703 Gopāla Tāpinī Upaniṣat; PM; 51B, 33; SKT, D.

0707 Gopāla Tāpinī Upaniṣat; PM; 51B, 37; SKT, D.

1143 Gopīcandanopaniṣat, etc.; PM; 104, 21; SKT, D.

0439 Gopī Gītā with Ṭīkā (Bhāgavata Purāṇa); *Kṛṣṇa Dvaipāyana Vyāsa*; B; 42, 5; SKT, BL; 1858 A.D.

1433 Govindalīlāmṛta; *Kṛṣṇadāsa Kavirāja*; PM; 119, 2; SKT, D.

0376 Govinda Līlāmṛta (Dvitīya Khaṇḍa); *Kṛṣṇa Dāsa Kavirāja Gosvāmī*; B; 40, 5; SKT H, D; 1965 A.D.

0457 Govinda Līlāmṛta (Sanskrit) (with Bengali Versification); *Kṛṣṇa Dās Kavirāj Gosvāmī*; B; 42, 23; SKT BL, BL; Baṅgābda 1303.

0383 Govinda Līlāmṛta and Padyāvalī Bhāṣā; *Śītala Dāsa* and *Śivapada*; B; 40, 12; H, D; 1963 A.D.

1445 Govindalīlāmṛta with Ṭīkā; *Kṛṣṇadāsa Kavirāja*; PM; 119, 14; SKT, D.

1220 Govindāṣṭakam; *Śaṅkarācārya*; PM; 107, 8; SKT, D.

0363 Grantha Ratna Pañcaka (Śrī Rādhā Kṛṣṇa Gaṇoddeśa Dīpikā: I Part); *Rūpa Gosvāmī*; B; 39, 24; SKT H, D; 1954 A.D.

0366 Grantha Ratna Pañcaka (Śrī Saṅkalpa Kalpadruma; V Part); *Viśvanātha Cakravarti*; B; 39, 27; SKT H, D; 1954 A.D.

0365 Grantha Ratna Pañcaka (Śrī Gaura Gaṇoddeśa Dīpikā: III Part); *Kavikarṇapūra*; B; 39, 26; SKT H, D; 1954 A.D.

0364 Grantha Ratna Pañcaka (Śrī Kṛṣṇa Līlā Stava: II part); *Sanātana Gosvāmī*; B; 39, 25; SKT H, D; 1954 A.D.

0367 Grantha Ratna Pañcaka (Braja Vilāsa Stava: V Part); *Raghunātha Dās Gosvāmī*; B; 39, 28; SKT H, D; 1954 A.D.

1456 Grantharatnatrikam (Contains, (1) Śṛṅgāracūḍāmaṇi Grantham, (2) Bhāgavatāmṛta Kaṇikā, (3) Rasasiddhānta Cintāmaṇi Grantha) with Hindi Translation; *Viśvanātha Cakravartī*; B; 120, 7; H SKT, D.

0146 Gṛhya Pariśiṣṭa; *Āśvalāyana*; PM; 6, 19; SKT, D.

0586 Gulazār Caman, Ānanda Caman, Bihār Caman; *Mahant Śītaladās*; B; 49, 26; H UR; D; 1912 A.D.

1344 Gurubhaktimandākinī; *Puruṣottamācārya*; PM; 109, 11; SKT, D.

0241 Guru-Bhāva-Prakāśikā and Rukmiṇīśa-Vijaya with Ṭīkā; *Vādirāja Tīrtha*; B; 34, 10; SKT, D; 1892 A.D.

1027 Gurubhāvaprakāśikā (Part I); *Śuddhasattvam Lakṣmaṇācārya*; PM; 91, 4; SKT, TE.

1028 Gurubhāvaprakāśikā (Part II); *Śuddhasattvam Lakṣmaṇācārya*; PM; 91, 5; SKT, TE.

1029 Gurubhāvaprakāśikā (Part III); *Śuddhasattvam Lakṣmaṇācārya*; PM; 91, 6; SKT, TE.

1488 Gurubhāvaprakāśikā Part I; *Śuddhasattvam Lakṣmaṇācārya*; PM; 123, 4; SKT, TE.

1489 Gurubhāvaprakāśikā Part II; *Śuddhasattvam Lakṣmaṇācārya*; PM; 123, 5; SKT, TE.

1490 Gurubhāvaprakāśikā Part III; *Śuddhasattvam Lakṣmaṇācārya*; PM; 123, 6; SKT, TE.

0646 Gurubhāvaprakāśikā with Vyākhyā; *Lakṣmaṇācārya*; PM; 51A, 3; SKT, D.

1252 Guru Caritra; *Jagannātha Dāsa*; PM; 107, 40; SKT, D.

1306 Gurudeva Māhātmyam; PM; 108, 47; SKT, D.

1293 Gurumantra Vidhi; PM; 108, 34; SKT, D.

1145 Guru Paraṁparā; PM; 104, 23; SKT, D.

1290 Guru Paramparā; PM; 108, 31; SKT, D.

1457 Guruparamparā Navaratnanirṇaya with Hindi translation; *Harirāmavyāsagosvāmī*; B; 120, 8; SKT H, D.

1509 Guruparamparāprabhāva; *Alahiya Perumāljīyar*; PL; 125, 2; TA, GR.

1146 Guru Paramparā Stotra; PM; 104, 24; SKT, D.

0317 Guruparamparā (Nimbārka) Stotra with Ṭīkā; PM; 37, 12; SKT, D.

1304 Guru Paramparā Vandana Stotra; PM; 108, 45; SKT, D.

1195 Haṁsadūta; *Rūpa Gosvāmī*; PM; 106, 16; SKT, D.

1181 Haṁsadūta with Commentary; *Rūpa Gosvāmī*; PM; 106, 2; SKT, D.

0370 Haṁsa-Dūta with Ṭīkā and Translation; *Rūpa Gosvāmī*; B; 39, 31; SKT H, D; 1957 A.D.

1132 Hanumad Kavacam; *Kṛṣṇa Dvaipāyana Vyāsa*; PM; 104, 10; SKT, D.

1245 Hanumāna Bāhuka; *Tulasīdāsa*; PM; 107, 33; H, D.

1133 Hanumat Kavaca; *Kṛṣṇa Dvaipāyana Vyāsa*; PM; 104, 11; SKT, D.

0466 Hari Bhakti Vilāsa Rasāmṛta; B; 42, 32; SKT BL, BL; Baṅgābda 1297.

0594 Hari Bhakti Vilāsa with Bhāṣā-Ṭīkā; *Gopāla Bhaṭṭa*; B; 50A, 1; SKT H, D; 1908 A.D.

0593 Hari Bhakti Vilāsa with Bhāṣā-Ṭīkā; *Gopāla Bhaṭṭa Gosvāmī*; B; 49, 33; SKT H, D; 1908 A.D.

1185 Hari Bhakti Vilāsa with Ṭīkā; *Gopāla Bhaṭṭa Gosvāmī*; PM; 106, 6; SKT, D.

1233 Hari Guru Caraṇa Dhyāna Tattvaprakāśī Stotra; PM; 107, 21; SKT, D.

1152 Harināmamālā; *Śaṅkarācārya*; PM; 104, 30; SKT, D.

0978 Haripāramyacandrikā; PL; 63, 1; SKT, GR.

0187 Hariścandropākhyāna of Mahābhārata (Āraṇya Parva); *Kṛṣṇa Dvaipāyana Vyāsa*; PM; 6, 60; SKT, D.

1247 Hari Tālikā Vratam; PM; 107, 35; SKT, D.

1556 Harivaṁśa; *Śrīśuka*; PL; 130, 5; SKT, GR.

1411 Harivaṁśapurāṇa; *Kṛṣṇa Dvaipāyana Vyāsa*; PM; 117, 2; SKT, D.

1483 Harivaṁśapurāṇa with Hindi Ṭīkā; *Kṛṣṇa Dvaipāyana Vyāsa,* (c) *Jvālāprasāda*; B; 122, 1; SKT H, D.

1482 Harivaṁśapurāṇa with Hindi Ṭīkā; *Kṛṣṇa Dvaipāyana Vyāsa,* (c) *Jvālāprasāda*; B; 121, 20; SKT H, D.

0216 Harivaṁśa with Ṭīkā, (Contains Viṣṇuśatanāma Stotram from Viṣṇupurāṇa, and Santānagopāla Mantrānuṣṭhāna Vidhiḥ); *Kṛṣṇa Dvaipāyana Vyāsa*; B; 31, 3; SKT, D; 1954 A.D.

0179 Hautram; PM; 6, 52; SKT, D.

1426 Hita Caurāsī (Caturāsī); *Hita Harivaṁśa*; PM; 118, 11; H, D.

0638 Īkṣatyadhikaraṇavicāraḥ; *Anantārya*; PM; 50B, 20; SKT, D.

1008 Irukāmyavilakkam; *Aritātar*; PL; 63, 31; TA, TA.

1587 Īśādidaśopaniṣad Bhāṣyam; *Gopālānandasvāmi*; B; 133, 14; SKT, D.

1060 Īśādidaśopaniṣad Bhāṣyam; *Gopālānandasvāmi*; B; 99, 13; SKT, D.

0107 Īśāvāsya Bhāṣya Ṭīkā; *Jayatīrtha*; PM; 5, 18; SKT, TU.

0138 Īśavāsya Bhāṣya Ṭīkā-Vivaraṇa (of Ānandatīrtha's Yajñīya Mantra Bhāṣya); *Jayatīrtha*; PM; 6, 11; SKT, D.

0064 Īśāvāsya Bhāṣya Ṭīkā Vivṛtiḥ; *Raghunātha Tīrtha*; B; 3, 39; SKT, D; 1907 A.D.

0296 Īśāvāsyādyupaniṣad Saptaka; PM; 36, 25; SKT, D.

1519 Īśāvāsyopaniṣad and Māṇḍūkyopaniṣad Bhāṣya, Varāhopaniṣad Mūla; *Vedāntācārya* and *Vādhūlavaradācārya*; PL; 125, 12; SKT, GR.

1064 Īśāvāsyopaniṣadbhāṣya; Vedāntadeśika, (c) *Kūranārāyaṇamuni* and *Śrīraṅgācārya*; B; 100, 2; SKT, D.

1073 Īśāvāsyopaniṣad, Kenopaniṣad, Kaṭhopaniṣad (c) *Vedāntadeśika, Kūranārāyaṇamuni* and *Raṅgarāmānuja*; 100, 11; B; SKT TA, D TA.

1609 Īśāvāsyopaniṣad with Three Bhāṣya-s; *Vedāntadeśika, Kūranārāyaṇamuni* and *Śrīraṅgācārya*; B; 135, 2; SKT, D.

0409 Īśāvāsyopaniṣat (with Vyākhyā and Hindi Translation); B; 40, 39; SKT H, D; 1953 A.D.

1618 Īśāvāsyopaniṣat Kenopaniṣat and Kaṭhopaniṣat with Commentary; Vedāntadeśika, *Kūranārāyaṇamuni* and *Rāmānuja*; B; 135, 11; SKT, D.

0001 Īśāvāsyopaniṣat Khaṇḍārtha (with text); *Rāghavendra Yati*; B; 1, 1; SKT, D.

0358 Īśopaniṣad with Bhāṣya; B; 39, 19; SKT H, D; 1965 A.D.

0828 Īśvarasaṁhitā; PM; 57, 7; SKT, GR.

0469 Jagannātha Ballabha Nāṭakam with Translation; *Rāmānanda Rāy*; B; 42, 35; SKT BL, BL; Baṅgābda 1282.

1391 Jamunājī ke Cālīsapada; *Paramānandadāsa, Kṛṣṇadāsa, Kumbhanadāsa, Biṭṭhala,* etc.; PM; 114, 3; SKT, D.

0361 Jagannātha Vallabha Nāṭaka with Translation; *Rāmānanda Rāya*; B; 39, 22; SKT H, D; 1964 A.D.

1131 Jānakī Stavarāja; PM; 104, 9; SKT, D.

0645 Jijñāsādarpaṇaḥ; *Śrīnivāsa*; PM; 51A, 2; SKT, TE.

1308 Jñāna Svaroda; *Caraṇa Dāsa*; PM; 108, 49; H, D.

0644 Jñānayāthārthyavādaḥ; *Anantācārya*; PM; 51A, 1; SKT, D.

0342 Jugalśatapada Bhūṣaṇa; *Śyāmadāsa*; PM; 39, 3; H, D; c. 1854 A.D.

0686 Kabīr Sāhab kī Sākhī; *Kabīr Dās*; PM; 51B, 16; H, D.

1495 Kaivalyaśatadūṣaṇī; *Kuruka Śrī Śailayogīśa*; PM; 123, 11; SKT, TE.

1034 Kaivalyaśatadūṣaṇī; *Kurukaśrīśailayogīśa*; PM; 91, 11; SKT, TE.

0640 Kaivalyasthānanirṇayaḥ; *Varadasudarśana*; PM; 50B, 22; SKT, GR.

0415 Kalki Purāṇa, (with Hindi Translation by Baladeva Prasad Mishra); B; 41, 5; SKT H, D; 1906 A.D.

0468 Kalki Purāṇam (Sanskrit Mūla with Bengali Translation); *Kṛṣṇa Dvaipāyana Vyāsa*; B; 42, 34; SKT BL; BL; Baṅgābda 1315.

0698 Kandarpārka Prakāśam; *Rāmacandra*; PM; 51B, 28; SKT, D.

0075 Kapilagītā (with Ṭīkā and Artha in Kannada); *Kṛṣṇa Dvaipāyana Vyāsa*; B; 4, 9; SKT, D; Śaka 1836, 1914 A.D.

0831 Kapiñjala Saṁhitā; PM; 57, 10; SKT, GR.

0994 Kapiñjalasaṁhitā; PL; 63, 17; SKT, GR.

0834 Kapiñjalasaṁhitā; PM; 57, 13; SKT, GR.

0990 Kāraṇamālāśatakakṣyā; PL; 63, 13; SKT, GR.

1577 Kāraṇavyākhyānam-Śivaparatvakhaṇḍana; PL; 133, 4; SKT, GR.

1050 Kāraṇavyākhyānam-Śivaparatvakhaṇḍana; PL; 99, 3; SKT, GR.

0997 Kārikādarpaṇaḥ; *Varadakavi*; PL; 63, 20; SKT, GR.

0839 Kārikādarpaṇaḥ; *Varadakavi*; PM; 57, 18; SKT, GR.

0841 Kārikādarpaṇaḥ; *Varadakavi*; PM; 57, 20; SKT, GR.

0186 Karma Nirṇaya Ṭīkā; *Jayatīrtha*; PM; 6, 59; SKT, D.

0266 Karma Nirṇaya Pañcikā with Vivaraṇa; *Jayatīrtha* and *Śrīnivāsa Tīrtha*; B; 35, 25; SKT D; 1900 A.D.

0250 Karma Nirṇaya; *Madhva/Ānandatīrtha*; PM; 35, 9; SKT, TU.

0184 Karmanirṇaya; *Madhvācārya/Ānandatīrtha*; PM; 6, 57; SKT, D.

1305 Karṇahara Stotra; *Keśava Śarman*; PM; 108, 46; SKT, D.

0840 Kārpaṇyadarpaṇam; *Śaṭhakopācārya*; PM; 57, 19; SKT, D.

0532 Kārttika Māhātmya (From Padma Purāṇa with Hindi Ṭīkā Bhāṣāśabda Prakāśikā); *Kṛṣṇa Dvaipāyana Vyāsa*; B; 48, 2; SKT H, D; 1885 A.D.

0674 Kārttika Māhātmya; *Kṛṣṇa Dvaipāyana Vyāsa*; PM; 51B, 6; SKT, D.

1474 Kāśīmāhātmya (from Brahmavaivarta Purāṇa) with Ṭīkā; *Kṛṣṇa Dvaipāyana Vyāsa*; B; 121, 12; SKT, D.

0995 Kāśyapottarasaṁhitā; PL; 63, 18; SKT, GR.

0996 Kāśyapottarasaṁhitā; PL; 63, 19; SKT, GR.

0986 Kāśyapottarasaṁhitā; PL; 63, 9; SKT, GR.

0056 Kāṭhaka Upaniṣad Bhāṣya Ṭīkā; *Vyāsa Tīrtha*; B; 3, 31; SKT, D; 1905

0011 Kāṭhaka Upaniṣad Bhāṣya Ṭīkā; *Vedeśa Bhikṣu*; B; 1, 11; SKT, D; 1905 A.D.

0060 Kāṭhaka Upaniṣad Bhāṣya Ṭīkā (Padārthakaumudī); *Vedeśa Bhikṣu*; B; 3, 35; SKT, D; 1905 A.D.

0007 Kāṭhakopaniṣad Bhāṣya Ṭīkā; or Kāṭhakavyāsa Tīrthīya Ṭīkā; *Vyāsa Tīrtha*; B; 1, 7; SKT, D; 1905 A.D.

0101 Kāṭhakopaniṣad Khaṇḍārtha; *Rāghavendra Tīrtha*; PL, 5, 12; SKT, D.

0040 Kāṭhakopaniṣad Khaṇḍārtha; *Rāghavendra Yati*; B; 3, 15; SKT, D.

0002 Kāṭhakopaniṣat Khaṇḍārtha (with text); *Rāghavendra Yati*; B; 1, 2; SKT, D.

0154 Kaṭhalakṣaṇa Vivaraṇam; *Jayatīrtha*; PM; 6, 27; SKT, TU.

0041 Kathā Lakṣaṇa Vivaraṇa; *Jayatīrtha Bhikṣu*; B; 3, 16; SKT, D.

1286 Kavaca Stavārtha Saṁgraha; PM; 108, 27; SKT, D.

1158 Kavitā Ratnamālikā; *Rāma Nārāyaṇa*; PM; 104, 36; H, D.

0613 Kāvyadīpikā; PM; 50B, 4; SKT, D.

0536 Kelimālā (with Life History of Svāmī Haridās by Sudarśana Siṁha); Svāmī Haridās; B; 48, 6; H, D; 1952 A.D.

1240 Khyāla Vilāsa, etc.; *Dhruva Dāsa*; PM; 107, 28; H, D.

0933 Kiraṇāgamaḥ; PM; 61, 21; SKT, GR.

0381 Kiśorī Dās kī Vāṇī; *Kiśorī Dās*; B; 40, 10; H, D; 1960 A.D.

1285 Krama Dīpikā; *Keśava Kaśmīrī Bhaṭṭa*; PM; 108, 26; SKT, D.

1175 Kramadīpikā with Ṭīkā; *Keśava Kaśmīrī Bhaṭṭācārya*; PM; 105, 15; SKT, D.

0838 Kriyākairavacandrikā; *Varāhadeśika*; PM; 57, 17; SKT, TE.

1096 Kriyākairavacandrikā; *Varāhaguru*; PL; 101, 8; SKT, GR.

1641 Kriyākairavacandrikā; *Varāhaguru*; PL; 137, 8; SKT, GR.

1231 Kṛṣṇa Baladevāṣṭakam; *Madhusūdana Dās*; PM; 107, 19; SKT, D.

0518 Kṛṣṇa Karṇāmṛta (with Three Commentaries); *Līlāśuka Bilva Maṅgala*; B; 44, 13; SKT, D.

0514 Kṛṣṇa Karṇāmṛta; *Bilva Maṅgala Līlā Śuka*; PM; 44, 9; SKT, D.

0465 Kṛṣṇa Karṇāmṛta Stotram; *Bilva Maṅgala Ṭhākur*; B; 42, 31; BL, BL; Caitanyābda; 415.

1652 Kṛṣṇakathāsāra (Kalyāṇa Kāṇḍa)-III; PL; 139, 7; KAN, KAN.

0141 Kṛṣṇāmṛta Mahārṇava; *Madhvācārya/Ānandatīrtha*; PM; 6, 14; SKT, D.

0837 Kṛṣṇāmṛtamahārṇavaḥ Savyākhyā; *Kṛṣṇācārya*; PM; 57, 16; SKT, D.

0725 Kṛṣṇāṣṭakam; PM; 51B, 55; H, D.

1227 Kṛṣṇa Stava Rāja; PM; 107, 15; SKT, D.

0490 Kṛṣṇa Stava Rāja (with Anvayārtha and Bhāṣānuvāda); B; 43, 12; SKT, H, D; 1965 A.D.

1350 Kṛṣṇastavarāja with Śrutyantasuradruma Ṭīkā; *Nimbārka*, (c) *Puruṣottama Prasāda*; PM; 110, 4; SKT, D.

1103 Kṛṣṇastavarāja with Ṭīkā Śrutyantasuradruma; *Nimbārka*, (c) *Puruṣottama Prasāda*; PM; 103, 4; SKT, D.

0711 Kṛṣṇa Stavarāja; with Śruti Siddhānta Mañjarī Ṭīkā; PM; 51B, 41; SKT, D.

0391 Kṣaṇadā Gīti Cintāmaṇi; *Manohara Dās*; B; 40, 21; H, D; 1960 A.D.

0641 Kudṛṣṭibhaṅga; *Appagoṇḍācārya*; PM; 50B, 23; SKT, D.

1071 Kudṛṣṭidhvāntamārtaṇḍa-I; *Raṅgācāryasvāmi*; B; 100, 9, SKT, D.

1616 Kudṛṣṭidhvāntamārtaṇḍa-I; *Raṅgācāryasvāmi*; B; 135, 9; SKT, D.

0230 Kūrma Mahāpurāṇa; *Kṛṣṇa Dvaipāyana Vyāsa*; B; 33, 7; SKT, D; 1926 A.D.

0836 Kurukeśagāthānukaraṇam; PM; 57, 15; SKT, TE.

0357 Laḍileyāṣṭaka (from Grantha Ratnatraya); *Nārāyaṇa Bhaṭṭa*; B; 39, 18; SKT, D; 1960 A.D.

1120 Laghubhāgavatāmṛta; *Rūpagosvāmī*; PM; 103, 21; SKT, D.

1367 Laghubhāgavatāmṛta; *Rūpagosvāmī*; PM; 110, 21; SKT, D.

0377 Mādhava Dās Jī kī Vāṇī tathā Ādarśajīvanī; B; 40, 6; H, D; 1963 A.D.

0199 Mādhava Stava Rāja of Vāyupurāṇa; *Kṛṣṇa Dvaipāyana Vyāsa*; PM; 7, 5; SKT, D.

0558 Madhu Keli Vallī, Śrī Rādhā-Kunda Stava, Śrī Rūpa-Sanātana Stotram; *Govardhana Bhaṭṭa*; B; 48, 28; SKT, D; 1955 A.D.

0380 Mādhurī Vāṇī (Braja Bhāṣā); *Mādhurī* (Disciple of Rūpa Gosvāmī); B; 40, 9; H, D; 1965 A.D.

1365 Mādhuryalaharī; *Kṛṣṇadāsa*; PM; 110, 19; H, D.

1118 Mādhuryalaharī; *Kṛṣṇadāsa*; PM; 103, 19; H, D.

0470 Madhva Gauḍeśvara Sampradāya; *Dr. Priyācaraṇ Śaraṇ Dās*; B; 42, 36; H, D; 1961 A.D.

0247 Madhva-Siddhānta Sāra (Padārtha Saṅgraha Vyākhyāna); *Padmanābha Tīrtha*; B; 35, 6; SKT, D; 1893 A.D.

0284 Madhva Vijaya Bhāvaprakāśikā Ṭīkā; *Nārāyaṇa Paṇḍita Ācārya*; B; 36, 13; SKT, D; 1925 A.D.

0239 Madhva Vijaya with Ṭīkā Bhāvaprakāśikā and Mandopakāriṇī; *Nārāyaṇa Paṇḍita Ācārya* (s/o Trivikrama Paṇḍita Ācārya); B; 34, 8; SKT, D.

1384 Mahābhārata; *Kṛṣṇa Dvaipāyana Vyāsa*; PM; 112, 2; SKT, D.

1382 Mahābhārata; *Kṛṣṇa Dvaipāyana Vyāsa*; PM; 111, 11; SKT, D.

1383 Mahābhārata; *Kṛṣṇa Dvaipāyana Vyāsa*; PM; 112, 1; SKT, D.

1387 Mahābhārata; *Kṛṣṇa Dvaipāyana Vyāsa*; PM; 113, 2; SKT, D.

0212 Mahābhārata (Bhīṣmaparva and Droṇaparva); *Kṛṣṇa Dvaipāyana Vyāsa*; PL; 7, 18; SKT, TU.

0213 Mahābhārata (Śānti Parva); *Kṛṣṇa Dvaipāyana Vyāsa*; PL; 7, 19; SKT, TU.

0111 Mandāra Mañjarī on Jayatīrtha's Tattvavivekaṭīkā; *Vyāsatīrtha*; PM; 5, 22; SKT, TU.

0115 Mandāra Mañjarī on Jayatīrtha's Mithyātvānumānakhaṇḍana; *Vyāsayati*; PM; 5, 26; SKT, TU.

0113 Mandāra Mañjari on Jayatīrtha's Upādhikhaṇḍanaṭīkā; *Vyāsayati*; PM; 5, 24; SKT, TU.

0112 Mandāra Mañjarī on Māyāvādakhaṇḍanaṭīkā; *Vyāsayati*; PM; 5, 23; SKT, TU.

0009 Māṇḍūkya Bhāṣya Ṭīkā; *Vyāsa Tīrtha Muni*; B; 1, 9; SKT, D; 1904.

0017 Māṇḍūkya Upaniṣad Bhāṣya Vivṛti-Padārthadīpikā; *Śrīnivāsa Tīrtha*; B; 1, 17; SKT, D; 1904 A.D.

0099 Māṇḍūkya Upaniṣad Khaṇḍārtha; *Rāghavendra Tīrtha*; PL; 5, 10; SKT, NA.

0202 Māṇḍūkyopaniṣad Bhāṣya; *Ānandatīrtha*; PM; 7, 8; SKT, D.

0137 Māṇḍūkyopaniṣad and Kaṭhalakṣaṇa; *Madhvācārya*; PM; 6, 10; DKT, D.

0197 Māṇḍūkyopaniṣad and Kaṭhalakṣaṇa by Ānandatīrtha; *Madhvācārya*; PM; 7, 3; SKT, D.

1402 Māṇḍūkyopaniṣad with Māṇḍūkyopaniṣadarthaprakāśa; PM; 115, 7; SKT, D.

0279 Maṇimañjarī; *Nārāyaṇa Paṇḍita Ācārya*; B; 36, 7; SKT, D; 1925.

0568 Mañjarī Svarūpa Nirūpaṇa; *Kuñjabihārī Dās Bābājī*; B; 49, 8; BL, BL; Gaurābda 478.

0479 Manośikṣā; *Premānanda Dās Mahānubhāva*; B; 43, 1; BL, BL; Baṅgābda 1304.

0527 Mantra Bhāgavata; B; 47, 2; SKT, D; 1903 A.D.

0678 Mantra Mahodadhi; *Mahīdhara*; PM; 51B, 10; SKT, D.

0563 Mantra Rahasya Ṣoḍaśī with Vyākhyā; *Nimbārka*; B; 49, 3; SKT, D; 1937 A.D.

0086 Māyāvāda Khaṇḍana Vyākhyā Mandāra Mañjarī; *Vyāsarāja* (Tīrtha); PL; 4, 20; SKT, NA.

0763 Māyibhaṅga with Telugu Ṭīkā; *Appagoṇḍācārya*; PM; 53, 15; SKT, D.

0087 Mithyātvānumānakhaṇḍana Mandāra Mañjarī; *Vyāsarāj* (Tīrtha); PL; 4, 21; SKT, NA.

0965 Mṛgendrāgamavṛtti; *Bhaṭṭa Nārāyaṇa*; PM; 62, 22; SKT, D.

1229 Mudāṣṭakam; *Madhusūdana Dās*; PM; 107, 17; SKT, D.

1444 Muktācarita (Braja Bāsī-Bhāva-Nirūpaṇa); *Nārāyaṇadāsa*; PM; 119, 13; BL, D.

1401 Mukundaśaraṇāpattistotra; *Anantarāma*; PM; 115, 6; SKT, D.

1511 Mumukṣuppadivyākhyāna; *Śrīvaravaramuni*; PL; 125, 4; TA, TA.

0696 Muṇḍakopaniṣat with Commentary; PM; 51B, 26; SKT, D.

1560 Nācciyār Tirumoli Vyākhyāna; *Parakālasvāmi*; PL; 130, 9; TA, GR.

0486 Nāgarī Dās Vānī Aṅka (Śrī Sarveśvara kā Viśeṣāṅka); B; 43, 8; H, D; 1965 A.D.

0143 Nakhastuti and Harivāyustuti (Vyākhyā); *Viśvapati Tīrtha*; PM; 6, 16; SKT, TU.

1393 Nāmaratna; *Raghunāthagosvāmī*; PM; 114, 5; SKT, D.

0680 Nāmatraya Kalpa (Extract from Sanatkumāra Saṁhitā); PM; 51B, 12; SKT, D.

0578 Namranivedana and Kucch Samīkṣā; *Kṛṣṇadās Bābā* (Kusumsarovar); B; 49, 18; H, D; 1946 A.D.

0733 Nānārthakalpavallī; *Veṅkaṭabhaṭṭar*; PM; 52, 1; SKT, GR.

1452 Nandamahotsava (From Bhāgavata); *Kṛṣṇa Dvaipāyana Vyāsa*; B; 120, 3; H, D.

1323 Nārada Niyamānanda Goṣṭhī Rahasya Ṭīkā; PM; 108, 64; SKT, D.

0848 Ṇatvopapattibhaṅgavādaḥ; *Tirumalācārya*; PM; 57, 17; SKT, GR.

0664 Navakoṭiḥ with Daśakoṭi Ratnamālikā; *Kuṇiṅgala Rāmāśāstri Aṇṇaṅgarārya*; PM; 51A, 21; SKT, GR.

0227 Nayacandrikā; *Traivikramācārya*; B; 33, 4; SKT, D.

0657 Nayadyumaṇi; *Meghanādāri*; PM; 51A, 14; SKT, D.

0660 Nayadyumaṇidīpikā; *Śrīnivāsācārya*; PM; 51A, 17; SKT, D.

0659 Nayamaṇikalikā; PM; *Śrīnivāsācārya*; 51A, 16; SKT, GR.

1606 Nayamayūkhamālikā; *Appayyadīkṣita*; B; 134, 17; SKT, D.

0655 Nayamayūkhamālikā; *Appayyadīkṣita*; PM; 51A, 12; SKT, GR.

0808 Nikṣepacintāmaṇiḥ; *Gopāladeśika*; PM; 56, 19; SKT, GR.

1631 Nikṣeparakṣā with Nikṣepacintāmaṇi; *Vedāntadeśika*, (c) *Siṁhadeva*; BL 135, 24; SKT, GR.

0850 Nikṣeparakṣāvyākhyā; *Nṛsiṁhārya*; PM; 57, 29; SKT, GR.

1086 Nikṣeparakṣā with Nikṣepacintāmaṇi-I; *Vedāntadeśika*, (c) *Gopālasūri*; B; 100, 24; SKT, GR.

1211 Nikuñja Darpaṇa; Anurāgamālā; Sudarśanāṣṭaka; Siddhāntadarpaṇa; Ācāryanāmāvalī; Aparādhakṣamāpaṇa; Ātmabodha; Chadmayoginīlīlā; Bhavaśveta Vedānta; Sudarśana Dās; PM; 106, 32; H SKT, D.

0478 Nikuñja Rahasya Stava (with Ṭīkā and Bengali Versification); *Rūpa Gosvāmī*; B; 42, 44; SKT BL, BL; 1902 A.D.

1163 Nīlakaṇṭha Stotra; PM; 105, 3; SKT, D.

1136 Nimbārkācārya Caritra; *Nārāyaṇa Devācārya*; PM; 104, 14; SKT, D.

1272 Nimbārkācārya Prādurbhāva; *Kṛṣṇa Dvaipāyana Vyāsa*; PM; 108, 13; SKT, D.

1301 Niyamānandapañcaratna; PM; 108, 42; SKT, D.

0528 Nṛsiṁha Campū; *Keśava Bhaṭṭa*; B; 47, 3; SKT, D; 1764 A.D.

0133 Nṛsiṁhakavacamālāmantra from Nṛsiṁhapurāṇa; *Kṛṣṇadvaipāyana Vyāsa*; PM; 6, 6; SKT, D.

1409 Nṛsiṁhaparicaryā (Translated into Bengali by Vidyaratna Rāmanārāyaṇa); *Kṛṣṇadevācārya*; B; 116, 4; SKT BL, BL.

1410 Nṛsiṁhaparicaryā (Translated into Bengali by Vidyāratna Rāmanārāyaṇa); *Kṛṣṇadevācārya*; B; 117, 1; SKT BL, BL.

0294 Nṛsiṁha Stuti; *Trivikrama Paṇḍitācārya*; B; 36, 23; SKT, D, 1902 A.D.

0142 Nṛsiṁha Stuti Vyākhyā; *Viśvapati Tīrtha*; PM; 6, 15; SKT, D.

0300 Nṛsiṁha Stuti with Vyākhyā by Nārāyaṇa; *Trivikrama Paṇḍitācārya*; B; 36, 29; SKT, D; 1904 A.

0661 Nyāyakuliśam; *Rāmānujācārya*; PM; 51A, 18; SKT, D.

0804 Nyāyamandāraḥ; *Vīrarāghava*; PM; 56, 15; SKT, D.

0093 Nyāyamauktikamālā; *Śrī Vijayīndra Tīrtha*; PM; 5, 4; SKT, D; c. 1580 A.D.

0667 Nyāyapariśuddhivyākhyā-Nikaṣā; *Śrīnivāsaśaṭhakopa*; PM; 51A, 24; SKT, GR.

0662 Nyāyapariśuddhivyākhyā-Nyāyasāra; *Śrīnivāsadāsa*; PM; 51A, 19; SKT, TE GR.

0748 Nyāya Pariśuddhi Vyākhyā-Sannyāyadīpikā; *Kṛṣṇatātācārya*; PM; 52, 16; SKT; D.

0259 Nyāya Ratnāvalī; *Padmanābha Tīrtha Bhaṭṭāraka*; B; 35, 18; SKT, D.

0735 Nyāyaratnāvalī; *Vedāntācārya*; PM; 52, 3; SKT, D.

0734 Nyāyaratnāvalī; *Vedāntācārya*; PM; 52, 2; SKT, D.

0910 Nyāyaratnāvalī; *Vedāntācārya*; PM; 60, 23; SKT, D.

1319 Pada Saṅgraha; PM; 108, 60; H, D.

0676 Pada Saṅgraha; PM; 51B, 8; H, D.

1127 Pada Saṅgraha; PM; 104, 5; H, D.

1135 Pada Saṅgraha; PM; 104, 13; H, D.

1670 Padmapurāṇam; PL; 141, 3; SKT, GR.

1562 Pādma Saṁhitā; PL; 131, 9; SKT, TE.

1563 Pādma Saṁhitā; PL; 132, 1; SKT, TE.

0867 Pādmasaṁhitātantram; PM; 58, 17; SKT, D.

1645 Padmatantram; PL; 138, 14; SKT, GR.

1646 Padmatantram; PL; 139, 1; SKT, GR.

0869 Pādmatantram; 59, 1; PM; SKT, GR.

0862 Pādmatantram; PM; 58, 12; SKT, D.

0868 Pādmatantram; PM; 58, 18; SKT, GR.

1662 Padukāsahasra and others; *Vedāntadeśika*; PL; 140, 7; SKT, GR.

1194 Padyāvalī; *Rūpa Gosvāmī*; PM; 106, 15; SKT, D.

0384 Padyāvalī Bhāṣā; *Śivapada*; B; H, D; 40, 13; (Continues 0383).

0697 Padyāvalī; Compilation from Jayadeva and Bilvamaṅgala; PM; 51B, 27; SKT, D.

0505 Padyāvalī with Hindi Bhāṣāṭīkā—Padyāvalī Prakāśikā; *Rūpa Gosvāmī*; B; 43, 27; SKT H, D; 1959 A.D.

1434 Padyāvalī with Ṭīkā; *Rūpagosvāmī*; PM; 119, 3; SKT, D.

0807 Pañcamāmnāyasāraḥ; *Samarapuṅgava*; PM; 56, 18; SKT, TE.

0737 Pañcamāmnāyasāraḥ; *Samarapuṅgava*; PM; 52, 5; SKT, TE.

1517 Pañcarahasyaṅgal; *Śrīlokācārya*; PL; 125, 10; TA, GR.

0937 Pañcaratnavyākhyā: (a) Tantrasāraprakāśikā, (b) Tārakadīpikā, (c) Śivatattvaprakāśikā, (d) Śrutyarthaprakāśikā, (e) Smaratattvaprakāśikā; *Vīraṇārādhya*; PM; 61, 25; SKT, D.

0745 Paramukhacapeṭikā; *Śrīkṛṣṇatātācārya*; PM; 52, 13; SKT, GR.

0854 Paramukhacapeṭikā; *Śrīśailakṛṣṇatātācārya*; PM; 58, 4; SKT, GR.

0492 Parapakṣa Girivajra (Fourth Part); *Mādhava Mukunda*; B; 43, 14; SKT, D.

0858 Parārthayajanādhikāranirvāhaḥ; *Sundaravīrarāghava*; PM; 58, 8; SKT, GR.

1565 Parāśara Saṁhitā; PL; 132, 3; SKT, GR.

1515 Pārāśaryavijaya; *Doḍḍayācārya*; PL; 125, 8; SKT, GR.

1623 Pārāśaryavijaya; *Mahācārya/Rāmānujadāsa*; B; 135, 16; SKT, D.

1078 Pārāśaryavijaya; *Mahācārya*; B; 100, 16; SKT, D.

0629 Paratattvanirṇayaḥ; PM; 50B, 12; SKT, GR.

0849 Paratattvanirṇayaḥ; PM; 57, 28; SKT, GR.

0746 Paratattvaprakāśikā; *Śrīnivāsadāsa*; PM; 52, 14; SKT, GR.

0082 Para Tattva Prakāśikā; *Śrī Vijayīndra Tīrtha*; PL; 4, 16; SKT, NA.

0744 Parikaravijayaḥ; *Doḍḍayyācārya*; PM; 52, 12; SKT, D.

0857 Parikaravijayaḥ; *Mahācārya*; PM; 58, 7; SKT, D.

0104 Parimala: (on Nyāya Sudhā of Jayatīrtha); *Rāghavendra Tīrtha*; PL; 5, 15; SKT, D.

0122 Pavamāna Sūkta; PM; 5, 33; SKT, D.

1558 Periyālvār Tirumoli; *Periyavāccān Pillai*; PL; 130, 7; TA, GR.

1524 Periyālvār Tirumolivyākhyāna; *Śrī Varavaramuni*; PL; 126, 3; TA, TA.

1551 Periyatirumoli Vyākhyāna 1 to 5 Śataka; *Periyavāccān Pillai*; PL; 129, 7; TA, TA.

1523 Periyatirumolivyākhyāna Arumbada; *Periyavāccān Pillai*; PL; 126, 2; TA, TA.

0262 Pramāṇa Paddhati with Ṭippaṇī (Bhāvadīpa); *Jayatīrtha*; B; 35, 21; SKT, D; 1897 A.D.

0875 Pramāṇasaṅgraha; *Lakṣmaṇa*; PM; 9, 7; SKT, D.

0873 Pramāṇasaṅgraha; *Saumyajāmātṛmuni*; PM; 59, 5; SKT, GR.

0874 Pramāṇasāra Prakāśikā; *Govindaguru*; PM; 59, 6; SKT TA, GR.

0121 Prameya Dīpikā on Madhva's Gītābhāṣya; *Jayatīrtha*; PM; 5, 32; SKT, TU.

0756 Prameyamālā; *Varadasūri*; PM; 53, 8; SKT, GR.

0545 Prameya Ratnāvalī; *Baladeva Vidyābhūṣaṇa*; B; 48, 15; SKT BL, D; 1927 A.D.

1343 Prameyaratnāvalī; *Baladevavidyābhūṣaṇa*; PM; 109, 10; SKT, D.

0554 Prameya Ratnāvalī with Kāntimālā Ṭīkā; *Baladeva Vidyābhūṣaṇa*; B; 48, 24; SKT H, D; Caitanyābda 455.

1522 Prameyaśekhara, Tirumantra Vivaraṇa, Mumukṣuppadi, Tattvatraya, Prapannaparitrāṇa and Navaratnamālā; *Śrī Pillailokācārya*; PL; 126, 1; TA, TA.

0736 Praṇavadarpaṇaḥ; *Śrīnivāsācārya*; PM; 52, 4; SKT, TE.

0741 Praṇavadīpikā; *Gopālasudhī*; PM; 52, 9; SKT, D.

0801 Praṇavadīpikā; *Gopālasudhī*; PM; 56, 12; SKT, D.

0738 Prapañca Mithyātvakhaṇḍanam; *Varadanātha*; PM; 52, 6; SKT, GR.

0045 Prapañca Mithyātvānumāna Khaṇḍana (Mandāramañjarī) (Bhāvaprakāśikā); *Vyāsa Yati*; B; 3, 20; SKT, D; Śaka 1818, 1896 A.D.

0303 Prapañca Mithyātvānumāna Khaṇḍana Ṭīkā; *Jayatīrtha Bhikṣu*; B; 36,32; SKT, D; 1896 A.D.

1099 Prapannadharmasārasamuccayaḥ; PL; 101, 11; SKT, GR.

1644 Prapannadharmasārasamuccayaḥ; PL; 137, 11; SKT, GR.

0806 Prapannāmṛtam; *Pillailokācārya*; P; 56, 17; SKT, GR.

0872 Prapannavijayaḥ; *Raṅgācārya*; PM; 59, 4; SKT, GR.

0130 Prapañca Mithyātvānumāna Khaṇḍana (Pañcikā) Bhāvaprakāśikā; *Vyāsatīrtha*; PM; 6, 3; SKT, D.

0049 Prapañca Mithyātvānumāna Khaṇḍana Pañcikā; *Śrīnivāsa tīrtha*; B; 3, 24; SKT, D; Śaka 1818, 1896 A.D.

0622 Prapañcamithyātvakhaṇḍanam; PM; 50B, 12; SKT, GR.

0800 Prapañcamithyātvakhaṇḍanam; PM; 56, 11; SKT, D.

0196 Prapañca Mithyātvānumāna Khaṇḍana Pañcikā Bhāva Prakāśikā; *Vyāsa Yati*; PM; 7, 2; SKT, D.

0046 Prapañca Mithyātvānumāna Khaṇḍana Vivaraṇa; *Jayatīrthabhikṣu*; B; 3, 21; SKT, D; Śaka 1818, 1896 A.D.

0876 Prapatyadhikāri Viśeṣaṇatva Niṣkarṣaḥ; PM; 59, 8; SKT, GR.

0441 Praśna Muṇḍaka Māṇḍūkya: three Upaniṣads and Ṭīkā and Translation, with Anvaya, Mukha Vyākhyā and Bengali Translation; B; 42, 7; SKT BL, BL.

0522 Praśnopaniṣad (with Vaiṣṇava Bhāṣya and Bhāṣābhāṣya); B; 44, 17; SKT H, D; 1942 A.D.

0755 Praśnopaniṣadvyākhyā; *Narasiṁhācārya* (Mudumbai); PM; 53, 7; SKT TE.

0723 Praśnottara Mālā; *Śukadeva*; PM; 51B, 53; SKT, D.

0726 Praśnottara Ratna Mālā; *Tulasī Dās*; PM; 51B, 56; SKT H, D.

0699 Praśnottara Ratna-Mālā; *Śuka Yatendriya*; PM; 51B, 29; SKT, D.

0281 Prātaḥ Saṅkalpa Gadya; *Rāghavendra Tīrtha*; B; 36, 9; SKT, D; 1971 A.D.

0878 Pratiṣṭhāpradīpaḥ; *Narasiṁhavājapeyin*; PM; 59, 10; SKT, GR.

0877 Pratiṣṭhātantram; PM; 59, 9; SKT, GR.

0880 Prāyaścittapaṭalam; PM; 59, 12; SKT, GR.

0879 Prāyaścittasaṅgraha; PM; 59, 11; SKT, GR.

1129 Prema Bhakti Candrikā; *Narottama Dās*; PM; 104, 7; BL, D.

0448 Prema Bhakti Candrikā; *Narottama Dās Ṭhākūr*; B; 42, 14; BL, BL; Baṅgābda 1281.

0388 Prema Bhakti Candrikā; *Vṛndāvan Dās*; B; 40, 17; H, D; 1950 A.D.

0362 Premāmṛta Rasāyana Stotra; *Kṛṣṇacaitanyadeva*; B; 39, 23; SKT H, D; 1967 A.D.

0442 Premānanda Varṣiṇī; *Bāṅke Bihārilāla* (Bāṅke Piyā); B; 42, 8; H, D; 1932 A.D.

1436 Premasaṁpuṭa; *Viśvanātha Cakravarti*; 119, 5; SKT, D.

0552 Preyobhakti Rasārṇava; *Nayanānanda Ṭhākur*; B; 48, 22; BL, BL; Caintanyābda 463.

0671 Priyājī kī Nāmāvalī; PM; 51B, 3; H, D.

1246 Puruṣa Sūkta; PM; 107, 34; SKT, D.

0743 Puruṣasūktacaramārthaniṣkarṣa; *Rāmānujācārya*; PM; 52, 11; SKT, D.

0802 Pūrvottaramīmāṁsaikakaṇṭhyam; PM; 56, 13; SKT, D.

0742 Pūrvottaramīmāṁsaikakaṇṭhyam; PM; 52, 10; SKT, D.

0430 Puṣṭimārgīya Siddhānta or Śuddhādvaita Mūlatattva; *Paṭavārī Raṇachoḍa Dāsa Vandrāvana Dāsa*; B; 41, 20; GUJ, GUJ; 1853 A.D.

0598 Rādhāballabha Bhaktamālā; *Priyādās Śukla*; B; 50A, 5; H, D; 1929 A.D.

1230 Rādhāgopālāṣṭakam; *Madhusūdana Dās*; PM; 107, 18; SKT, D.

1224 Rādhā Kavacam; PM; 107, 12; SKT, D.

1200 Rādhā Kṛpā Kaṭākṣastotram; *Kṛṣṇa Dvaipāyana Vyāsa*; PM; 106, 21; SKT, D.

1126 Rādhā Kṛṣṇa Sagāratha Līlā; *Nanda Kavi*; PM; 104, 4; H, D.

0566 Rahasya Prakāśikā; *Haṁsa Dās*; B; 49, 6; H, D; 1913 A.D.

0577 Rahasya Prakāśikā and Godanā Līlā; *Haṁsa Dās*; B; 49, 17; H, D; 1941 A.D.

0897 Rahasyarakṣā; *Vedāntadeśika*; PM; 60, 10; SKT, D.

0896 Rahasyarakṣā; *Veṅkaṭadeśika*; PM; 60, 9; SKT, D.

1564 Rahasyarakṣā-Stotrādhikāra; *Śrī Vedāntadeśika*; PL; 132, 2; SKT, GR.

0542 Rahasya Siddhānta Grantha Mālā (First Part); B; 48, 12; SKT, D; 1920 A.D.

0892 Rahasyatrayakārikādarpaṇam; PM; 60, 5; SKT, TE.

0889 Rahasyatrayakārikā Savyākhyā; PM; 60, 2; SKT TA, GR TA.

0893 Rahasyatrayamīmāṁsābhāṣya Kaṭhina Padadīpikā; PM; 60, 6; SKT TA, GR.

0891 Rahasyatrayamīmāṁsābhāṣyam; *Rāmānujadāsa*; PM; 60, 4; SKT, TE.

1549 Rahasyatrayasāra; *Śrīvedāntācārya*; PL; 129, 5; SKT, TE.

0821 Rahasyatrayasārādhikārasaṁgraha with Vyākhyā; *Śrīnivāsācārya*; PM; 56, 32; SKT, TE.

0894 Rahasyatrayasārapramāṇa Saṁgrahaḥ; *Śrīnivāsācārya*; PM; 60, 7; SKT, D.

0895 Rahasyatrayavyākhyātātparyadīpikā; *Virarāghava*; PM; 60, 8; SKT TA, GR TA.

0900 Rahasyatrayavyākhyā-Tātparyadīpikā; *Vīrarāghava*; PM; 60, 13; SKT TA, GR.

0291 Rājarājeśvarī Lalitā Sahasranāma Stotra from Brahmāṇḍa Purāṇa; *Kṛṣṇa Dvaipāyana Vyāsa*; PM; 36, 20; SKT, D.

1266 Rākṣasakāvyam with Ṭīkā by Premadhara; PM; 108, 6; SKT, D.

0424 Rāma Candra Stava Rāja Stotram (from Sanat

0386 Rasacandrikā; *Hara Deva*; B; 40, 15; H, D; 1965 A.D.

0579 Rāsa Līlānukaraṇa and Śrī Śrī Nārāyana Bhaṭṭa; *Kṛṣṇadās* (Kusumasarovar); B; 49, 19; H, D; 1946 A.D.

1334 Rasa Mañjarī; *Sudarśana Dās*; PM; 109, 1; SKT H, D.

1333 Rasa Mañjarī; *Sudarśana Dās*; PM; 108, 74; SKT H, D.

0438 Rāsa Pañcādhyāya (with a Bengali commentary); *Dvija Pītāṁbara*; B; 42, 4; SKT BL, BL.

0511 Rāsa Pañcādhyāyī (A Portion of the Bhāgavata Purāṇa); *Kṛṣṇa Dvaipāyana Vyāsa*; PM; 44, 6; SKT, D.

1166 Rāsa Pañcādhyāyī; *Kṛṣṇa Dvaipāyana Vyāsa*; PM; 105, 6; SKT, D.

0349 Rāsa-Pañcādhyāyī (from Bhāgavataṁ with Rasikāhlādinī Ṭīkā); B; 39, 10; SKT, D; 1964 A.D.

0395 Rasika Jīvanī; *Manohar Dās* (Compiler); B; 40, 25; H, D; 1962 A.D.

0269 Ratna Saṅgraha; *Raghunātha*; PM; 35, 28; SKT, TU.

0035 Ṛg Bhāṣya; *Madhva/Ānanda Tīrtha*; B; 3, 10; SKT, D; Śaka 1824, 1902 A.D.

0097 Ṛgbhāṣya Ṭīkā; *Jayatīrtha*; PM; 5, 8; SKT, D; c. 14th Century.

0036 Ṛg Bhāṣya Ṭīkā; *Jayatīrtha Bhikṣu*; B; 3, 11; SKT, D; Śaka 18123, 1901 A.D.

0037 Ṛg Bhāṣya Ṭīkā Vivṛti; *Chalārī Narasiṁhācārya*; B; 3, 12; SKT, D; Śaka 1824, 1902 A.D.

0246 Ṛg Bhāṣya with Ṭīkā; *Madhva/Ānandatīrtha*; PM; 35, 5; SKT, KAN.

0238 Ṛg Bhāṣya with Ṭīkā; *Madhvācārya*; B; 34, 7; SKT, D; 1901 A.D.

0251 Ṛg Veda Caturthāṣṭakaḥ; PM; 35, 10; SKT, TU.

0272 Ṛg Veda Mantra Saṁhitā; B; 35, 31; SKT, D; 1924 A.D.

0273 Ṛg Veda Mantra Saṁhitā; B; 36, 1; SKT, D; 1924 A.D.; (Continuation of 35, 31).

0946 Śaivadīkṣāvidhiḥ with Commentary; PM; 62, 3; SKT, D.

0948 Śaivalakṣaṇam with Telugu Meaning; PM; 62, 5; SKT, TE.

0961 Śaīvaparibhāṣā; *Śivāgrayogin*; PM; 62, 18; SKT, D.

0787 Sajjanāmṛtam; *Appagoṇḍācārya*; PM; 55, 9; SKT, D.

0982 Sajjanāmṛtam; *Appagoṇḍārya*; PL; 63, 5; SKT, TE.

1331 Śakunāvalī: Kṛṣṇa Kathā Dvādaśādhyāya; *Sudarśana Dās*; PM; 108, 72; H, D.

1263 Śakuntala Prākṛta Vivṛti; PM; 108, 3; SKT, D.

1573 Śāligrāmalakṣaṇādi; PL; 132, 11; SKT, GR.

1574 Śāligrāmalakṣaṇādi; PL; 133, 1; SKT, GR.

1165 Śāligrāma Stotra; *Kṛṣṇa Dvaipāyana Vyāsa*; PM; 105, 5; SKT; D.

0463 Samāja Gāyana Sṛṅkhalā (Anthology of Haridāsī Songs); B; 42, 29; H, D; 1974 A.D.

1215 Samāja Gāyan Śṛṅkhalā; PM; 107, 3; H, D.

0985 Sāmānādhikaraṇyavādaṭippaṇī; *Anantācārya*; P; 63, 8; SKT, GR.

1019 Samāsavādaḥ; *Anantārya*; PL; 78, 9; SKT, GR.

0414 Sāmaveda Saṁhitā; B; 41, 4; SKT, D; 1910 A.D.

1316 Samaya Prabandha; *Rasika Govinda*; PM; 108, 57; H, D.

1317 Samaya Vibhāga Evaṁ Utsava Vidhi; PM; 108, 58; H, D.

0939 Saṁhitāratnākara; PM; 61, 27; SKT, TE.

0926 Saṁhitāratnākaraḥ; PM; 61, 14; SKT, TE.

0927 Saṁhitāratnākaraḥ; PM; 61, 15; SKT, TE.

1603 Sampradāya Akaradi; B; 134, 14; TA, TE.

0382 Sampradāya Bodhinī; *Manohar Dās*; B; 40, 11; SKT H, D; 1959 A.D.

0928 Sampradāya Candrikā; *Veṅkaṭānandasūri*; PM; 61, 16; SKT, TE.

0929 Sampradāyacandrika; *Veṅkaṭānandasūri*; PM; 61, 17; SKT, D.

0934 Sārasaṅgrahaḥ; PM; 61, 22; SKT, D.

0079 Śārīraka Mīmāṁsā (Rāmānuja Bhāṣya Anusārī); *Vijayīndra Bhikṣu*; PM; 4, 13; SKT, D.

1022 Śārīrakārthacintā; *Śrīśailayogirāja*; PL; 78, 12; SKT, GR.

1605 Śārīrakasāstrārtha Dīpikā; *Raṅgarāmānujamuni*; B; 134, 16; SKT, D.

0772 Śārīrikamīmāṁsābhāṣyasaṅgrahaḥ; *Nṛsiṁhārya*; PM; 54, 5; SKT, GR.

0781 Sārīrikasāstradīpikā; *Raṅgarāmānujasvāmin*; PM; 55, 3; SKT, TE.

0780 Sārīrikasāstrārthasaṅgrahaḥ; *Raṅgarāmānujasvāmin*; PM; 55, 2; SKT, D.

0276 Sarva Mūla Granthāḥ, contains Bhāgavatatātparyanirṇaya; *Madhva*; B; 36, 4; SKT, D.

0788 Sarvārthasiddhivyākhyā; *Nṛsimhadeva*; PM; 55, 10; SKT, GR.

0786 Sarvārthasiddhivyākhyā; *Saumyavaradarāmānujamuni*; PM; 55, 8; SKT, GR.

0793 Sarvārthasiddhivyākhyā; *Śrīnivāsācārya*; PM; 56, 4; SKT, GR.

1018 Sarvārthasiddhivyākhyā-Ānandavallarī; *Nṛsiṁhadeva*; PL; 78, 8; SKT, GR.

0372 Sarvasaṁvādinī; *Jīva Gosvāmī*; B; 40, 1; SKT, D; 1965 A.D. (continues 0371).

0371 Sarvasaṁvādinī; *Jīva Gosvāmī*; B; 39, 32; SKT, D; 1965 A.D.

1164 Sarvavidyā Mantrāgamotkīlanam; PM; 105, 4; SKT, D.

0434 Sarvopaniṣat Sāra Saṅgrahaḥ; *Govindānanda Svāmī* (Compiler); B; 41, 24; SKT, D; 1929 A.D.

0435 Sarvopaniṣat Sārasaṅgrahaḥ; *Govindānanda Svāmī*; B; 42, 1; SKT, D; 1929 A.D; (continues 0434).

1392 Sarvottamastotra, Vallabhāṣṭaka Premāmṛta; *Agnikumāra* (Viṭṭhaleśvara); PM; 114, 4; H, D.

1594 Śatadūṣaṇī-IV with Commentary Caṇḍamāruta; *Vedānta Deśika,* (c) *Mahācārya*; B; 134, 5; SKT, D.

0977 Śatadūṣaṇīvyākhyā; *Rāmānujadāsa*; PL; 62, 34; SKT, GR.

1123 Sata Pañcāśikā; *Rāma Caraṇa*; PM; 104, 1; H, D.

0732 Sata Pañcāśikā; *Rāma Caraṇa*; PM; 51B, 62; H, D.

0949 Satkriyākalpamañjarī; PM; 62, 6; SKT, TE.

0690 Sat Nāma (Pṛthī Khaṇḍa); *Dharma Dās*; PM; 51B, 20; H, D.

0055 Ṣaṭpraśna Bhāṣya Ṭīkā; *Jayatīrtha*; B; 3, 30; SKT, D.

0015 Ṣaṭpraśna Bhāṣya Ṭīkā Vivaraṇa; *Maṅkāla Dharmācārya*; B; 1, 15; SKT, D; 1907 A.D.

0061 Ṣaṭpraśna Bhāṣya Ṭīkā Vivaraṇam; *Maṅkāla Dharmācārya*; B; 3, 36; SKT, D; 1907 A.D.

0118 Ṣaṭpraśnopaniṣadbhāṣyaṭīkā; *Jayatīrtha*; PM; 5, 29; SKT, TU.

0003 Ṣaṭpraśnopaniṣat Khaṇḍārtha (with text); *Rāghavendra Tīrtha*; B; 1, 3; SKT, D.

0102 Ṣaṭ Praśna Upaniṣad Khaṇḍārtha; *Rāghavendra Tīrtha*; PL; 5, 13; SKT, D.

0491 Ṣaṭsandarbhanāmaka Bhāgavata Sandarbha; *Jīva Gosvāmī*; B; 43, 13; SKT, D.

0506 Ṣaṭ Sandarbha Nāmakabhāgavata Sandarbha; *Jīva Gosvāmī*; B; 44, 1; SKT, D.

1324 Satsaṅga Mahimā; *Kiśorī Alī*; PM; 108, 65; SKT, D.

0280 Sat-Tattva-Ratna-Mālā; *Madhva/Ānandatīrtha*; B; 36, 8; SKT, D.

0070 Sattattvaratnamālā Vyākhyā; *Ānandatīrtha* s/o *Śrīmadviṭṭhalācārya*; B; 4, 4; SKT, D; 1918 A.D.

1660 Sāttvika Brahmavidyāvilāsaḥ; PL; 140, 5; SKT, GR.

0932 Sātvatāmṛtam; *Yogānanda*; PM; 61, 20; SKT, GR.

0931 Satvatantrabhāṣyam; *Alasiṅgabhaṭṭa*; PM; 61, 19; SKT, GR.

0607 Satya Nārāyaṇa Vrata Kathā (Extracted from Skanda Purāṇa); *Kṛṣṇa Dvaipāyana Vyāsa*; PM; 50A, 14; SKT, D.

0693 Savaiyā Sundara Dāsjī ke; *Sundara Dās*; PM; 51B, 23; H, D.

0308 Saviśesanirviśeṣa Kṛṣṇastavarāja with Ṭīkā; *Nimbārkācārya*; PM; 37, 3; SKT, D; c. 1973.

0307 Saviśeṣanirviśeṣa Śrī Kṛṣṇastata; *Nimbārka* with *Bhāvaprakāśikā Ṭīkā* by *Śitaladās*; 37, 2.

0428 Śeṣa Upaniṣad; B; 41, 18; SKT, D; (Continues 41, 17).

0909 Seśvaramīmāṁsā; *Vedāntadeśika*; PM; 60, 22; SKT, GR.

0498 Sevā Sukha; *Harivyāsadevācārya*; B; 43, 20; H, D; 1965 A.D.

1496 Siddhadharma Vijayamaṅgala Dīpikā; PM; 123, 12; SKT, TE.

1035 Siddhadharmavijaya Maṅgaladīpikā; PM; 91, 12; SKT, TE.

1016 Siddhāntacintāmaṇiḥ; *Śrīnivāsācārya*; PL; 78, 6; SKT, TE.

0561 Siddhānta Darpaṇa; *Baladeva Vidyābhūṣaṇa*; B; 49, 1; SKT BL, D BL; Gaurābda 457.

0496 Siddhānta Darpaṇa and Ṭīkā with Bengali Translation; *Baladeva Vidyābhūṣaṇa*; B; 43, 18; SKT BL, D BL.

0560 Siddhānta Darpaṇa with Ṭippaṇī by Nanda Miśra; *Baladeva Vidyābūṣaṇa*; B; 48, 30; SKT BL, D; Gaurābda 457.

1354 Siddhāntajāhnavī; *Devācārya*; PL; 110, 8; SKT, GR.

1107 Siddhānta Jāhnavī (Commentary on Pārijāta Saurabha, of Nimbārka) I Taraṅga; *Devācārya*; PM; 103, 8; SKT, D.

0973 Siddhāntanyāyacandrikā; *Devarāja*; PL; 62, 30; SKT, GR.

1249 Siddhānta Paddhati; *Rāghavānandajī*; PM; 107, 37; SKT, D.

1236 Siddhānta Puṣpāñjalī Bhāṣya; PM; 107, 24; SKT, D.

0487 Siddhānta Ratnākara; B; 43, 9; H, D; 1956 A.D.

0355 Siddhānta Ratnam or Govinda Bhāṣya Pīṭhakam (with Ṭippaṇī); Baladeva Vidyābhūṣaṇa; B; 39, 16; SKT, D; 1965 A.D.

0976 Siddhāntaratnāvaliḥ; *Veṅkaṭācārya*; PL; 62, 33; SKT, GR.

0908 Siddhāntasāraḥ; *Appagoṇḍācārya*; PM; 60, 21; SKT, D.

1015 Siddhāntasārāvaliḥ; *Trilocanaśivācārya*; PL; 78, 5; SKT, TE.

1105 Siddhāntasetuka (Commentary on Siddhānta Jāhnavī of Devācārya); *Sundara Bhaṭṭa*; PM; 103, 6; SKT, D.

1106 Siddhāntasetuka (Commentary on Siddhānta Jāhnavī of Devācārya); *Sundara Bhaṭṭa*; PM; 103, 6; SKT, D.

1352 Siddhāntasetuka (Commentary of Siddhānta Jāhnavī of Devācārya); *Sundara Bhaṭṭa*; PM; 110, 6; SKT, D.

1353 Siddhāntasetuka (Commentary on Siddhānta Jāhnavī of Devācārya); *Sundarabhaṭṭa*; PM; 110, 7; SKT, D.

0983 Siddhāntasiddhāñjanam; *Anantācārya*; PL; 63, 6; SKT, GR.

0972 Siddhitrayam; *Yāmunācārya*; PL; 62, 29; SKT, GR.

0782 Siddhitrayam; *Yāmunācārya*; PM; 55, 4; SKT, D.

0968 Siddhitrayam; *Yāmunācārya*; PM; 62, 25; SKT, GR.

1494 Siddhopāyasudarśanam; PM; 123, 10; SKT, TE.

1033 Siddhopāyasudarśanam; PM; 91, 10; SKT, TE.

0942 Śiṣṭabhūṣaṇam; *Rāmānujācārya*; PM; 61, 30; SKT, GR.

0194 Śiṣṭatātparya Candrikā; *Raghunātha Yati*; PM; 6, 67; SKT, D.

0195 Śiṣṭatātparya Candrikā; *Raghunātha Yati*; PM; 7, 1; SKT, D.

1552 Śrī Bhāgavata; PL; 130, 1; SKT, GR.

0378 Śrī Bhāgavata Bhāṣā (Dūsrā Khaṇḍa, 10th, 11th, 12th Cantos); *Rasajāni Vaiṣṇava Dās*; B; 40, 7; H, D; 1953 A.D.

0215 Śrī Bhāgavata-Ṭippaṇī; *Satyadharma Yati*; B; 31, 2; SKT, D; 1936 A.D.

1571 Śrī Bhāgavata Vyākhyāna (Tenth Skandha, 50th Adhyāya); Śrīdhara; PL; 132, 9; SKT, GR.

1541 Śrī Bhāgavata Vyākhyāna (Twelve Adhyāyas); *Śrīdhara*; PL; 128, 9; SKT, GR.

0416 Śrī Bhakta Māla (with Bhakti Rasa Bodhinī Ṭīkā); *Śrī Nārāyaṇa Dās* (Nābhā Dās); B; 41, 6; H, D; 1910 A.D.

0581 Śrī Bhakta Nāmāvalī; *Śrī Hita Dhruvadāsa*; B; 49, 21; H, D.

0206 Śrī Bhāṣya; *Rāmānujācārya*; PM; 7, 12; SKT, D.

1588 Śrī Bhāṣya with Śruta Prakaśikā; *Bhagavad Rāmānuja*, (c) *Sudarśana Sūri*; B; 133, 15; SKT, D.

1061 Śrībhāṣya I with Śrutaprakāśikā; *Bhagavad Rāmānuja*, (c) *Sudarśanasūri*; B; 99, 14; SKT, D.

1062 Śrībhāṣya II with Śrutaprakāśikā; *Bhagavad Rāmānuja*, (c) *Sudarśanasūri*; B; 99, 15; SKT, D.

1589 Śrī Bhāṣya-II with Śrutaprakāśikā; *Bhagavad Rāmānuja*, (c) *Sudarśana Sūri*; B; 133, 16; SKT, D.

1590 Śrībhāṣya with Śrutaprakāśikā; Bhagavad Rāmanuja; (c) *Sudarśana Sūri*; B; 134, 1; SKT, D.

1675 Śrī Bhāṣya with Śrutaprakāśikā (Jijñāsādhikaraṇa only); *Bhagavad Rāmānuja*; B; 141, 8; SKT TA, GR TA.

1053 Śrībhāṣyādi Sūkti Sādhutva Mālikā; PL; 99, 6; SKT, GR.

1580 Śrī Bhāṣyādisūkti Sādhutvamālikā; PL; 133, 7; SKT, GR.

0967 Śrībhāṣyādyantabhāgaḥ; PM; 62, 24; SKT, GR.

1638 Śrībhāṣyam; *Bhagavad Rāmānuja*; PL; 137, 5; SKT, GR.

0524 Śrī Guru Paramparā; B; 44, 19; SKT H, D.

0544 Śrī Guru Śaraṇāgati (with Translation in Hindi); *Kiśora Dās*; B; 48, 14; SKT H, D; 1934 A.D.

0390 Śrī Hari Līlā; *Brahma Gopāla Gosvāmī*; B; 40, 19; H, D; 1948 A.D.

1122 Śrīharivyāsajaśāmṛtasāgara; *Rūpa*; PM; 103, 23; SKT, D.

1370 Śrīharivyāsarasāmṛtasāgara; PM; 110, 24; H, D.

0584 Śrī Harivyāsa Yaśāmṛta; *Rūpa Rasika Deva*; B; 49, 24; H, D; 1925 A.D.

0571 Śrī Hita-Vṛndāvana Vilāsa; *Yugala Ballabha 'Nirmohī'*; B; 49, 11; H, D; 1940 A.D.

0575 Śrī Karuṇā Velī; *Cācā Vṛndāvana Dās*; B; 49, 15; H, D.

0263 Śrī Kṛṣṇāmṛta Mahārṇava; *Madhva*; B; 35, 22; SKT, D; 1881 A.D.

0471 Śrī Kṛṣṇārcana Paddhati; *Muralīmohan Gosvāmī* (Advaita Vaṁśya); B; 42, 37; BL, BL; Bangābda 1300.

0730 Śrī Kṛṣṇa Sahasranāma Stotram from Sarvottama Māhātmya Tantra; PM; 51B, 60; SKT, D.

0683 Śrī Kṛṣṇa-Stavarāja (From Brahmavaivarta Purāṇa); *Kṛṣṇa Dvaipāyana Vyāsa*; PM; 51B, 15; SKT, D.

0722 Śrī Kṛṣṇa Stavarāja (with Ṭīkā-Śrutisiddhāntamañjarī); *Nimbārkācārya*; PM; 51B, 52; SKT, D.

1150 Śrīmad Bhagavad Gītā Mālā Mantra, etc.; *Kṛṣṇa Dvaipāyāna Vyāsa*; PM; 104, 28; SKT, D.

0127 Śrīmad Bhāgavata (Canto 9 & 10); *Kṛṣṇa Dvaipāyana Vyāsa*; PM; 5, 38; SKT, TU.

0128 Śrīmad Bhāgavata; *Kṛṣṇa Dvaipāyana Vyāsa*; PM; 6, 1; SKT, TU; Continues 5, 38.

0319 Śrīmadbhāgavata; *Kṛṣṇa Dvaipāyana Vyāsa*; PM; 37, 14; SKT, D.

0320 Śrīmadbhāgavata; *Kṛṣṇa Dvaipāyana Vyāsa*; PM; 38, 1; SKT, D; (Continuation of 37, 14)

0530 Śrīmad Bhāgavata (with Bhāṣā Ṭīkā, Five Commentaries); *Kṛṣṇa Dvaipāyana Vyāsa*; B; 47, 5; SKT H, D; 1966 A.D.

0339 Śrīmadbhāgavata (with Ṭīkā Bhāvārthadīpikā); *Kṛṣṇa Dvaipāyana Vyāsa*; PM; 38, 20; SKT, D; c 1834 A.D.

0340 Śrīmadbhāgavata (with Ṭīkā Bhāvārthadīpikā); *Kṛṣṇa Dvaipāyana Vyāsa*; PM; 39, 1; SKT, D; c 1834 A.D.

0309 Śrīmadbhāgavata Bhāṣā; *Rasajānī*; PM; 37, 4; H, D.

1453 Śrīmadbhāgavata Līlākalpadruma; *Govindaśāstrī*; B; 120, 4; SKT, D.

0026 Śrīmad Bhāgavatam; *Kṛṣṇadvaipāyana Vyāsa*; B; 3, 1; SKT, D; Śaka 1850, 1928 A.D.

1388 Śrīmadbhāgavatam (Skandha-s 1-9) with Bhāgavatasiddhānta Pradīpa Vyākhyā; *Kṛṣṇa Dvaipāyana Vyāsa*; (c) *Śukasudhī*; PM; 113, 3; SKT, D.

1389 Śrīmadbhāgavatam (Skandha-s 1-9) with Bhāgavata Siddhānta Pradīpa Vyākhyā; *Kṛṣṇa Dvaipāyana Vyāsa*, (c) *Śukasudhī*; PM; 114, 1; SKT, D.

0525 Śrīmad Bhāgavata Purāṇa with Bhāvārthadīpikā; *Kṛṣṇa Dvaipāyana Vyāsa*; B; 44, 20; SKT, D; 1861 A.D.

1451 Śrīmadbhāgavata Purāṇa with Bhāvārthadīpikā; *Kṛṣṇa Dvaipāyana Vyāsa*, (c) *Śrīdharsvāmin*; B; 120, 2; SKT, D.

0033 Śrīmad Bhāgavata Ṭippaṇī; *Śrīnivāsa Tīrtha*; B; 3, 8; SKT, D; Śaka 1850, 1928 A.D. 0034 Ṛk Sūcī: Alphabetical Index of Mantras from Mantrārtha Mañjarī; B; 3, 9; SKT, D; Śaka 1874, 1907 A.D.

0032 Śrīmad Bhāgavata Ṭippaṇī-Mandabodhinī; Śeṣa (Disciple of Chalārī Narasiṁhācārya); B; 3, 7; SKT, D; Śaka 1850, 1928 A.D.

0030 Śrīmad Bhāgavata Ṭippaṇī-Mandanandinī; *Vyāsatattvajña Tīrtha*; B; 3, 5; SKT, D; 1928 A.D.

0031 Śrīmad Bhāgavata Ṭippaṇī-Padamuktāvalī; *Liṁverī Śrīnivāsa*; B; 3, 6; Śaka 1850, 1928 A.D.

0531 Śrīmad Bhāgavata with Bhāṣā Ṭīkā; *Kṛṣṇa Dvaipāyana Vyāsa*; B?; 48, 1; SKT, D; 1966 A.D; (Continues 0530)

0066 Śrīmad Brahma Sūtra Bhāṣya Ṭīkā Tattva Prakāśikā; *Jayatīrtha*; PM; 3, 41; SKT, D.

0067 Śrīmad Brahma Sūtra Bhāṣya Ṭīkā Tattva Prakāśikā; *Jayatīrtha*; PM; 4, 1; SKT, D; (Continuation of 0066).

0405 Śrīmad Vaiṣṇava Siddhānta Ratna Saṅgraha; *Syāmlāl Hakīm* (Compiler); B; 40, 35; SKT H, D; 1953 A.D.

0221 Śrī Mahā-Bhāgavata; *Kṛṣṇa Dvaipāyana Vyāsa*; B; 32, 3; SKT, D; 1913 A.D.

0406 Śrī Mahā Mantra Mīmāṁsā; *Gopāla Dās Kavi* (Compiler); B; 40, 36; SKT BL, BL; 1746 Baṅgābda.

0679 Śrī Mahāprabhujī ke Śrī Gusāījī ke Sevya Svarūpa; PM; 51B, 11; H, D.

0038 Śrīman Mantrārtha Mañjarī; *Rāghavendra Tīrtha*; B; 3, 13; SKT, D; Śaka 1824, 1902 A.D.

0228 Śrīman Nyāya-Sudhā-Ṭippaṇī; *Rāmacandra Bhikṣu*; B; 33, 5; SKT, D.

0076 Śrīmat Saṁgraha Rāmāyaṇa (with Vyākhyā); *Nārāyaṇa Paṇḍita Ācārya*; PM; 4, 10; SKT, D; c. 1830 A.D.

0287 Śrī Nārāyaṇahṛdaya and Lakṣmīhṛdaya; B; 36, 16; SKT, D; 1881 A.D.

1466 Śrīnāthajī kī Kathā; *Ananya Rasika Vaiṣṇava Dās*; B; 121, 4; H, D.

0431 Śrī Nāthajīnī Prākaṭya Vārtā; *Govardhana Lāljī Mahārāj*; B; 41, 21; GUJ SKT, GUJ D; 1920 A.D.

0595 Śrī Nikuñja Keli Mādhurī; *Mādhava Dās* (Upanāma Alimādhurī); B; 50A, 2; H, D; 1926 A.D.

0588 Śrī Nikuñja Prema Mādhurī; *Mādhava Dās* (Upanāma: Alīmādhurī); B; 49, 28; H, D; 1934 A.D.

0543 Śrī Nimbārka Sampradāya kī Sādhana Praṇālī; *Kiṣora Das*; B; 48, 13; H, D; 1937 A.D.

1470 Śrī Śrī Bhakti Rasāmṛta Śeṣa; *Jīvagosvāmī*; B; 121, 8; SKT BL, BL.

0476 Śrī Śrī Navadvīpa Darpaṇa Grantha Pariśiṣṭa (Dvitīya Khaṇḍa); *Vraja Mohan Dās*; B; 42, 42; BL, BL; Baṅgābda 1327.

0460 Śrī Śrī Rāsalīlā Tattva; *Śrīśacandra Rāya Caudhurī* (Compiler); B; 42, 26; SKT BL, BL; Baṅgābda 1343.

1467 Śrī Śrī Śruti Ratna Mālā (Twelve Upaniṣads—Īśa, Kena, Kaṭha, Praśna, Muṇḍaka, Māṇḍūkya, Taittirīya, Aitareya, Chāndogya, Bṛhadāraṇyaka, Śvetāśvatara and Kauṣītakī; Compiled by *Niśikānta Sannyāla*; B; 121, 5; SKT BL, BL.

1469 Śrī Śrī Suratakathāmṛtam with Ṭīkā and Translation; *Viśvanātha Cakravarti Ṭhākur*; B; 121, 7; SKT BL, BL.

0436 Śrī Śrī Vṛndāvana Mahimāmṛta and Saṅgraha with Anuvāda by Śrī Bhagavant Mudit; *Vamśī Dāsa Prabodhānanda Sarasvatīpāda* (Compiler); B; 42, 2; H, D.

1427 Śrīsvāmiharidāsjī kī Vāṇī; *Haridās Svāmī*; PM; 118, 12; H, D.

0945 Śrītattvaratnam; PM; 62, 2; SKT, D.

0451 Śrī Tiruppāvāvaisvāpadeśaḥ (with Commentary in Sanskrit); *Godāmbājī*; B; 42, 17; SKT, D; 1950 A.D.

1546 Śrīvacanabhūṣana Arumbada; PL; 129, 2; TA, GR.

1095 Śrīvacanabhūṣaṇa Rahasyajālam; *Pillai Lokācārya*; PL; 101, 7; Maṇipravālam; GR.

1640 Śrīvacanabhūṣaṇarahasya Jālam; *Pillai Lokācārya*; PL; 137, 7; Maṇipravalam; GR, TA.

1525 Śrīvacana Bhūṣaṇa Vyākhyāna; *Śrī Varavaramuni*; PL; 126, 4; TA, TE.

1653 Śrī Vaiṣṇava Dharma Pramāṇa Saṅgrahaḥ; PL; 139, 8; SKT, GR.

0400 Śrī Vaiṣṇava Matābja Bhāskara (Śrī Rāmārcana Paddhati Sahitaś ca); *Rāmānanda Svāmī*; B; 40, 30; H, D; 1927 A.D.

1026 Śrutaprakāśikātūlikā; *Vādhūla Śrīnivāsācār*; PM; 91, 3; SKT, TE.

1487 Śrutaprakāśikā Tūlikā; *Vādhūla Śrīnivāsācārya*; PM; 123, 3; SKT, TE.

0790 Śrutaprakāśikāvivaraṇam-Tātparyadīpikā; PM; 56, 1; SKT, GR.

0981 Śrutaprakāśikāvyākhyā; *Raṅgarāmānuja*; PL; 63, 4; SKT, GR.

1020 Śrutaprakāśikāvyākhyā; PL; 78, 10; SKT, GR.

0783 Śrutaprakāśikāvyākhyā; *Campakeśācārya*; PM; 55, 5; SKT, GR.

0975 Śrutaprakāśikāvyākhyā-Bhāvaprakāśikā; *Raṅgarāmānuja*; PL; 62, 32; SKT, GR.

0784 Śrutaprakāśikāvyākhyā-Gurubhāvaprakāśika; *Lakṣmaṇārya*; PM; 55, 6; SKT, D.

1025 Śrutaprakāśikāvyākhyānam; *Lakṣmaṇamuni* (Embar Svāmi); PM; 91, 2; SKT, TE.

1486 Śrutaprakāśikā Vyākhyānam; *Lakṣmaṇa Muni* (Embar Svāmi); PM; 123, 2; SKT, TE.

0979 Śrutaprakāśikāvyākhyā-Tūlikā; PL; 63, 2; SKT, GR.

1322 Śrutyanta Kalpavallī; *Puruṣottama prasāda*; PM; 108, 63; SKT, D.

0677 Stava Mālā with Commentary; *Rūpa Gosvāmī*; PM; 51B, 9; SKT, BL.

1650 Stotrakadambam; *Ālvārs* and *Ācāryas*; PL; 139, 5; SKT TA, TE GR.

0597 Subodhinī Ṭīkā on Rāsa Pañcādhyāya of Śrīmad Bhāgavatam; *Kṛṣṇa Dvaipāyana Vyāsa*; B; 50A, 4; SKT, D; 1923 A.D.

1130 Sudarśana Kavaca; PM; 104, 8; SKT, D.

0936 Sudarśanaprapattiḥ; PM; 61, 24; SKT, TE.

0935 Sudarśanasaṁhitā; PM; 61, 23; SKT, T.

0940 Sudarśanasaṁhitā; PM; 61, 28; SKT, TE.

0553 Śyāma Candrodaya; *Jagadānanda Ṭhākur*; B; 48, 23; H, BL; Caitanyābda 463.

0182 Taittirīya Caula Prayoga and Upanayana Prayoga; PM; 6, 55; SKT, D.

0236 Taittirīya Saṁhitā; B; 34, 4; SKT, D; 1899 A.D.

0016 Taittirīya Upaniṣad Bhāṣya Ṭīkā; *Śrīnivāsa Tīrtha*; B; 1, 16; SKT, D; 1905 A.D.

0063 Taittirīya Upaniṣad Bhāṣya Vivaraṇa; *Vyāsa Tīrtha*; B; 3, 38; SKT, D; 1905 A.D.

0103 Taittirīya Upaniṣad Khaṇḍārtha; *Rāghavendra Tīrtha*; PL; 5, 14; SKT, D.

0654 Taittirīyopaniṣadbhāṣyam; *Kūranārāyaṇadāsa*; PM; 51A, 11; SKT, D.

1649 Taittirīyopaniṣadbhāṣyam; *Raṅgarāmānujamuni*; PL; 139, 4; SKT, GR.

0650 Taittirīyopaniṣadbhāṣyavṛtti-Mitākṣarā; *Govindarāja*; PM; 51A, 7; SKT, D.

0656 Taittirīyopaniṣadvyākhyā; *Narasiṁhācārya*; PM; 51A, 13; SKT, TE.

0059 Talavakāra Upaniṣad Bhāṣya Vivaraṇa; *Vyāsatīrtha*; B; 3, 34; SKT, D; 1907 A.D.

0010 Talavakāra Upaniṣad Bhāṣya Vivaraṇa; *Vedeśa Tīrtha Bhikṣu*; B; 1, 10; SKT, D; 1907 A.D.

0058 Talavakāra Upaniṣad Bhāṣyavivaraṇam; *Vedeśa Tīrtha Bhikṣu*; B; 3, 33; SKT, D; 1907 A.D.

0057 Talavakāropaniṣadkhaṇḍārthaḥ; *Rāghavendra Yati*; B; 3, 32; SKT, D; 1907 A.D.

0052 Talavakāropaniṣadkhaṇḍārthaḥ; *Rāghavendra Yati*; B; 3, 27; SKT, D; Śaka 1819, 1897 A.D.

0176 Tantra Dīpikā; *Rāghavendra Tīrtha*; PM; 6, 49; SKT, D.

0256 Tantra Dīpikā; *Rāghavendra Tīrtha*; PM; 35, 15; SKT, TU.

0906 Tattvabhāskaraḥ; *Pelapūrdīkṣita*; PM; 60, 19; SKT, D.

1673 Tattvadīpam with Dīpa Prakāśa; *Alahiya Maṇavāla Jīyar* (Vādi Keśari); B; 141, 6; SKT, TE.

0904 Tattvadīpaprakāśaḥ; *Saumyajāmātṛmuni*; PM; 60, 17; SKT, GR.

0844 Tattvadīpikā; *Śrīnivāsācārya*; PM; 57, 23;SKT, GR.

1057 Tattvamārtāṇḍa I; *Śrīnivāsācārya* (Sūrapuram); B; 99, 10; SKT, D.

1058 Tattvamārtāṇḍa II; *Śrīnivāsācārya* (Sūrapuram); B; 99, 11; SKT, D.

1584 Tattva Mārtāṇḍa-I; *Śrīnivāsārya* (Sūrapuram); B; 133, 11; SKT, D.

1585 Tattva Mārtāṇḍa-II; *Śrīnivāsācārya* (Sūrapuram); B; 133, 12; SKT, D.

0666 Tattvāmṛtam; *Appagoṇḍācārya*; PM; 51A, 23; SKT, D.

0652 Tattvamuktākalāpaḥ; *Veṅkaṭanātha*; PM; 51A, 9; SKT, GR.

0653 Tattvamuktākalāpavyākhyā-Sarvārthasiddhi; *Vedāntadeśika*; PM; 51A, 10; SKT, GR.

1056 Tattvanirṇaya; *Vātsya Śrīvaradācārya*; B; 99, 9; SKT, D.

1583 Tattvanirṇaya; *Vātsyaśrīvaradācārya*; B; 133, 10; SKT, D.

0847 Tattvanirṇaya; *Varadācārya*; PM; 57, 26; SKT, GR.

0647 Tattvanirṇayaḥ; *Appagoṇḍācārya*; PM; 51A, 4; SKT, D.

0907 Tattva Nirṇayaḥ; *Kandādai Appagoṇḍācārya*; PM; 60, 20; SKT, D.

0649 Tattvanirṇayaḥ; *Varadācārya*; PM; 51A, 6; SKT, GR.

0905 Tattvaniṣkarṣaḥ; *Kandādai Appagoṇḍācārya*; PM; 60, 18; SKT, D.

0126 Tattvaprakāśikā; *Jayatīrtha*; PM; 5, 37; SKT, TU.

0073 Tattvaprakāśikā Vākyārthamañjarī; *Śrīnivāsatīrtha*; B; 4, 7; SKT, D.

0062 Tattvasaṁkhyāna Ṭippaṇī; *Satyadharma Yati*; B; 3, 37; SKT, D.

0901 Tattvasaṅgrahaḥ; PM; 60, 14; SKT, D.

0648 Tattvasaṅgrahaḥ; *Śrīraṅgarājayajvan*; PM; 51A, 5; SKT, GR.

0275 Tattva Saṅkhyāna Ṭīkā-Bhāvadīpa, (also Contains Tattva Saṅkhyāna Śrīnivāsatīrthīya Ṭippaṇī by Śrīnivāsa); B; 36, 3; SKT, D; 1896 A.D.

0050 Tattva Saṁkhyāna Vivaraṇa; *Jayatīrtha Bhikṣu*; B; 3, 25; SKT, D.

1443 Tattvasandarbha Ṭippaṇī; *Baladeva Vidyābhūṣaṇa*; PM; 119, 12; SKT, D.

0114 Tattvasaṅkhyāna Ṭippaṇī; *Upādhyāya*; PM; 5, 25; SKT, TU.

0327 Tattvasiddhāntabindu; *Anantarāma*; PM; 38, 8; SKT, D; c. 1848.

0651 Tattvatrayaculukārtha Saṁgraha; *Varadanātha*; PM; 51A, 8; SKT, D.

0902 Tattvatrayaculukārthasaṅgrahaḥ; *Varadanātha*; PM; 60, 15; SKT, D.

1501 Tattvatraya Vyākhyāna; *Śrīvaravaramuni*; PL; 124, 5; TA, GR.

1041 Tattvatraya Vyākhyāna; *Śrīvaravaramuni*; PL; 92, 6; TA, GR.

0131 Tattvaviveka (Pañcikā) (Bhāvaprakāśikā); *Vyāsatīrtha/Vyāsayati*; PM; 6, 4; SKT, D.

0132 Tattva Viveka (Pañcikā) Ṭīkā (Bhāvaprakāśikā); *Vyāsatīrtha/Vyāsayati*; PM; 6, 5; SKT, D.

0047 Tattva Viveka Vivaraṇam; *Jayatīrthabhikṣu*; B; 3, 22; SKT, D; Śaka 1818, 1896 A.D.

0139 Tattvodyota; *Madhvācārya/Ānandatīrtha*; PM; 6, 12; SKT, D.

0255 Tattvodyota Ṭīkā; *Jayatīrtha*; PM; 35, 14; SKT, TU.

0098 Tattvodyota Ṭippaṇī; *Vijayīndra Tīrtha*; PM; 5, 9; SKT, D; c. 1600 A.D.

0624 Tirodhānānupapattiḥ; PM; 50B, 12; SKT, GR.

0665 Tirodhānānupapatti with part of Prapañcamithyātvakhaṇḍanam, Āśrayānupapatti and Svarūpānupapatti; PM; 51A, 22; SKT, GR.

0123 Tīrtha Prabandha; *Vādirāja Tīrtha*; PM; 5, 34; SKT, TU.

1518 Tirukkurundaṇḍakam Vyākhyāna; *Periyavāccānpillai*; PL; 125, 11; TA, TA.

1570 Tirumālai 6000 Padi; *Alahiya Maṇavāla Perumāl Nāyanār*; PL; 132, 8; TA, TE.

1529 Tirumālai Vyākhyāna; *Periyavāccān Pillai*; PL; 126, 8; TA, TA.

1007 Tirupati-vaṇṇa-viruttam; PL; 63, 30; TA, TA.

1512 Tiruppallāṇḍu, Kaṇṇinum Siruttāmbu, Amalanadipirān Tiruppallielucci—Vyākhyāna; *Periyavāccānpillai*; PL; 125, 5; TA, TA.

1672 Tiruppallāṇḍu, Vaiṣṇavasamayācāra niṣkarṣa and others; *Periyālvār*; B; 141, 5; TA, GR.

1510 Tiruppāvai Svāpadeśavyākhyāna; PL; 125, 3; TA, TA.

1521 Tiruppāvai Vyākhyānārumpada, 36000 Padi Vyākhyāna; *Annan-Appa, Periyavāccānpillai*; PL; 125, 14; TA, TA.

1667 Tiruvāimoli; *Nammālvār*; PL; 140, 12; TA, GR.

1668 Tiruvāimoli; *Nammālvār*; PL; 141, 1; TA, GR.

1661 Tiruvāimoli Nuttandādivyākhyā; PL; 140, 6; Maṇipravālam, GR.

1055 Tiruvāimoli Vyākhyā I; *Nammālvār, Tirukkurukai Pirān Pillan* and others; B; 99, 8; TA, TE.

1582 Tiruvāimoli with Vyākhyā-I; *Nammālvār,* (c) *Tirukkurukaipirān Pillan* and others; B; 133, 9; TA, TE.

1527 Tiruviruttam Vyākhyānam—Īdu; *Nambillai*; PL; 126, 6; TA, TA.

0984 Upādānatvasamarthanam; *Śrīnivāsa*; PL; 63, 7; SKT, TE.

1561 Upadeśaratnamālāvyākhyāna; *Pillai Lokam Jīyar*; PL; 130, 10; TA, GR.

0088 Upādhi Khaṇḍana Mandāra Mañjarī; *Vyāsarāja* (Tīrtha); PL; 4, 22; SKT, NA.

0285 Upādhi Khaṇḍana Mandāra Mañjarī; B; 30, 14; SKT, D; 1896 A.D.

0110 Upādhikhaṇḍana Ṭīkā on Tattvaprakāśa by Ānandatīrtha; *Jayatīrtha*; PM; 5, 21; SKT, TU.

0051 Upādhikhaṇḍana Vyākhyāvivṛti; *Śrīnivāsa Tīrtha*; B; 3, 26; SKT, D; Śaka 1818, 1896 A.D.

1654 Upaniṣaddīpikā; PL; 139, 9; SKT, NA.

0254 Upaniṣad-s and Commentaries; *Madhva*; PM; 35, 13; SKT, D.

0639 Upaniṣanmaṅgalābharaṇam (Twenty-four Upaniṣads); PM; 50B, 21; SKT, D.

0642 Upaniṣanmaṅgalābharaṇam; *Mādhavayogin*; PM; 50B, 24; SKT, D.

0243 Upanyāsaratnamālā; *Vādirāja Tīrtha*; B; 35, 2; SKT, D; 1954 A.D.

0835 Upayuktāṁśasaṁgrahaḥ; PM; 57, 14; SKT, GR.

1001 Upendrasaṁhitā; PL; 63, 24; SKT, GR.

0792 Upendrasaṁhitā; PM; 56, 3; SKT, D.

0833 Ūrdhvāmnāya Saṁhitā; PM; 57, 12; SKT, D.

0830 Utsavasaṁgraha; PM; 57, 9; SKT, TE.

0832 Utsavasaṁgraha with Telugu Ṭīkā; PM; 57, 11; SKT, TE.

1596 Vacassudhāvicāra; *Śrīnivāsa Narasiṁhācārya* (Kuppanna Iyengar); B; 134, 7; SKT, TE.

0084 Vāda Mālikā; *Śrī Vijayīndra Tīrtha*; PL; 4, 18; SKT, NA; c. 1600 A.D.

0244 Vaikuṇṭha Varṇana; *Vādirāja Tīrtha*; B; 35, 3; KAN, D; 1893 A.D.

1203 Vairāgya Śatakam; *Bhartṛhari*; PM; 106, 24; SKT, D.

0604 Vaiṣṇava Dharma Mīmāṁsā (Saṅkṣepa); *Ananta Rāma*; PM; 50A, 11; SKT, D.

1478 Vaiṣṇavadharma Mīmāṁsā; *Ananta Rāma*; B; 121, 16; SKT, D.

1368 Vaiṣṇavadharma Suradrumamañjarī; *Saṅkarṣaṇa Śaraṇa*; PM; 110, 22; SKT, D.

0515 Vaiṣṇava Dharma Suradruma Mañjarī with Hindi Ṭīkā; *Saṅkarṣaṇa Śaraṇa Deva*; B; 44, 10; SKT H, D; 1929 A.D.

0299 Vaiṣṇavānām Ṛgvedīya Śrāddhaprayoga; B; 36, 28; SKT, D; 1925 A.D.

0574 Vaiṣṇava Nitya Karma; *Hīrālāl Durgāśaṅkara* (ed.); B; 49, 14; SKT GUJ, D GUJ.

0925 Vaiṣṇavaprasādādipratiṣṭhāvidhiḥ; *Mohanarāyaguru*; PM; 61, 13; SKT, GR.

1461 Vaiṣṇavāvadhāna (Extract from Bhāgavata); *Nityānanda Bhaṭṭa*; B; 120, 12; SKT H, D.

0497 Vaiṣṇava Vaibhava (Bhāga 2); B; 43, 19; SKT H, D; 1924 A.D.

1448 Vaiṣṇava Vandanā; *Vṛndāvana Dāsa*; PM; 119, 17; BL, D.

0392 Vallabha Rasika Jī kī Vāṇī; B; 40, 22; H, D; 1948 A.D.

0562 Vallabha Rasikajī kī Vāṇī; *Vallabha Rasikajī*; B; 49, 2; H, D; 1948 A.D.

1321 Vaṁśīvaṭ Vilāsa Mādhurī; *Mādhurī Dās*; PM; 108, 62; H, D.

0570 Vañjārauvelī and Vāraha Māsa Vinoda Velī; *Cācā Vṛndāvan Dās*; B; 49, 10; H, D; 1931 A.D.

1207 Varma nārāyaṇa Kavaca; *Kṛṣṇa Dvaipāyana Vyāsa*; PM; 106, 28; SKT, D.

1357 Vedāntaratna Mañjūṣā; *Puruṣottamācārya*; PM; 110, 11; SKT, D.

1419 Vedāntaratnamañjūṣā; *Puruṣottamācārya*; PM; 118, 4; SKT, D.

1110 Vedāntaratnamañjūṣā; *Puruṣottamācārya*; PM; 103, 11; SKT, D.

0336 Vedānta Ratna Mañjūṣā; *Puruṣottamācārya*; PM; 38, 17; SKT, D; c. 1809 A.D.

1157 Vedānta Ratna Mañjūṣā; *Puruṣottamācārya*; PM; 104, 35; SKT, D.

1643 Vedāntaśāra; *Bhagavad Rāmānuja*; PL; 137, 10; SKT, GR.

1528 Vedāntasāra; *Śrī Rāmānujācārya*; PL; 126, 7; SKT, GR.

1098 Vedāntasāra and Vedānta Dīpa; *Bhagavad Rāmānuja*; PL; 101, 10; SKT, GR.

0326 Vedāntasārapadyamālā; *Anantarāma*; PM; 38, 7; SKT, D; c. 1848.

1404 Vedāntasiddhānta Jāhnavī (Prathama Taraṅga); *Devācārya*; PM; 115, 9; SKT, D.

0797 Vedāntasiddhāntakaumudī; PM; 56, 8; SKT, GR.

1239 Vedānta Siddhānta Ratnāñjalī; PM; 107, 27; SKT, D.

1339 Vedānta Siddhānta Ratnāñjalī; *Hari Vyāsa Devācārya*; PM; 109, 6; SKT, D.

0323 Vedāntasiddhāntaratnapadyamālā with Ṭīkā; *Anantarāma*; PM; 38, 4; SKT H, D.

0322 Vedānta Siddhāntaratna Padyamālā with Ṭīkā; *Anantarāma*; PM; 38, 3; SKT H, D.

1109 Vedānta Tattva Bodha; PM; 103, 10; SKT, D.

0334 Vedāntatattvabodha; *Anantarāma*; PM; 38, 15; SKT, D; c. 1833 A.D.

0332 Vedāntatattvabodha; *Anantarāma*; PM; 38, 13; SKT, D; c. 1893 A.D.

1361 Vidvanmaṇḍanam; *Viṭṭhaleśvara*; PM; 110, 15; SKT, D.

1013 Vijayīndraparājayaḥ; *Tātācārya*; PL; 78, 3; SKT, GR.

0963 Vijayottarasaṁhitā; PM; 62, 20; SKT, GR.

1572 Vilakṣaṇamokṣādhikāranirṇaya; PL; 132, 10; TA, GR.

1614 Vilakṣaṇa Mokṣādhikārinirṇayam; *Erumbiyappa*; B; 135, 7; TA, TE.

1069 Vilakṣaṇamokṣādhikārinirṇayam; *Erumbiyappa*; B; 100, 7; TA, TE.

0482 Vilāpa Kusumāñjalī; *Vṛndāvanavāsa Jī and Raghunāthadāsa Gosvāmī*; B; 43, 4; SKT H, D; 1950 A.D.

0387 Vilāpa Kusumāñjalī (Braj Bhāṣā translation by Vṛndāvana Dās); *Raghunātha Dās Gosvāmī* (Mūla); B; 40, 16; H, D; 1950 A.D.

1329 Vinaya Patrikā; *Sudarśana Dās*; PM; 108, 70; H SKT, D.

0449 Vinaya Patrikā; *Tulasī Dāsa Gosvāmī*; B; 42, 15; H, D; 1887 A.D.

0956 Vīramāheśvarācārasaṅgrahaḥ; *Nīlakaṇṭhanāganātha*; PM; 62, 13; SKT, D.

0952 Vīraśaivāhnikam with Telugu Meaning; *Vīraśaivadīkṣāvidhānam*; PM; 62, 9; SKT, D.

0947 Vīraśaivāhnikam with Telugu Meaning; PM; 62, 4; SKT, TE.

1014 Viṣayatāvādaḥ; *Anantācārya*; PL; 78, 4; SKT, GR.

1066 Viṣayavākyadīpikā; *Raṅgarāmānujamuni*; B; 100, 4; SKT, D.

1611 Viṣayavākyadīpikā with Ṭippaṇī; *Raṅgarāmānujamuni*, (c) *Lakṣmaṇadāsa*; B; 135, 4; SKT, D.

1620 Viśiṣṭādvaita Siddhāntamu; *Sampatkumāra Varadaveṅkaṭa Raṅgācārya* (Nallān Cakravarti); B; 135, 13; TE,TE.

0310 Viṣṇusahasranāma with Ṭīkā; *Kṛṣṇadvaipāyana Vyāsa*; PM; 37, 5; SKT, D.

0911 Viṣṇusaṁhitā; *Nārāyaṇamuni*; PM; 60, 24; SKT, GR.

0081 Viṣṇu Stuti Vyākhyā; *Vijayīndra Yati*; PM; 4, 15; SKT, D.

0124 Viṣṇustuti with Vyākhyā (Viṣṇusaṁstavasadvyākhyāpradīpaḥ); *Trivikrama Paṇḍitācārya*; PM; 5, 35; SKT, TU.

0912 Viṣvaksena Saṁhitā; PM; 60, 25; SKT, GR.

1091 Viṣvaksenasaṁhitā-II; PM; 101, 3; SKT, TE.

1636 Viṣvaksenasaṁhitā-II; PM; 137, 3; SKT, TE.

0501 Viṭhal Bipul Dev Jī kī Vāṇī; *Svāmī Viṭhalbipuladeva*; PM; 43, 23; H, D; c. 1781 A.D.

1376 Vivekatrayaratna; *Rāmānujācārya Dās*; PM; 111, 5; SKT, D.

0606 Vraja Siddhānta Jyotsnā; *Dhanīrāma*; PM; 50A, 13; SKT, D; c. 1893.

0494 Vraja Vinoda; *Lāl Balabīr* and *Prema Sakhī* (Brothers); B; 43, 16; H, D; 1969 A.D.

0702 Vrata Nirṇaya (Also contains Rādhājanmakathā from Harilīlāmṛtatantra); *Gopāla Kṛṣṇa*; PM; 51B, 32; SKT, D.

1142 Vrata Nirṇaya, Pañca Saṁskāra; PM; 104, 20; SKT, D.

0710 Vrata Nirṇaya with Śakunāvalī; PM; 51B, 40; SKT, D.

1216 Vratārka; *Bhaṭṭaśaṅkara*; PM; 107, 4; SKT, D.

1371 Vṛndāvanamahimāmṛta; *Prabodhānanda Sarasvatī*; PM; 110, 25; SKT, D.

1372 Vṛndāvana Mahimāmṛta; *Prabodhānandasarasvatī*; PM; 111, 1; SKT, D.

1421 Vṛndāvanamahimāmṛta; *Prabodhānanda Sarasvatī*; PM; 118, 6; SKT, D.

1156 Vṛndāvana Rasāmṛta; *Prabodhānanda Sarasvatī*; PM; 104, 34; SKT, D.

1312 Yoga Śāstra; PM; 108, 53; SKT, D.

1309 Yoga Śāstra with Ṭīkā Rājamārtaṇḍa; *Patañjali*; PM; 108, 50; SKT, D.

1311 Yoga Sūtra; *Patañjali*; PM; 108, 52; SKT, D.

1310 Yoga Sūtra with Ṭīkā Rājamārtaṇḍa; *Patañjali*; PM; 108, 51; SKT, D.

1345 Yogopāyakathanam; PM; 109, 12; SKT, D.

1212 Yugalabadhāi; PM; 106, 33; H, D.

1213 Yugalabadhāi; PM; 107, 1; H, D.

1196 Yugala Kiśora Sahasra Nāma; *Kṛṣṇa Dvaipāyana Vyāsa*; PM; 106, 17; SKT, D.

0673 Yugala Rasa Mādurī; *Rasika Govinda*; PM; 51B, 5; H, D.

0540 Yugala Saneha Patrikā; *Vṛndāvan Dās*; B; 48, 10; H, D; 1928 A.D.

1455 Yugalāṣṭakam (Hindi Bhāṣānuvāda); *Mādhavendra Purīcaraṇa*; B; 120, 6; H, D.

0729 Yugala Stavarāja from Maheśvara Gaurī Tantra; PM; 51B, 59; SKT, D.

LETTER*

THE LIBRARY OF CONGRESS
WASHINGTON, D.C. 20540-4810

ASIAN DIVISION

Southern Asia Section
LJ 150
Washington, DC 20540-4810
tel. 202-707-3732
fax. 202-707-1724
email: athr@loc.gov

September 7, 2001

Dear Charles,

Many thanks for the copy of the catalog *The Adyar Library and Institute for Vaiṣṇava Studies Microfilm Collection of Vaiṣṇava Literature.* We will be cataloging it and adding it to the Library's permanent collections. This is a very valuable collection of material on a family of religious movements

---

* The copy below is the letter, solicited from Dr. Allen W. Thrasher, Senior Reference Librarian of the Southern Asian Section of the Library of Congress, as a review of the Catalogue at the time that he wrote it. It is his professional opinion and is not meant as any form of endorsement of this project by the Library of Congress. We hope that the collection of old Vaiṣṇava books and manuscripts and the bibliographic rescue, represented in this Catalogue, will be of use to the interested scholarly community.

than which there is no more influential one in India. I am very happy to hear that American University is going to make archival copies of the microfilms and keep them in its permanent collections.

As I said, I searched all the items on four randomly chosen pages by author and title, including various guesses of alternative forms. The total of the items searched was 78, and of these only 15 appeared in any form in the Library of Congress online catalog. This is but 19% of the total. Of the 15 seven were printed books, but LC had only 2 of these in the edition filmed. The remaining 8 were manuscripts of which LC had printed editions or another manuscript copy. These figures illustrate the rarity of the materials.

I might add that very few Indian texts have had truly critical editions, and the capturing of multiple manuscript or printed editions in film is a major contribution to making truly critical editions possible. Commercial printed editions are significant testimonia to regional versions of the texts or to lost manuscripts. At LC we have not shrunk from acquiring multiple editions of works in both the classical and the modern languages.

I also think this material will in fact get used. I regularly have inquiries about Vaisnava texts that are not in LC and do not appear in the online union catalog OCLC, which includes most of the research libraries in North America and a steadily growing number elsewhere.

As I mentioned I think the catalog as it is should be supplemented by alphabetical indexes of authors and titles. Another obvious thing would be to put the indexes list on a website and to make a CD-ROM of it. (I am a firm believer in continuing to put information in paper which in my opinion is a lot more permanent than websites, and CD-

ROMs which are some by some real but unspecifiable degree more permanent.)

Sincerely,

Allen W. Thrasher, Ph.D.
Senior Reference Librarian
Southern Asia Section

PROF. CHARLES S.J. WHITE
Professor Emeritus of Religion and Philosophy,
American University
4400 Massachusetts Ave. N.W.
Washington, DC 20016-8056
Tel. (202) 885-2925 Off.